# MARY MCALEESE

## *The Outsider*

# Mary McAleese

## The Outsider

An unauthorised biography

## Justine McCarthy

BLACKWATER PRESS

Editor
*Anna O'Donovan*

Design/Layout/Cover
*Liz Murphy*


ISBN
1 84131 441 2

© Justine McCarthy 1999


Produced in Ireland by
Blackwater Press
c/o Folens Publishers
Hibernian Industrial Estate,
Greenhills Road,
Tallaght, Dublin 24.

*For Bride McCarthy*

# Introduction

Mary McAleese did not assist me in researching this book. Nor did she give it her blessing – rather the opposite. For that, I am grateful. As a sceptic of authorised biography, I specifically did not seek her imprimatur.

To those who did help, thank you. More than 100 people provided interviews, advice, valuable insights and, above all, their time and patience. Some of them did not wish to be quoted or to have their part publicly acknowledged. In many cases, this was because the events recorded are still relatively fresh and sores have yet to heal. To avoid embarassing any of those people, I have decided it is safer not to name any names. You know who you are and I hope I have not let you down.

*Justine McCarthy*
*October 1999.*

# Contents

# 1

# Bridge of Sighs

THE CONCIERGE STEPPED OUT of the elevator and steadied the breakfast tray in his hands. Most of the guests had not yet begun to stir as he padded past their bedroom doors. Day would break in another hour, dappling Dublin Bay with its silvery light and the wave foam rippling onto the strand beneath the four-star Portmarnock Hotel & Golf Links.

Dermot Keenan made a final inspection of the tray he carried. The meal was modest: toasted brown bread, fruit salad and freshly-brewed coffee. A lanky, boyish Dubliner with a native charm, he had been elected the night before to deliver this morning's VIP room service. He felt honoured to have been chosen; a bit player in history, memorising his lines. Three words that would herald a new dawn.

Stopping outside room 307, he knocked on the door. It opened to reveal a tall, slim, bleary-eyed woman. The concierge guessed she was not long awake. The tell-tale signs of sleep were everywhere. The drawn curtains, the stifled yawn, the towelling robe that swaddled her. He marvelled at her calm as he set the breakfast tray down and turned to greet her.

'Good morning, President,' he grinned, mentally chalking up the moment. One day, he promised himself, he would tell his grandchildren how he had been the first person to address her as President on the day she was installed as the eighth incumbent of Ireland's highest office.

The previous night, he and several of his colleagues had spent more than an hour in the bar with the McAleese family, chatting easily and nursing soft drinks. A thank-you gesture by the President-elect. The hotel had been her home-from-home for three weeks, once the nerve-centre for the climax of her election campaign and a refuge from the bruising political battle for non-political office. It had been her sanctuary since she and her husband, Martin, vacated the apartment they owned in the affluent embassy belt of Ballsbridge a week before polling day. She had eschewed the two luxury suites in the adjoining nineteenth-century home of the Jameson whiskey distillery family, choosing instead one of the £225-a-night executive rooms in the modern extension looking onto Portmarnock Beach and Ireland's Eye and, beyond, to the Hill of Howth.

The view from her bedroom window reminded her of her home in Rostrevor, she had told the hotel manager, Shane Cookman, a 35-year-old Donegal man from Raphoe on the Derry border. A place, like herself, straddling history.

On this auspicious morning, as she poured her breakfast coffee in room 307, Mary McAleese existed in a virtual no-man's land. Less than a two-hour drive from the border and her own hinterland with its bloody history, she prepared to make the 12-mile journey to Dublin Castle as incoming first citizen of a country which had denied her a vote in her own election as president. Once ensconced there, she would have to seek permission from the government whenever she wished to return to the postcard-pretty village in Northern Ireland that she called home. Despite the hardships, she had single-mindedly set out to land the plum position in the Phoenix Park, prepared to take a drop in income for the £112,273-a-year president's emolument.

Since her victory at the polls 12 days earlier, she had worked on her inauguration speech, tapping out the words on a laptop in the room next-door, number 306, which the hotel had converted into an office with a bank of telephones and fax machines. Her predecessor in Áras an Uachtaráin, Mary Robinson, had entranced the nation seven years earlier by quoting Paul Durcan poetry and inviting the global diaspora to come dance with her in Ireland. Robinson, now the United Nations High Commissioner for Human Rights in Geneva, had gone on to become one of the most popular heads of state in the world; a class act her successor had begged to follow. The two women had worked together in Trinity College more than a decade earlier and their paths had criss-crossed over the years, sometimes on the same side, more often than not on opposite sides of the political fence.

Mary McAleese had already been dubbed Mary Mark II, a disparaging yellow-pack label weighted with cynicism and coined by a gallery of commentators who viewed her election candidacy as one of breath-taking opportunism. That did not bother her unduly. She had often been accused of the uniquely female sin of ambition in her career and, besides, her victory at the polls had been emphatic. Still, as a woman and an academic lawyer, she would have to prove herself even more worthy of her new-found position than had the mould-breaking Mary Robinson whose gender and legal career had copperfastened her status as an icon.

Because she shared the female gender, a christian name, and a legal career with her predecessor, Mary McAleese knew that she would have to carve out her own distinct precedents to signal a new presidency. And so, she had written in her speech of her delight in being the first person from Ulster to take up residency in Áras an Uachtaráin. Looking out at the Irish Sea beyond her window, she had composed her new job description as that of a bridge builder, someone who would span the gulf between the past and the future, the violence of old and the peace to come, the North and the South.

The gargantuan leap she was about to take was littered with ironies. Here she sat in this slumbering seaside hotel, the former Mary Patricia Leneghan from north Belfast, now, at the age of 46 and one of the most successful Northern Ireland nationalists of her generation, about to embark on a prodigal homecoming to a city where she had previously found life to be 'a shocking experience'.

She was not impervious to the hostility within the capital's intelligentsia who had branded her a social outcast, depicting her as a crypto-terrorist and the bishops' tout. Even her accent had grated on their sensitivities. Nor was she immune to the suspicions she aroused at several levels of the establishment. The post-Catholic liberal wing viewed her as a mouthpiece for the institutional Roman Catholic Church, unaware that some of her harshest critics were to be found among the clergy and even the hierarchy. The media, which had once ousted her from its jealously-guarded ranks, still bristled after its tetchy encounter with her on the election campaign trail. Sections of the body politic fretted that her elevation could alienate Northern Ireland's unionists at a crucial, delicate juncture in the progress to peace. Yet, she was aware that her election – even as it was being welcomed by most Northern nationalists as affirmation of their kinship with the south – would not sit so easily with some of their civic leaders back home.

There was no time to ponder the past now though. By 7.30am, the hotel room she shared with Martin was invaded by a battalion of assistants. Her wardrobe adviser, Helen Cody, a sultry beauty who had once been engaged to marry the son of Conor Cruise O'Brien, the man Mary McAleese blamed substantially for one of the most miserable periods of her life, arrived to oversee the final fitting of the pewter velvet gown and evening coat she would wear to that night's banquet. Its designer, Mary Gregory, had worked through the weekend to finish the outfit, the shimmering coat-lining imprinted with the Christopher Logue poem she would recite in her inauguration speech:

> Apollinare said: 'Come to the edge'.
> 'It's too high'.
> Apollinare said: 'Come to the edge'.
> 'We might fall'.
> 'Come to the edge'.
> And they came.
> And he pushed them.
> And they flew.

A second dress designer, Miriam Mone, carefully removed the wrapping off another outfit, the fabric having been specially flown in from Germany to create the caramel velvet suit and flowing cashmere coat which would be the insignia of her inauguration at Dublin Castle.

By the time the rest of the hotel guests had made their way downstairs for breakfast, a dozen people were crammed into the McAleeses' room. The woman who had been her media guru on the campaign trail and whom she had chosen to be her special adviser, Eileen Gleeson, talked rapidly on her mobile phone, fine-tuning the precision timing of the inauguration ceremony. Mary

Bruton from Reds hair salon in Dublin applied the president-elect's make-up and teased her newly tawnied hair into a wispy fringe. Top-ranking garda detectives came and went, speaking hurriedly into tiny mouthpieces. At one stage, Justin McAleese, one of the 12-year-old twins, barrelled into the room to tell his mother excitedly about the cavalcade of gleaming garda motorbikes waiting to escort her. His animation gladdened her. Only four days before, Martin had gone to collect their three children from their last day at school in Rostrevor to find Emma (14), Justin and Saramai (both 12), in floods of tears. Martin had tried to comfort the children. Dear solid, calm Martin, who had sacrificed so much for his wife's dreams. And to think she had nearly married someone else. How different her life would have been.

She seemed oblivious to the fuss all around her. Reading over her speech, fixing the cadences and nuances in her mind, obliging whenever a voice urged: turn round, lift your chin, head down... At last the attendants sighed their satisfaction. Their work done. Pleased with the elegant, radiant result.

'It was like the morning of a wedding,' remembered Helen Cody, 'when everybody is rushing around and the bride is the only unruffled person in the place. We were all calling her "President" that morning but she was unfazed. Serene. She was ready. This was what she'd worked for, and she was ready.'

She had checked into the hotel with Martin several weeks before as plain Mr and Mrs McAleese, now, as she left it for the last time, she found the elevator frozen in place, waiting to waft her down to the lobby, as elevators around the world would await her for the next seven years.

Downstairs, the staff had lined up on both sides of a red carpet unfurled for her departure. A child stepped forward and pressed a bunch of wild flowers into her hand. On the tarmac outside, the brass buttons of her aide-de-camp glinted in the chill November sunshine as he stood in ramrod military salute for the new Commander-in-Chief of the defence forces.

It was Armistice Day – Tuesday, November 11, 1997 – when Mary McAleese made the most significant journey of her life into the heart of Dublin, a city which had once cruelly rejected her. 'It will be my most profound privilege to be President of this beautiful, intriguing country,' she would tell the distinguished audience gathered in the castle's Throne Room. Yet she was a woman whose sense of displacement had been painfully underscored when she fled the heartbreak of her homeplace to a city she had always seen as her spiritual capital – only to find a more insidious tormentor there. The daughter of the ghetto was coming home, again. Coming home, this time, as the premier citizen of the Republic. The first among equals.

As the cavalcade swung into the Upper Yard at Dublin Castle, the old seat of British dominion, the cries of hundreds of children splintered the sunlit morning. 'Mary, Mary, Mary,' they screamed, before the Army Number One Band struck up 'The Star of the County Down'.

Home, at last.

Mary McAleese had arrived.

# 2

# The Worst of Times

THE SCREAMS PIERCED THE black winter evening. Roars of hatred threatened to drown them out, but the screams went on and on. They seemed to grow more piteous with every dull thud, the sound of something heavy hitting its target.

Inside the walls of number 657 on the Upper Crumlin Road, Belfast, 21-year-old Mary Leneghan listened with her parents and her younger siblings to the commotion outside their house. They dared not go out to help. Instead, they consoled one another that it would end soon; that it was just another flash of the street violence that had stalked their neighbourhood for the past three years. Ever since the Troubles had begun.

They went on listening. Waiting for the disturbance to move off. Eventually, they heard the sound of feet running away. The screams weakened, turning to muffled moans. Now they were joined by a scratching sound at the front door. Somebody was out there, desperate to get in. Mary, the eldest of the nine Leneghan children, went into the front hall and tentatively eased the door ajar. At first she did not recognise the bloodied bundle on the doorstep; not until the human shape crawled past her into the hallway. And collapsed.

'Oh, God, John,' she cried, kneeling down to wipe the blood from her brother's face. 'It's John!'

John Leneghan nearly died that day in 1972. He was rushed to hospital by ambulance. Doctors told his family he had suffered severe head injuries. They said he would be lucky to survive. Mary, his big sister, was heart-broken. There had always been a special bond between her and John. She, the first born. He, born a few years later, profoundly deaf. Now, a 16-year-old teenager on the threshold of life, he lay broken and lacerated in a hospital bed, close to death.

His sister's anguish turned to anger as John made a slow recovery over the next three weeks in hospital, regaining sufficient strength to tell his family what had happened. He had been on his way home from a club for the deaf in north Belfast when he was approached by three men wielding bottles and a heavy, blunt instrument he could not identify. The men had demanded to know if he was a Catholic or a Protestant, before battering him savagely and repeatedly cutting him with the bottles.

The attack was reported to the police, complete with eye-witness evidence. A neighbour had seen the whole thing, recognising one of the attackers, but nobody was ever prosecuted for the vicious assault, sowing the seeds of the lamentable legend in the Leneghan family that the attacker seen by their neighbour went on to murder another man. Afterwards, Mary admitted that she had wanted her brother's assailants 'lynched'.

John Leneghan survived. But the innocence of his family died that day. They knew they had been marked out. There could be no misunderstanding. This had been a direct attack on their doorstep. Their home was situated in one of those Belfast areas that would become known in time as the city's 'interfaces'. Sterile shorthand for a flash point, sandwiched between Protestant and Catholic strongholds, vulnerable to easy access and a quick getaway. The broad uphill sweep of the Crumlin Road was split down the centre. Here, Catholic and Protestant homes, solid semi-detached and stand-alone houses, faced one another in a tense undeclared war zone. But, while the Leneghans lived on the 'Catholic' side of the road, their house was situated on a corner site, adjoining Hesketh Road which led to the predominantly loyalist Glenbryn housing estate.

They were an easy target. That message was driven home to them the day their local newsagent was murdered.

Gerry Kelly was a 58-year-old married man with two grown up children. His daughter was married and lived away from north Belfast but his son was still at home, helping his father in the shop. In August 1972, the premises were badly damaged by a bomb. Father and son carried out repairs and re-opened for business, only to be bombed again in October. On Saturday, November 11, Gerry Kelly was in his shop, untying bundles of newspapers and joking with three local children who delivered the papers for him in the area. As the newsagent and the children chatted, two unmasked men walked in and killed Gerry Kelly, pumping six bullets into him. The gunmen ran from the shop followed by the fleeing, screaming children.

Gerry Kelly had been a friend of the Leneghans and they took his death hard. Within three weeks, however, it would be their turn.

It was a dank, wintry night. The family was at home, some watching television, others of the children poring over their homework. Suddenly, all hell broke loose. The noise was deafening. The Leneghans cowered together, behind the security screens they had recently fitted to their windows to protect them from petrol bombs. They put their hands over their ears, trying to block out the terrifying noise. The roars of men bent on destruction in their front garden. Glass shattering. Wood buckling and smashing. Gradually, they realised what was happening. A mob of between 30 and 40 men was tearing paving slabs out of the ground and hurling them at number 657.

Mary Leneghan, a law student in her third year at Queens University, ran to the telephone and called the police. Then she waited in the terrifying darkness with her family, watching their front door burst at the seams. 'I understood then what it meant to be petrified,' she recalled years later. 'I literally couldn't move.'

By the time the Royal Ulster Constabulary arrived at two o'clock in the morning, several hours after she had made the first of numerous phone calls for help, the mob had long gone. No one was ever charged with the attack.

In reply to questions put 27 years later, the RUC press office stated that, as only specific records are retained beyond a 10-year cut-off point, 'no means exist now of checking if the assaults (on John Leneghan and the house at 657 Crumlin Road) were reported'.

A month before the mob attack on their home, a bomb had exploded outside 'The Long Bar' in Leeson Street, off the Lower Falls, a pub owned by Mary's father, Paddy Leneghan. Passers-by had noticed four men sprinting from a Vauxhall Viva parked up the street from the pub. As the car slowly began to move forward, pedestrians on the street idly surmised that the handbrake must have been left off. When the car blew up at 5.30pm on October 7, 1972, it killed a 22-year-old mother of three small children, Olive McConnell, the sister of a friend of Mary's. She died in the ambulance, 10 minutes after a chunk of the exploding car struck her neck and broke it as she had been trying to gather up her little girl in the safety of her arms.

Paddy Leneghan was convinced the bomb had been intended for him or, at least, for his business. Grief and guilt over Olive McConnell's death overwhelmed him, plunging him into a state of near despair.

He found some solace in his faith. Paddy and Claire Leneghan were traditional, devout Catholics who had reared their large family to respect their inherited faith. On December 8, 1972, the entire family attended mass at Holy Cross Monastery on the Crumlin Road for the annual Feast of the Immaculate Conception. The monastery was an intrinsic part of life for Catholics in north Belfast. Its twin spires, a landmark. Its priests an exotic but familiar sight in their flowing black robes, the wooden crosses hanging around their necks, rosary beads swinging from black leather belts, open-toed sandals and the little birettas they used to wear on their heads.

In 1869, The Bishop of Down and Conor had invited the Passionist priests to take over the pastoral care of the 2,000 Catholics living in the linen mill houses here. By 1935, the Catholic population had more than trebled, with a substantial number living in the isolated enclave of Ardoyne. After the British Army tanks rolled into north Belfast on August 15, 1969 to quell the sectarian violence, the priests in the monastery, 20 of them in all, arranged with their parishioners that, if they ever came under attack, they would ring the church bell to sound the alarm.

'There isn't a family that hasn't had somebody killed or wounded or imprisoned here so there's an intimacy in a place like this,' explained Fr Myles Kavanagh, a Dubliner from Harolds Cross who came to Belfast in the early 1960s.

There was no time to ring the church bell on Friday, July 7, 1972 when a 1,000lb bomb exploded in the monastery grounds at midnight. Though nobody was hurt, the force of the explosion blew the stained glass windows out of the church and left a 10-foot wide crater inside the perimeter wall.

Five months later, the Leneghan family walked together down the road to Holy Cross, filling a pew in the middle of the church. It was two weeks to Christmas, and they were looking forward to it, hoping that the holiday would help dim the awful memories of the past year. A year that had started with the horror of Bloody Sunday on January 30 when 14 civilians were shot dead on the streets of Derry by the British Army's Parachute Regiment. For Mary Leneghan, it was the year her family's friend was murdered in what police described as 'a motiveless killing', her deaf brother had been twice assaulted in the space of two weeks, her home had been besieged and a friend's sister had died in an explosion outside her father's pub. As the year was drawing to its close, it had already secured its ignoble place in history as the worst year for fatalities in Northern Ireland's 30-year conflict. Exactly 470 people would have died violently by New Year's Eve – 322 citizens, 131 soldiers and 17 police officers. Little did the Leneghan family suspect, as they offered their responses to the mass in Holy Cross on that Feast of the Immaculate Conception, that this would be their last Christmas in north Belfast. By January, they too would have joined the ranks of the dispossessed.

Their fate was starkly evident when they walked back up the hill from Holy Cross after mass to find their home riddled with bullet holes. There were bullets embedded in the walls, the tables, the chairs and the mattresses on the beds. The windows were shattered; the doors splintered. Shards of glass carpeted the floor. Neighbours told the distraught family that, while they had been in church, two men had come and emptied a pair of machine guns into their house. Nearly 30 bullets were counted in all.

*The Irish News* ran the story on its front page the following Tuesday, not naming the family nor giving their address; a measure of the fear that gripped the community. The newspaper story quoted Paddy Leneghan anonymously.

'There are nine children in the family,' the father said. 'As far as the gunmen who attacked the house were concerned we were all inside. We were very lucky. Several of the family would undoubtedly have been killed had we been at home.'

This was ethnic-cleansing Irish-style. Official reports show that between August 1969 and February 1973, between 30,000 and 60,000 people, almost 12 per cent of the city's population, were forced out of their homes in Belfast. Of those, 80 per cent were Catholics. Eleven people of that 80 per cent statistic were the Leneghans from the Crumlin Road.

Twelve years after she fled her home with her mother, her father and her eight younger brothers and sisters, Mary Leneghan claimed in a media interview: 'Nothing was ever done about any of these incidents, although the names were well known to the police.'

Soon after the horrors of 1972, she would quit Belfast and Northern Ireland, sickened to her soul by the unremitting death and barbarity. Leaving behind her big, close-knit family to find peace elsewhere, only to find that the events of 1972 would come back to haunt her. How brutally her life had been upended. A life which had started with such promise.

# 3

# In The Beginning...

AS A CHILD, SHE had the kind of face artists paint on cherubs. Big, baby-blue eyes and a perfect rosebud mouth, framed by a shock of wavy blonde hair. Everybody said that little Mary Leneghan was a gorgeous wain. When she used to visit her godmother, Auntie Una, in her hair salon next door to Hales Fruit Shop, customers would crane their necks under the whirring hairdryers, declaring to God that the little sun-bronzed girl in her flouncy summer frock was the spitting image of Princess Anne.

They were easy-going times. The years before the Troubles and the tyranny of political correctness when it was still considered a great compliment to liken a Northern Ireland Catholic child to a member of the English royal family. In the Catholic enclave of Ardoyne in north Belfast, where Mary Leneghan's maternal grandparents lived, people coped with the usual vagaries of life, sharing sorrow, laughter and solidarity like any normal community. Blissfully unaware of the decades of tragedy about to unfold.

But, beneath the surface, it was always simmering.

On the day Claire Leneghan gave birth to her first child, Wednesday, June 27, 1951, the political focus was on the blockade in far-off Korea and the increasing likelihood of war there. Eamon de Valera was the Taoiseach in the Republic of Ireland and Stormont the seat of government in the North. The Belfast Barmen's annual outing was to Dundalk that summer and Betty Grable was frolicking with Victor Mature in *Wabash Avenue* at the Imperial Cinema.

The veneer of normality had already begun to lose its lustre, however. On the day that Mary Patricia Leneghan came into the world, *The Irish News*, Northern Ireland's biggest-selling nationalist newspaper, reported the introduction of a 30 per cent tax on the North's betting pools. The editorial thundered against the 'Sabbatarian' measure in the 'Orange supremacist State', warning that the North's only voluntary hospital, 'that great Catholic institution, the Mater Infirmorum Hospital' would be penalised for running 'a very successful pool'.

They were still the best of times for Claire and Paddy Leneghan, enthralled by every burp and gurgle of their infant child at home in 61 Ladbrook Drive, on the outskirts of Ardoyne. Paddy Leneghan had come north to Belfast to find work at the age of 14, leaving his family's 15-acre farm holding in County Roscommon to live in digs with his aunt, his mother's sister, Nora McDruary, on the Crumlin Road. Miss McDruary ran a hairdressing business from her house with the help of an exceptionally pretty Ardoyne girl called Claire McManus.

Both of Claire's parents, Catherine and John McManus, hailed from Dromara, County Down. When they married they moved to Maghera in Derry, where nine of their ten children were born, including the sixth child, Claire. The tenth and last, Anne, was born in Belfast, when the family settled there permanently. The children's father, who had been a breadman in Maghera, worked sporadically in Scotland, before finally turning his love of gardening into a modestly profitable living. Long after his death, residents in Ardoyne remembered John McManus by the herbaceous borders and floral rockeries he had planted in their gardens.

When Paddy Leneghan met Claire McManus in Nora McDruary's hair salon, the darkly handsome Roscommon barman was bewitched.

As they exchanged solemn vows on their wedding day, he vowed too to give his young bride a good life. He had seen his own mother continually struggle against the privation thrown up by the stony Roscommon soil, supplemented by her husband's meagre earnings as a labourer with the county council. She had waved goodbye to her only daughter and her three sons as, one by one, they left home in search of something better.

Paddy Leneghan resolved that his wife would want for nothing. He found work with the east Belfast drinks company, RP Culley

Ltd, selling wine and spirits to pubs in the west of the city. As his earnings increased, his growing family moved into bigger houses: from Ladbrook Drive, to Balholm Drive, to Mountainview Gardens, to Woodvale Road until, finally, they arrived in the Crumlin Road in the 1960s, to the house at number 657, down the hill from the courthouse.

It was a halcyon childhood for Mary, part of a huge extended family who would provide her with 59 first cousins on her mother's side alone. Her McManus grandparents' house in Ardoyne's Duneden Park was like a second home and there were regular holidays back in her father's homeplace at Croghan, a few miles inside the Roscommon county border from the picturesque Carrick-on-Shannon.

She remembered her Granda Leneghan as 'a deeply religious man but a strong adherent of the school of lamentation and martyrdom'. In her book, *Reconciled Being: Love In Chaos*, published in 1997, she wrote: 'The world was always miserable for him. He was the sole martyr who had to put up with it. He was afflicted especially by the fact that his son, my father, had gone off to the "black North", married there and had children whose credentials as Catholics would always be suspect because of their proximity to those of the other persuasion.'

Mary Leneghan's was not the typical working-class lifestyle one might expect of a child who, looking back on it in adulthood, has tended to depict her family as a sometimes impecunious, embattled clan. While the name of Ardoyne became a byword for strife in the 1970s, it is technically incorrect to say that she spent the early years of her life there. Her family, in fact, lived on the fringes and, by the time most of the children were born, they were part of the new Catholic middle class which largely comprised publicans, bookmakers and undertakers. Yet she was born into a distinct Ardoyne culture, spawned by the area's religious and socio-political isolation at a time when members of her Church were treated as second-class citizens by the Protestant-governed statelet.

As a young girl, Mary used to go to Ardoyne to visit her grandparents or to attend McAleers School of Irish Dancing. On Saturdays, she swam at Peter's Hill Public Baths and played badminton in Holyrood Hall or Woodvale Tennis Club, near the home of two of her closest friends, brothers Myles and Tony O'Reilly. There were Sunday ice-creams in Pat Collins' Castle Creamery and teenage meetings with her pals in Freddy Fusco's chip shop. Her father owned a car, unlike most of her friends' fathers, and visitors often called to the house on Crumlin Road for the luxury of watching television on one of the rare sets in the neighbourhood. There were family holidays too, other than in Roscommon, like that in 1961 when 10-year-old Mary Leneghan won a talent contest for singing at Butlins Holiday Camp.

Though she had been called a 'Fenian' for the first time at the age of six, the burgeoning conflict was remote from her life. One of her favourite annual activities was collecting planks of wood and old mattresses with her Protestant and Catholic friends for the eve of The Twelfth bonfire commemorating the routing by King William of Orange of the Jacobites at the Battle of the Boyne in 1690, its legacy combusting nearly 300 years later in Northern Ireland's civil war.

At the end of an uneventful primary education in the Convent of Mercy, then housed in the grounds of the Mater Hospital on Crumlin Road, Mary Leneghan passed her 11-plus exams, qualifying for a much-coveted scholarship to grammar school. Only pupils of grammar schools had any hope of reaching third-level education under Northern Ireland's education system and many parents viewed it as an escape hatch for their children from the straitjacket of their predestined circumstances. She started at St Dominic's High School on the Falls Road in the autumn of 1962, taking the direct bus from Crumlin Road, proudly wearing her new maroon uniform with its 'Veritas' ('Truth') school crest. (In the years to come, school authorities in the city would grant their pupils special dispensation to remove their school badges to protect them against sectarian attacks). The imposing redbrick convent, founded in 1870 and standing opposite the Royal Belfast Hospital for Sick Children, was to have a profound effect on her development. The Dominican nuns, who also ran Belfast's other prestigious Catholic girls' school at Fort William, promoted a genteel but radical ethos, teaching its charges to respect their own intelligence. This was a time when children were expected to be seen rather than heard and women were more accustomed to saying 'I feel' than 'I think'. In short, Dominican girls were taught to think for themselves.

It was a discipline embraced by the young Mary Leneghan. Asked in history class one day, 'Where are the British Isles?', she replied: 'Somewhere between Europe and Ireland.' The choices that awaited her when she would leave St Dominic's were spectacularly embodied by two of her classmates. Like Mary Leneghan, both would make their mark on society. One, a young girl named Anna Carraher, would go on to become head of broadcasting with the BBC in Northern Ireland. The name of the other girl would become part of the history of the Troubles. She was Doloures Price who, with her sister, Marian, was convicted of a car bombing in London and went on hunger-strike in 1973 for the right to serve out their sentences in Ireland. The sisters' fast, which was interrupted by forced feeding, would last for more than 200 days.

Despite her sharp-witted description of the British Isles, Mary Leneghan never looked likely to choose the same path as Doloures Price. While she was not academically outstanding, she had a keen intelligence and a hunger for knowledge, immersing herself in her three favourite school subjects – English, History and Spanish. She was made school prefect and captain of the debating team. A familiar figure in the St Dominic's chapel between classes, she founded the school's first conference of the Society of St Vincent de Paul.

'As the eldest,' she once said, 'a lot of ambition rests on you, a lot of other people's ambition rests on you.' But, even at that age, her own ambition required little encouragement. She had decided to be a lawyer, a noble but unlikely profession in those times for someone with two obvious handicaps – she was female, and she was the child of a labourers' lineage. Two facts forcefully impressed upon her by her Dublin-born parish priest on the Crumlin Road. Mary announced her intention one evening while the cleric was enjoying her father's hospitality and his baby Powers whiskey in the house. Appalled by her lofty notions, the cleric spluttered indignantly: 'You can't because you're a woman; you can't because no one belonging to you is in the law.' With that, her mother, gentle, quiet-spoken Claire who had assiduously tutored her children to respect – if not revere – the clergy, propelled the priest to the front door and yelled: 'You – out!' Then, turning to her first-born, she cautioned: 'And you – ignore him!'

One of Claire Leneghan's favourite sayings was that 'sometimes the worst thing that can happen is for the Lord to answer your prayers'. In 1969, at the age of 17, it looked as if her daughter need have no fear of having her wish granted; of going to university to study law. As she prepared to sit her crucial A-level exams other pressures associated with being the eldest were beginning to bear down on her. By now, she had three sisters and four brothers. John, because of his deafness, had special needs. Another brother, Damien, would have a cancerous tumour removed from his face, requiring painful reconstructive surgery. The last of the Leneghans was born in 1969, a fifth son given the name Clement.

Paddy Leneghan had bought the pub in Leeson Street and was working hard to make it a success. Competition for business was fierce in the Lower Falls, with nearly 20 pubs fighting for custom in an area measuring one square mile. With her mother weakened by childbirth and its consequent broken nights, it fell to Mary to mind the baby when she was home from school and to get her other siblings up and out of the house in the mornings. She filled a surrogate matriarchal role in the household, particularly for her three sisters – Claire, Kate and Nora. In St Dominic's, Mary's English teacher, Miss May O'Friel, an aunt of Anna Carraher, noticed the girl's pallor of exhaustion. She questioned her and, upon discovering the adverse circumstances at home, determined to help her in so far as she could. From that day on, Mary was driven to school every morning by the kindly Miss O'Friel in her battered Morris Minor.

She sat her A-level exams in June, a fortnight before her 18th birthday. This was an era when the 21st birthday was recognised as a young person's coming-of-age, marked by the handing over of the front-door key. Instead, it was her 18th birthday that heralded the end of innocence for Mary Leneghan. The celebrations were dampened by the death, five days earlier, of her favourite priest at Holy Cross Monastery. County Meath-born Fr Justin Coyne had arrived in Ardoyne in 1961. A history teacher who instructed Passionist seminarians, he knew every child in the district by name. On June 22, 1969, he was found dead in his bed having suffered a brain haemorrhage.

Mary Leneghan had adored Fr Justin. His sudden death was the first real bereavement in her life. It was to be the first of many, and one of the most peaceful. The bloody conflict she would later dub 'the slow-burning civil war' was about to be unleashed. On August 15, the British Army arrived on the streets of Belfast.

The troops were initially welcomed by Northern Catholics, the women showering them with bearhugs and kisses, tea and cakes, believing the young English soldiers to be their saviours. It was not to last.

'From the first day of the Troubles I turned my face away from taking any part,' Mary told the Belfast journalist, Fionnuala O'Connor, in her book, *In Search of a State: Catholics in Northern Ireland*, published in 1993. 'I watched the B Specials walk up the Crumlin Road with a Protestant crowd intent on burning out Catholic homes. And, having seen these forces of law and order behaving in an extraordinary, totally unacceptable way, I turned my face against that and set out to become a lawyer, not a revolutionary...'

Belfast was teetering on the brink of civil turmoil when Mary Leneghan received formal notification that she had passed her A-levels in English, History and Spanish, qualifying for a place in the law school at Queens University – the first in her family to do so. She was jubilant. To celebrate, the new parish priest at Holy Cross Monastery, Fr Honoris, an awesome preacher with a booming voice, took her out to dinner with another young student called Eileen Gilmartin. The trio dined in style at the Knocknagoney Hotel in Belfast's leafy, peaceful eastern suburbs. But the scene that greeted them when they returned home to the Crumlin Road could not have been a starker contrast. Members of the notorious B Specials were running rampant. The place was in uproar. It presented the young Mary with her moment of truth – a truth she would struggle with for the rest of her life.

'We came back that night and our lives had changed utterly,' she told *The Irish Times* in an interview 30 years later. 'The men were out with hurleys and marbles trying to emulate the sound of gunfire to fight off what was a uniformed police force attacking Catholic houses. I was 18 and I was angry. I went into the house to get milk bottles to throw.'

Her father followed her into the house. Paddy Leneghan could see his daughter's rage seething as he watched her frantically search the kitchen for useful missiles. 'I did not rear a rebel,' his clear, stern voice cut through her fury. That, she said afterwards, was the instant she consciously rejected the compulsion to join the fight.

The tests of that dictum came fast and furious. Mayhem piled upon mayhem. Kidnappings, hijackings, gang beatings, shootings, bombings and killings took a stranglehold on the city. The Crumlin Road would be set aflame. The IRA was to emerge as a paramilitary force set to become one of the most feared in the world. Churches were attacked. Men were pistol-whipped. Catholic girls who dated policemen or soldiers were tarred and feathered and left tied to lamp-posts in ritualistic public humiliation. Internment was introduced, giving license for widespread, indiscriminate arrests, mainly of Catholic fathers, sons and brothers whose womenfolk often did not know where they were being held. In the 24 years between 1969 and 1993, 600 people would die in Ardoyne, while north Belfast would account for one-third of all the deaths in the Troubles.

The GAA club grounds of the Ardoyne Kickhams, where Mary Leneghan played unremarkable camogie as a girl, would become something of a shrine to the unfolding events. The club, located just 400 yards from where the Ulster Defence Association was founded in the Shankill, would lose more than 20 of its members – the equivalent of an entire squad. The first man to die was Frank Corr. He was the secretary of South Antrim GAA and a county committee member. Aged in his late 40s, he had served the Ardoyne Kickhams for 37 years. At 11.30 one night in 1972, after failing to return home from a match, Frank Corr was found dead in the boot of his burning Austin Cambridge car, a bullet wound in his head. The charred body of another man lay in the back seat.

In the Catholic-dominated Falls, the street where Paddy Leneghan ran his pub became known as 'a gunny street' for the number of gun battles fought there. Situated beside Kelly & McCartan bookmakers in the artisan terrace of Leeson Street, the Long Bar – so called because of its narrow bar-room extending onto Cyprus Street at the back – acquired a reputation as the chief drinking haunt of the Official IRA. Paddy Leneghan had no truck with the men of violence. He was respected in the area, an affable Southerner who ran a convivial public house. One of his best friends was Jim Sullivan, chairman of the Citizens Defence Committee who would become a Workers Party councillor for West Belfast. Other associates of Jim Sullivan who frequented the pub were the future Workers Party councillor, Dessie O'Hagan, and Liam McMillan, OC of the Official IRA who would be shot dead by the INLA, a splinter republican paramilitary group aligned with the Irish Republican Socialist Party.

The upstairs rooms above the pub were routinely used for separate meetings by the GAA, the Workers Party and the Civil Rights Movement.

Leeson Street was a dangerous place where British Army tanks, giant rolls of barbed wire, tear gas and the search lights of military helicopters became a part of life. Loyalists attempted to bomb the Bush Bar, 75 yards down the street from Paddy Leneghan's pub, and, when they failed, returned to machine gun the premises.

Trouble flared frequently in the street. On March 5, 1971, soldiers swooped on the Long Bar, looking for two Sandy Row men who had been kidnapped at gunpoint the night before. Local women banged their bin lids to warn of the soldiers' advance but several men were rounded up and taken away. The troops returned later that day, this time dressed in riot gear. Stones and bin lids were thrown at the army Land Rovers and lorries. The soldiers fired rubber bullets at the rioters. A city bus, hijacked earlier in Grosvenor Road, was placed across the street, about 50 yards from the Long Bar, forming a barricade.

Four months later, at eight o'clock on the night of July 21, troops came under fire after carrying out a search of the Long Bar. Nothing had been found. A crowd of about 60 lobbed stones at the soldiers, who responded by firing rubber bullets. A nail bomb was thrown and, according to a report of the incident in *The Belfast Telegraph*, three shots were fired. A woman, Mrs Bridget McGaughey of Abercorn Street North, was wounded when a .45 bullet struck her in the shoulder.

For Paddy Leneghan, it culminated a year later in the fatal car bomb explosion outside his pub when 22-year-old Olive McConnell lost her life. Years later, his eldest daughter – whom customers remembered occasionally seeing working behind the bar – would describe the bomb as having been 'designed to kill him'.

She would also claim that her father had lost his business as a result. 'We were quite poor during those years (after the bomb exploded outside the pub and the family was forced to evacuate the house at 657 Crumlin Road). It was an uncertain time.'

In fact, the damage to the Long Bar was not extensive. Paddy Leneghan sold it in 1973 to James O'Hare who ran a general provisions shop on the Falls Road. The pub continued trading into the 1980s when it was demolished for the total redevelopment of Leeson Street. Meanwhile, in July 1971, Paddy had bought a long lease on a second pub, the Red Barn in the city centre's Rosemary Street, in partnership with Thomas F Hunt. The pair let the property to John J McKenna, proprietor of the Centre Hall Bar on the Falls Road. On November 1, 1974, it too was damaged by an explosion after a 15-minute warning was given for a 20lb parcel bomb. Four years later, Paddy sold his share of the superior interest in the lease to his partner, Tom Hunt.

'My parents never, ever reacted angrily,' Mary recalled in an interview with *The Irish News*. 'It is a source of amazement to me now. They never got cross. They were hurt. They were really, really hurt. And they were baffled. A lot of the time they were just confused, but they were never, ever angry.'

After the machine-gun attack on their home in December 1972, the Leneghan family was split up, the children scattered to the homes of aunts and uncles. They were lucky. Most of their neighbours who had to flee could only find accommodation in a local school which had been adapted as a makeshift refugee centre. In the aftermath of the collapse of the Stormont government, the parliament of Westminster provided for a new fund known as SPED, the Scheme Purchase of Evacuated Dwellings, to assist people who had been intimidated out of their homes. Under the scheme, the Northern Ireland Housing Executive was to act as a neutral estate agent, buying houses from their fleeing owners at the market value, on receipt of written verification from the RUC. Over the years, the Housing Executive's average annual budget for the scheme worked out at about £3 million, rising to a phenomenal £9 million in 1998.

Two years before the Leneghan family home was attacked on the Crumlin Road, number 657 had been valued at £7,000. Saddled with a mortgage and forced to shell out rent money on alternative accommodation, Paddy Leneghan was scornful of an offer he considered derisory made by the Housing Executive for the Crumlin Road house. He held out until March 1975 when he finally sold the house to the agency.

In early 1973, he had moved his family across the city to the Falls, renting a house for two years from an order of nuns in Fruithill Park, a quiet residential road with a prosperous ambience connecting the Glen Road to Andersonstown. The Leneghans lived at number 20, formerly owned by a wealthy family of fruit importers, the Benners, and boasting a special cachet for local children who believed a snake had once escaped in the big garden. Across the road from number 20 lived Anna McCoy, the doyenne of Irish dancing in Belfast, who shared a house with her bachelor brother. Other neighbours included Brian Feeney, a prominent SDLP politician, and Bríd Brennan, the daughter of a Falls Road publican who would win a Tony Award in the 1990s for her acting role in Brian Friel's play, 'Dancing At Luaghnasa', on Broadway.

'The day we moved in, a crowd of teenagers broke 19 windows,' Mary Leneghan told Fionnuala O'Connor many years later. Her memory of that time appears faulty however. 'On the next day, the army came into the house,' she continued,' and searched the garden and found the tailfin of a rocket launcher. Thanks be to God they found it before some of our kids did – but, unfortunately, they had their photographs taken holding the tailfin. It exploded, one of them was killed and the other lost his sight.'

The incident she described is not recorded by any of Northern Ireland's newspapers. Nor does the RUC have any record of it. It may be that she was confusing it with an incident of similar detail but one which could not have occurred while the Leneghans were living in the Falls.

A 33-year-old colour sergeant, Stewart Middlemas, of the 1st Battalion, King's Own Scottish Borderers, died as he inspected the tailfin of a 3.5-inch rocket which had been found in Fruithill Park. *The Irish News* reported that two other soldiers were injured, one losing his eyes, when the rocket exploded at Fort Monagh army post in Andersonstown. The RUC press office confirmed this incident, adding that the booby-trapped rocket part exploded in the army camp at approximately 2.45 a.m. on December 10, 1972. That was at least a month before the Leneghans moved to Fruithill Park and was, in fact, less than 48 hours after their home on the Crumlin Road was attacked.

After two years in Fruithill Park, the Leneghans settled in the charming County Down seaside village of Rostrevor, living above Paddy's new pub, The Corner House. At one stage, he had considered buying a pub in Bray, County Wicklow, and moving back to the Republic he had left as a 14-year-old boy. But, when The Corner House came up for sale, it brought the family back to the home county of his wife's parents. The younger Leneghan children were sent to boarding school in nearby Newry so that 'they wouldn't be seduced into the language of hostility and bitterness'.

Mary Leneghan continued studying to be a lawyer at Queens University Belfast. She was undoubtedly scarred by what had happened to her family in that city, but she was determined not to be damaged by it. Those years had formed one of the foremost traits of her character. She once described it as '... my sense of who I was as a person was shaped by the stereotypes and pigeon-holing of people as Catholic, nationalist. That's one of the reasons why all of my life I have resisted very strongly all attempts to place me into other people's handy and sometimes rather lazy labels and pigeonholes.'

For the rest of her life, that intellectual defiance would be her trademark. Some people would love her for it. But not everyone.

# 4

# The Marriage That Nearly Never Was

MARTIN MCALEESE ARRIVED AT university in October 1969 with a vague interest in physics and, he would recall years later, 'a growing curiosity about a young law student named Mary Leneghan'.

He was a clean-cut, serious young man, thin as a greyhound and mild by nature. The sort of fellow who might blend unnoticed into a bustling student campus where the radicals of the new civil rights movement were the pin-ups of the day. Queens University Belfast was a veritable incubator of such new generation luminaries as Bernadette Devlin, Eamon McCann, Michael Farrell, the actor Stephen Rea, Nick Ross, who would go on to present the BBC's *Crimewatch* and David Montgomery of Mirror Group Newspapers.

'As an Englishman, it seemed astonishing to me how backward Northern Ireland was, how out of touch with the 1960s, and how deeply religious discrimination was officially embedded,' remembered former deputy president of the Students Union, Nick Ross, when he returned 30 years later to make a television documentary on the Troubles.

The long-simmering discontent had exploded into civil turmoil a year previously, on October 5, 1968, when the RUC baton-charged a civil rights march in Derry. The general outrage provoked by television pictures of the police brutality coincided with the start of a new academic year, igniting the torch of reform fervour in Belfast's student politics. For the rest of the world, it was the era of flower power and the Beatles, Vietnam protest rallies, the Prague

Spring and student riots in Paris when President de Gaulle admitted he was 'never more frightened' in his life. In the remote European outpost of Northern Ireland, a deadly struggle had begun and Queens University's leafy groves in south Belfast would play a pivotal early role under the auspices of the Peoples Democracy, the student branch of the Civil Rights Movement.

All that was beyond the experience of most first-year students, however, dazzled by the redstone splendour of their new surroundings and the awesome maze of university life. Martin had opted for a physics degree with some as yet unformed notion that he might like to work as a dentist. Meanwhile, the object of his extracurricular interest, Mary Leneghan, was setting out to prove her old parish priest wrong by studying law at a time when the ranks of the North's inner bar consisted exclusively of men. Not alone would she have to study hard, she would also have to learn about the archaic customs and fraternities which dominated her chosen profession. It was just as well, therefore, that the path of true love promised to run exceedingly smooth. For Martin Philip McAleese was already a hero in the eyes of Mary Patricia Leneghan.

They had first met more than a year before, when the girls of St Dominics debating team trounced the boys of St Mary's Christian Brothers grammar school from Barrack Street at the convent on the Falls Road. One of the vanquished debaters from St Marys was Martin McAleese. He was impressed that evening by the fiery passion of the girls' 17-year-old captain and the way she unselfconsciously flicked her thick mane of dark blonde hair, dominating the hall with every fibre of her 5 foot 8½ inch stature. The two teenagers had much in common, both products of the Catholic tradition and living with their families in exposed areas of Belfast. Martin's home was in Albertbridge Road, a staunchly Protestant main route connecting the city to the eastern suburbs housing Stormont Castle and backing onto Belfast's docklands where his father, Charlie, worked in the Shorts aircraft factory. The company, which manufactured state-of-the-art planes for sale around the world, had an abysmal track record as a sectarian employer and, as the Protestant churches prohibited their flocks from working on the Sabbath, Shorts expected the minority Catholics among its workforce to cover on Sundays. For men like Charlie McAleese, the son of north Antrim farming stock, that meant a six-and-a-half-day working week and a home for his wife, Emma, their daughter and four sons in the heart of loyalist Belfast.

When Martin received an invitation to Mary Leneghan's 18th birthday party four months before they both started at Queens University, he was thrilled. She was equally chuffed when he accepted because, to her – a fanatical supporter of gaelic games – Martin McAleese was a glamorous figure. He had already cornered his own patch of history that summer when the GAA county board, in an unprecedented move, had him flown home from a temporary job in England to captain the Antrim Minors in a first-round match of the Ulster football championships.

The romance blossomed at Queens where Mary Leneghan quickly developed a reputation as the college's foremost GAA groupie. She would happily spend freezing winter evenings at Martin's O'Donovan Rossa Club on the Falls Road, or cheering him on from the sidelines at club matches where the pitches were knee-deep in mud and the changing facilities non-existent, the players often togging out behind the cover of overgrown hedges. One of her proudest memories of those days was travelling by hired bus to University College Dublin's sports fields at Belfield in 1970. Martin was playing at right full-forward for Queens, roared on by his girlfriend in the terraces, an incongruous sight in a black velvet maxi coat and a white fur hat, finished off with a black-and-white frilly umbrella. When a UCD player kicked Martin in the groin and no penalty was given, his incensed girlfriend raced onto the pitch brandishing her brolly to remonstrate with the referee. The crowd cheered on the dervish in swirling black velvet and a blizzard of white fur until she was unceremoniously escorted off the field by two burly officials. Afterwards, *en route* back to Belfast in the minibus, Mary Leneghan was unanimously voted Man of the Match.

However, she was to miss one of Martin's finest hours when her parents prohibited her from travelling to Galway in 1971 for the final of the Sigerson Cup which Queens University won that year for only the third time. Martin McAleese, wearing the number 13 jersey, scored two points to pull off the victory at Pearse Stadium. At the celebration dinner that night in the Great Southern Hotel in Eyre Square, the ecstatic Queens right forward was seen dancing an approximation of a waltz with a member of the defeated team from University College Cork, a giant of a Kerryman called Moss Keane who would become a lifelong friend and a colossus of Irish international rugby.

Queens' Roman Catholic chaplain, Fr Ambrose McCauley, who had travelled with the team to Galway, phoned Mary from the hotel to relay the final score, light-heartedly assuring her that he was keeping an eye on Martin. She need not have worried, however, for Martin McAleese only had eyes for one girl. And, if she needed proof, she got it – when he presented her with his hard-won Sigerson medal suspended from a fine gold neck chain.

But those carefree days were about to end. On Monday, January 31 1972, the south Belfast campus of Queens University was shrouded in stunned grief. It was the day after Bloody Sunday. The student populace was bewildered by the deaths of 14 people in Derry the day before. The Students Union, which tended to attract activists from the largely Catholic areas west of the River Bann, called a halt to lectures for the day. But the gesture of mourning went unheeded by many of the teaching staff. Among them was Mary's lecturer in equity and land law, 27-year-old David Trimble, a rising star in the college firmament and soon to be deputy leader of William Craig's Vanguard Unionist Progressive Party.

Martin McAleese had been in Blackpool working at a summer job in his second year at Queens when the Troubles came crashing into his life. It was the night of August 9, 1971, the day internment was introduced in Northern Ireland, when 'a mob came and just burnt us out'. Charlie and Emma McAleese gathered up as much of their belongings as they could fit into three suitcases and fled with their other four children. Among the possessions they were forced to leave behind were the scorched remains of their family photograph albums.

The McAleeses moved to Rathcoole which was set to become the North's biggest public housing estate. Though traditionally a Catholic stronghold, its social demography was undergoing profound change even then as residents of the Protestant Shankill Road were resettled there by policy of the Stormont government. Among the Catholic families already moving out was that of Bobby Sands, the Provisional IRA man who would die a decade later on hunger-strike in Long Kesh jail. During the McAleeses' first week in Rathcoole, Martin's youngest brother was attacked near their new home by a loyalist gang who ghoulishly carved the letters, UVF, on his arm with a glass.

When Mary's home was raked with gunfire the following year and her brother was hanging to life by a thread after being viciously assaulted, Martin was there to comfort her. Their friends saw the couple as kindred spirits with similar orthodox Catholic backgrounds and a shared love of sport; her zeal tempered by his caution. They were opposite sides of the one coin: he the calm, gentle one; she the forthright, impassioned flip-side. 'Whenever Mary was getting worked up over something, Martin would tease her to bring her back down to earth,' recalled one of those friends. Both sets of parents approved of the relationship. The Leneghans and the McAleeses were rearing their families on the same principles of Catholic moral probity and they were satisfied to see that ethos reflected in the young couple.

Six months after the Leneghans fled the Crumlin Road, Mary received her honours degree parchment, to the strains of the RUC band playing 'God Save The Queen' in the university's Whitla Hall, dedicated to the memory of a long-dead slave trader. Her graduation was a proud day for the enormous extended family as they celebrated the first of their fold to secure a university education. She had already arranged to devil for a junior barrister for the next six months, the final on-the-job pupilage scheme she would have to complete under the Inn of Court before ultimately acquiring her certificate to practise. Only the previous December, another St Dominics old girl, Philomena Lucy Bateson, had penetrated the bastion by becoming the first woman admitted to the Northern Bar in more than 20 years. Mary Leneghan would be one of only three women who would be called to the Bar in 1974, including Ailish McDermott who would become the North's first woman Queen's Counsel.

Mary Leneghan was facing into adult life having achieved a seemingly impossible ambition but the dark clouds were already gathering, signalling the end of her uncomplicated childhood romance with Martin McAleese.

On graduation, Martin had decided that physics was not for him after all and opted to embark on an accountancy apprenticeship. He moved to Dublin where he joined the country's biggest practice, Stokes Kennedy Crowley, as an articled clerk to the firm's senior partner, Laurence Crowley. The physical distance soon put a strain on his relationship with Mary, no longer an everyday part of his life. Martin shared what he later called 'a grotty flat' in Grosvenor Road on Dublin's southside with a young Derry footballer, Seamus Mullin. In the upstairs flat of the same building lived Moss Keane, Martin's dance partner of three years earlier. Along with other friends from Kerry who were studying accountancy with Martin, the flat-dwellers lived a bachelor lifestyle, usually meeting up in the Rathmines Inn or Madigans pub for a drink after work. 'Martin could fit into any scene,' Moss Keane remembered, but his memory of Mary is vaguer. 'She was kept at arm's length in those days.'

Back in Belfast, another man was falling in love with Mary Leneghan. His name was Rory McShane, better known to his friends as 'Red Rory'. An attractive shopkeeper's son from south Armagh, he was a few years older than Mary and Martin and infinitely more worldly. As president of the Students Union at Queens in 1968, he was a founding member of the Peoples Democracy and a member of the Civil Rights Movement's executive committee. In January 1972, he chaired the anti-internment rally in Derry the day 10,000 people marched to the anthem, 'We Shall Overcome', and which will forever be remembered as Bloody Sunday. In its aftermath, it was 'Red Rory' who organised a massive protest march through Newry the following weekend in response to the 14 killings in Derry by the British Army.

Rory McShane never met Mary Leneghan at Queens. He had graduated with a commerce degree the summer before she entered law school. He did however know her father, from the time he used to help broadcast Radio Free Belfast from one of the upstairs rooms of Paddy's pub, the Long Bar. Since then, he had taken a career sabbatical, stood as an Independent candidate in the North's Assembly elections, narrowly failing to take a seat, and returned to Queens to qualify as a solicitor in 1973.

That was how he came to meet her. Mary had finished devilling with Peter Smith whose practice mostly dealt with personal injury and civil litigation. She would only remain at the Bar for little more than a year. 'She was very able but not very interested in the prosaic day-to-day practise,' recalled her former master who became chairman of the South Belfast branch of the Ulster Unionists Party in the 1980s. 'She told me with a remarkable lack of rancour that her family had been intimidated out of their home. The legal world in Belfast would not have been an easy place for her then. There was an endemic gender problem.'

In her book, *Reconciled Being: Love In Chaos*, she recalled her acute discomfort in that environment when she felt like 'a pair of rosary beads in an Orange Lodge' on her first day in court. 'I had all the unimportant paraphernalia, law degree, practising certificate, wig, gown, law books, I even had a client, God help him, but there was a couple of absolutely essential things missing,' she wrote. 'The first thing of paramount importance that I lacked was any idea of where I should sit....Even my client, a regular it seemed on the court circuit, knew where he should sit. He threw himself into the public gallery with the air of a man who owned the place, but I, the advocate on whom he was relying to impress the court, hung awkwardly around the lawyers' bench in the hope that an obvious space would open up which I could claim.'

The young advocate Rory McShane saw representing her criminal and family law clients in Belfast's High Court was a far more assured practitioner than the timorous debutante she has described. It was the confident cross-examiner with the razor-sharp intellect that the newly-qualified solicitor fell in love with and planned to marry. Nearly a quarter-of-a-century later and reluctant to discuss their relationship, he remembered her as 'a brilliant cross-examiner with a very good analytical mind. She wasn't very comfortable in the Northern Ireland courtroom but I always thought she could have had a great career there,' he said.

Rory McShane could hardly have been more different to Mary's old flame. Smaller and stockier than Martin, he exuded an urbanity that was absent in the younger man. He enjoyed a high profile, particularly after the Assembly elections, and, though he was not classically handsome, he exuded a strong magnetism. Having had only one long-term boyfriend before this, Mary began what was a heady romance by her standards. By the time Martin McAleese returned from Dublin to work in Stokes Kennedy Crowley's newly opened Belfast office, his childhood sweetheart was engaged to another man. Her parents, who had come to consider Martin as one of their own, were disappointed. A relation, visiting the Leneghan house in Rostrevor one day, witnessed an embarrassing encounter when Mary walked in from the garden and her mother confronted her: 'Mary,' she asked, 'why don't you get back with Martin again?' What Claire Leneghan did not realise was that her daughter had been strolling in the garden with Rory McShane, who now stood before her.

A date was set for the wedding and the bride-to-be began making plans with her fiancé. Then, out of the blue, she dropped a bombshell in the summer of 1975. She told Rory she had been offered a job in Dublin, the Reid professorship in Trinity College's law school; an irresistible career opportunity for a 24-year-old woman. He begged her not to go, arguing that the distance of more than 100 miles between Dublin and his growing law practice in Newry would put too great a strain on their impending marriage. But she had made up her mind. She went.

'I left (Belfast) because I couldn't stand the oppression any more, the hypocrisy and the danger,' she stated in an interview with the *Irish Independent* in 1984.

It was the beginning of the end of her romance with Rory McShane. Though the engagement continued, it grew increasingly fraught, absence only serving to drive the two ambitious careerists apart. Ultimately, it was she who ended it, creating shock waves when, within weeks, she walked down the aisle with her first love. Despite a legend which subsequently flourished in the Northern Ireland Catholic establishment to the effect that she went ahead and married Martin in the same church on the same day she had planned to marry Rory McShane, her former fiancé denies its veracity. 'That would not be fair to Mary,' he said.

Mary Leneghan and Martin McAleese were married in the quaint Catholic church in Rostrevor on Tuesday March 9, 1976, the bride's sisters acting as her attendants and her best friend, Ailish Farrell, a future head of the College of Music in Dublin, playing the violin, accompanied by her sister on the church organ. It was a big wedding, too big to be accommodated, as initially planned, in The Golden Pheasant, a popular restaurant located between Ballynahinch and Lisburn and run by her old friends from Ardoyne, Tony and Myles O'Reilly. The brothers, with whom she had played as a child in Ardoyne, promised that, as soon as they had finished serving lunch at the restaurant, they would attend the wedding reception at the venue of second choice, the Ardmore Hotel in Newry, owned by Damien Scallon whose future wife, the singer Dana, would one day be the bride's rival for the presidency. The Ardmore was one of the North's most frequently bombed hotels in the Troubles and, in a later media interview, Mary would recall that it had been blown up yet again by the IRA the day after her wedding. In fact, the conjunction of the two events was slightly less dramatic. Armed and masked men planted a bomb in the hotel foyer a fortnight after the wedding, causing minor damage to the building.

During the dancing that evening, Mary remarked to her new husband that the O'Reillys had never turned up. She thought little more about it in the flurry of her wedding day, looking forward to their honeymoon in Kerry, at the three-star Aghadoe Heights Hotel with its wraparound views of Killarney's famous lakes, the McGillicuddy Reeks, Slea Head and the Dingle Penninsula.

As she and Martin prepared to leave Newry for an overnight at Sachs Hotel in Dublin, her mother fussed over her like the typical mother-of-the-bride. 'Enjoy yourselves,' Claire Leneghan told them. 'Don't be looking at the news or reading the papers. Just relax.'

More than two hours later when the happy couple arrived in their Dublin hotel room and, by reflex, switched on the television news, they discovered why Claire Leneghan had warned them against it. Scenes of devastation filled the television screen, two names leaping out at them – Myles and Tony O'Reilly. A reporter was telling how the bodies of the brothers, aged 41 and 43 and married to two sisters, had been found in the rubble of their restaurant that afternoon. Some of their staff spoke tearfully about three armed and masked loyalists bursting into the Golden Pheasant shortly before lunchtime, shooting the brothers three times and setting off two bombs within moments of each other.

The bride of just a few hours sat in a far-off Dublin hotel room on the first night of her honeymoon, and wept.

# 5

# South of the Border

SHE WAS A WIFE NOW. Wedded to her childhood sweetheart at the age of 24. Had she been the heroine of a soppy romantic novel, she would have been luxuriating in marital bliss, swapping recipes with kindly neighbours and sharing cosy, intimate evenings with her husband. But that was not to be. The honeymoon was over for Mrs Martin McAleese as she unpacked her trousseau alone in her bachelor flat.

Dublin, with its population of a million people, was one of Western Europe's least cosmopolitan capital cities. Its streets bore the shabbiness of a relatively young under-confident nation. The preservation of architectural heritage had yet to come into vogue, resulting in haphazard planning and the sprouting of ugly, utilitarian commercial buildings. Shop windows displayed fashions that were several months behind London and Paris, and young people were vanishing in the ebb tide of emigration. Yet a whiff of bohemianism clung obstinately to the air, around places like the Dandelion Market on St Stephens Green where arty types peddled their wares and a struggling band of teenagers, going by the bizarre name of U2, strummed their guitars for Saturday shoppers. To anyone freshly arrived from the provinces, Dublin was big, exciting and, in the case of Mary McAleese, it must have been very, very lonely.

Martin had returned to Belfast after their fortnight in Kerry to resume his work as an accountant with Stokes Kennedy Crowley while his wife remained in her Wellington Road flat in Ballsbridge. The only signs of her new status were the gold band she wore on her ring finger and the adjustment to Trinity College's academic calendar, now showing the incumbent of the Reid chair as Professor Mary McAleese.

'She had glasses and lots of nice hair,' according to fellow lecturer, David Norris. 'She wore polo necks and trousers that weren't quite as baggy as they became later on. She was humorous, very direct, very positive.'

Mary Robinson, the woman she succeeded as Reid Professor of Criminal Law, Criminology and Penology, was by now a controversial member of Seanad Éireann and a lecturer at the European Law Centre in Trinity. Though spun from a bluestocking west-of-Ireland tapestry which consisted of a French finishing school and an episcopal dispensation to 'read' law at Trinity when Catholics were barred from the university by the formidable Archbishop McQuaid of Dublin, Robinson was emerging as the *enfant terrible* of the decade. She was seen as a dangerous intellectual feminist, pilloried for her liberal Contraceptive Bill in the Oireachtas and the recipient of more hate mail than any other public figure of the time. She had joined the Irish Women's Liberation Movement on the famous Belfast train when the euphoric sisterhood returned to Dublin carrying armfuls of condoms, which were banned in the Republic.

'I got the impression that McAleese thought of Robinson as the daughter of privileged aristocracy while she saw herself as the daughter of the Belfast ghetto,' assumed a student of both women who subsequently joined the staff of Trinity. 'Robinson had got the contraceptives in but I felt that McAleese thought: "Big deal – I've been machine-gunned in the Ardoyne". She used to dress very severely and she spoke trenchantly, an acerbic lecturer well able to put students in their place. The image was of the tough woman. She was a regular on the debating circuit in college, at the Hist and the Law Society, and I remember her speaking at a debate about gunfire raking her home. Her attitude seemed to me to be "Brits out".'

Another law student who became a full-time lecturer in Trinity in 1982, Gerard Hogan, remembered her differently. 'I heard her give a lecture organised by the Irish Council for Civil Liberties on the treatment of accused persons in Northern Ireland,' he said. 'It was a very serious, professional lecture which was critical in a lawyerly way. I was very impressed by it. I remember thinking to myself listening to that lecture: This is the new version of Mary Robinson – and maybe even better.'

The Reid endowment was granted to Trinity College Dublin in the 1880s as a temporary junior lectureship with commensurate pay but specifically designated a professorship. In effect, it was a far less exalted position than the job title suggested. Mary Robinson occupied the chair at the age of 25, following Matt Russell, the lawyer who took early retirement from the Attorney General's office in 1995 after the political crisis precipitated by the criminal prosecution of Fr Brendan Smyth for paedophile offences. In March 1975, the university instigated proceedings in the High Court to amend the Reid trust, obtaining an order to establish the position as full time and permanent. So, when Mary McAleese arrived in Trinity at the age of 24 and one of only two women on the full-time staff of the law school, she was the first person to hold the job under the new terms.

Though the conditions of the Reid professorship allowed her to practise at the Irish bar, she never again returned to a courtroom in a professional capacity after her year in Belfast. She chose instead to throw her energy and passion into other challenges.

A sea change was underway in the Republic during the latter years of the 1970s. Though loyalists from the North had bombed Dublin and Monaghan the year before her arrival south of the border, the Republic was preoccupied with reinventing itself as a separate 26-county entity. Two years into its membership of the European Economic Community, it had begun looking to Europe for part of its identity against the backdrop of new wave history revisionism. Mary McAleese recalled the atmosphere that prevailed when she told Fionnuala O'Connor in 1993: 'I went there first when Conor Cruise O'Brien was in the ascendant – and, if ever there was a culture shock, Conor Cruise O'Brien was to me. Here was this extraordinarily arrogant man in the process of revising everything that I had known to be a given and a truth about Irish history – who set in motion a way of looking at Northern Ireland that we are only now beginning to grow up and grow out of.'

She expanded on the theme in a *Late Late Show* interview. 'When I first came to Dublin in '75 I came expressly because I had found Belfast to be a hateful place and to be a place that I could no longer emotionally live in,' she explained, 'and I moved to Dublin for that reason. I had this idea – a typical Northern Catholic nationalist – that Dublin would be a spiritual home and when I'd arrive here I'd be welcomed with open arms and it would be a wonderful place. Well anyway, I came here and I was pretty traumatised by events that had happened to us. We had lost our home, we had lost our family business and it had been a really very difficult time. You get down and you're full of this story and people say, "well, what are things like up there?" and, like a big eejit of an innocent, I would start reciting the story. And about three-quarters of the way through, you'd realise switch-off had already taken place, eyes glazed over. Do not want to know anymore.

'I think it was that people just didn't want to enter your pain. Because to enter your pain or to enter into the problem you are coming from meant having to give something of themselves and having to take some responsibility for it and people didn't want to do that.'

By the time Martin moved back to Dublin in 1977 to work as the financial controller of the Aer Lingus holiday subsidiaries, Blueskies and Enterprise Travel, his wife had been absorbed into the capital's radical milieu of civil rights campaigners.

It was a phase of her life that would later confound those of her critics wont to brand her a right-wing, doctrinaire Roman Catholic. By co-founding the Campaign for Homosexual Law Reform with her fellow Trinity academic, David Norris, she was aligning herself with one of the most audacious causes on the liberal agenda. The Ireland of the late 1970s was a fundamentally conservative country where contraception was restricted to married couples by Health Minister Charles Haughey, sex education was unheard of, and women – who had only recently been allowed return to work in the civil service after marriage – were treated by the system as their husbands' chattels. The abolition of an obscure nineteenth-century statute outlawing homosexual lovemaking was way down the priorities list of even the most ardent reformers.

The Campaign for Homosexual Law Reform brought together a motley selection of the country's leading lights, led by Joycean scholar David Norris, who had already established the Irish Gay Rights Movement. Its patrons included Victor Griffin, the Anglican dean of St Patrick's Cathedral, playwright Hugh Leonard, former government minister Noel Browne and Victor Bewley, scion of the oriental café dynasty and a veteran champion of travellers' rights. Mary McAleese fitted comfortably into the small, committed group, regularly attending its press conferences and launching pamphlets.

The Campaign members used to meet in Buswells Hotel opposite Dáil Eireann or, more often than not, in David Norris' rooms at Trinity where his briefcase, stuffed with documents and half-a-drawer of the filing cabinet represented the full extent of the group's paperwork. Despite being lambasted as part of a sinister plot to undermine the very foundations of the State, the Campaign secured the services of a future Supreme Court judge, Donal Barrington, to write the legal opinion for its test case in the High Court. When he was subsequently appointed to the judiciary, the cudgel was taken up by another eminent senior counsel, Mary Robinson, who took it all the way to the European Court of Human Rights.

'As far as I was concerned, Mary McAleese was as radical as the rest of us,' recalled David Norris. 'It was a very courageous thing for her to do. Visionary and enlightened.

'At one stage, we were accused of being part of an international conspiracy funded by Jewish money from New York! We both had a good laugh at that.'

It would become apparent in time, as her stance on issues like abortion, contraception and divorce developed, that this woman could not be succinctly classified under any single ideology, the lasting legacy of her youth in Belfast when she resolved never to be pigeon-holed by anybody. Her attitudes and opinions were hugely informed by her own experiences, making inconsistency the abiding constant in her public life. Her commitment to the reform of homosexual law may, in fact, have had more to do with the personal than the political. John Leneghan, the brother she loved and almost lost when he was 16 and who had trained in London as a hairdresser, was also drawn to helping the gay community. After opening his own hair salon in Rostrevor, he would return to London as a voluntary worker with London Lighthouse, a project established to assist HIV sufferers, where he met Princess Diana on four different occasions.

The myriad committees and campaigns Mary McAleese signed up to had the added bonus of alleviating the mundanity of academic life. For an opinionated extrovert, the ivory tower bookishness of a university campus can be stultifying, particularly when that person thrives under the public spotlight. An unusual duality had evolved in her make-up, making her simultaneously cerebral and populist. Mind and heart battled it out for supremacy, the cold glint of steel colliding with the soft mallow of compassion.

'I don't think she was challenged by the Trinity environment,' Gerard Hogan suspected. 'She was very charming, very able and a very, very good lecturer but I don't know that she was hugely excited by the job. One key feature of academia is to publish and one would have expected more from her by way of published output.'

Another former colleague put it more bluntly. 'She was not a natural academic,' he said. 'She was bored by it. She wanted the limelight.'

Having lived briefly in a Grange Developments house in Dublin's Scholarstown Road when Martin returned to Dublin, the couple bought their first marital home in County Meath in the summer of 1977. Situated on Lagore Road in the townland of Mooretown, on the Ratoath side of Dunshaughlin, the modern bungalow, with its front and rear gardens, stood in a pastoral oasis a 90-minute drive from the border. They christened it 'Rostrevor'.

Martin's new job with Blueskies and Enterprise Travel, however, meant that he had to frequently fly abroad to the various holiday destinations promoted by the company, leaving Mary with time on her hands.

When the future Labour Party senator, Joe Costello, invited her to join the Commission of Inquiry into the Irish Penal System which he was organising under the umbrella of the Prisoners Rights Organisation, she readily accepted. It gave her an extra-mural outlet for her academic expertise and introduced her to a man she would come to consider as a great friend, the elderly senior counsel Dr Seán MacBride. The former IRA chief-of-staff and cabinet minister who was chosen to chair the Commission of Inquiry was the living embodiment of modern Irish history. The son of Maud Gonne, a ravishing beauty celebrated by the poet, William Butler Yeats, he had been awarded both the Lenin and Nobel peace prizes. Other members of the Commission included Michael D Higgins, chairman of the Labour Party and a sociology lecturer at University College Galway, Fine Gael senator Gemma Hussey and her party's spokesman on law reform, Michael Keating, the country's leading criminal law senior counsel, Patrick McEntee, the Jesuit priest, Dr Mícheál MacGréil and the prominent trade unionist, Matt Merrigan.

The Commission of Inquiry held three open days at the Jesuit-owned Milltown Park in Dublin in April 1979, hearing submissions from such interested parties as solicitors Pat MacCartan and Michael White, journalist Mairín De Búrca and Senator Mary Robinson, who delivered a paper on 'The International Dimension'.

'My outstanding memory of Mary McAleese during those three days,' recalled Joe Costello, 'was when a prisoner called Eddie Cahill gave his testimony. Eddie was a brother of Martin Cahill (the notorious Dublin criminal known as 'The General' who was shot dead in Ranelagh in 1994) and he had another brother, Gerard, who died in prison in the Curragh. He told the Commission how, at mealtimes, the prison warders would put all three courses of the meal – the soup, the main course and the dessert – into a plastic bag and slosh it all together. I remember looking at Mary as he was talking – and she was crying.'

For the next 18 months, the 11 members of the Commission met regularly at the Dublin home of Seán MacBride, Roebuck House in Clonskeagh. Their brief was broad and complex. By the end of the 1970s, Ireland's prison population of 1,200, plus 1,600 on probation, had risen by 200 per cent since 1960. It was the time of 'the heavy gang' – the garda brutality exposed in an official report by Judge Barra O'Briain. Prison suicides were a growing phenomenon and heroin abuse was escalating to such a level that, by 1982, it would be more widespread in the north inner-city of Dublin than in New York's Harlem, then acknowledged as the world's worst afflicted region.

When the MacBride Commission's report was published it was greeted with general indifference, and a few raised eyebrows. Among its recommendations were the provision of bail hostels and detoxification units in prisons, weekend tutorials on dangerous driving for traffic offenders, the introduction of community service, the abolition of solitary confinement and an independent inquiry into drug abuse in prisons. It also proposed that the government abandon its plans for a new women's prison, that the age of criminal responsibility be raised to 14 years, and that the crime of prostitution be revised allowing the law of Public Nuisance to be applied to prostitutes' clients.

'The report got a bad reception from the Minister for Justice, Gerry Collins, but it seminally influenced others, like the Whittaker Report in the 1980s,' said Joe Costello.

After her experiences in Belfast it seemed a natural progression for Mary McAleese to join the Irish Council for Civil Liberties, which she did in the late 1970s. Another of her fellow Trinity academics, South Africa-born law lecturer Kadar Asmal, who would return to Pretoria as a minister in Nelson Mandela's post-apartheid government, was a prominent member of the Council, becoming its president in 1980. But it was to be a short-lived alliance for the Reid Professor who declined an invitation to join the executive in 1983 in protest at the Council's decision to support the anti-amendment side of the 1983 abortion referendum.

'I understood she resigned because of differences of opinion with the Council,' said UCD lecturer and secretary of the ICCL, Ailbhe Smyth. 'It was a difficult time because a lot of issues were being discussed about Northern Ireland and whether we should take on those issues as a Republic-based organisation. There was a lot of discussion too about rape legislation and whether the complainant's sexual history should be admissible as well as the issue of abortion and whether we should row in behind the Pro-Choice Campaign, which we decided to do.'

Mary McAleese's orthodox views on so-called moral issues were beginning to emerge. This was a new side to the woman, surprising many of her friends in Dublin's intelligentsia who had bracketed her as an all-round liberal like themselves. They had good reason for holding that belief. On May 3, 1979, for instance, she argued passionately in favour of civil divorce at a debate held by the Incorporated Law Society of Ireland at its annual conference in Galway. 'We have so little to fear from permitting divorce and so much to be concerned about in continuing to forbid it,' she contended. 'Anti–divorce lobbyists often argue that divorce damages children, yet the truth is that what damages children is not the *de iure* dissolution of the marriage but the process of rows, scenes, violence, bitterness, recrimination and upheaval which *de facto* broke it up.'

She went on: 'There is no guarantee of a happy ending but divorce does at least hold out the possibility. Without it there remains the syndrome of breakdown, of frustrated people trapped in unsatisfactory relationships, of children soured by their experience at the hands of incompatible parents, of illegitimate children and illicit relationships which have their own form of inherent misery precisely because they cannot be legitimised.

'We need to stop thinking of marriage as a rigid structure alien to and isolated from the couple who make it function,' she urged. 'We must stop thinking of divorce as an inhuman monster who creeps in through open bedroom windows disseminating huge dollops of marital disharmony. It is to cherish the nation's children less than equally to expect and to coerce any one of them to live out his or her life in a loveless and embittering union.'

Two years after that debate, in the spring of 1981, Professor McAleese accepted an invitation to chair a public meeting in Liberty Hall organised as a platform for the Women's Right to Choose Group in the run-up to the abortion referendum. Its panel of five speakers included the journalists, Mary Holland and Anne Marie Hourihane, and the trade unionist, Ann Speed. Though she insisted afterwards that she had been led to believe both sides of the referendum campaign would be represented at the meeting and that she had, in fact, been lured there under false pretences, her liberal image persisted. The organisers of the Liberty Hall meeting denied her version of events, exclaiming disbelief that she could easily be 'conned'. To many, Mary McAleese was pro-divorce and pro-choice in terms of abortion and homosexuality – all the right-on credentials of a subscriber to radical chic.

That was the public woman. In private, however, she had been struggling with an internal dilemma for much of the 1970s. She described it like this in an interview with Gay Byrne on *The Late Late Show* in March 1993: 'During the '70s, I – like a lot of people – went through troubles with what were called the big moral questions of the day: divorce, abortion, contraception and all that kind of stuff.' While she was agonising over the moral teachings of her Church, she had, she told a friend, 'never moved away from God'. 'By the late '70s, I had had it with the Church,' she confided to this friend, 'and the Pope's visit (in 1979) was a low point for me.'

Several people who knew her in Dublin during the late 1970s and into the 1980s suspect that the experience of childbirth was her Damascus. Having suffered two miscarriages, her first child was born at Mount Carmel Hospital in Dublin in September 1983. The child was named Emma, after Martin's mother who had died suddenly during Mary's pregnancy. She described the magic of first-time motherhood in *Reconciled Being: Love In Chaos* as follows.

> I had had babies up to my tonsils throughout my teenage life. My mother and her siblings had taken to heart the gospel call to increase and multiply and fill the earth, except that they thought they had to do it single-handedly. Between them they had 60 children, most of them younger than me. If the truth be told, I had a relatively underwhelmed attitude to babies generally. I was surprised therefore to find myself so completely overwhelmed and totally smitten by my own daughter. I loved her to bits.

David Norris noticed the change in his old ally from the Campaign for Homosexual Law Reform when, soon after Emma's birth, he was invited to dinner in Ratoath.

'She and Martin were very charming hosts. We had drinks in the garden that evening before going inside for dinner. I became aware that she was taking a different tack to the rest of us on abortion that night. She indicated this was an experience of motherhood, that it had crystallised her views. I may be wrong but it certainly was my impression that they were fairly amorphous before that. I'm not suggesting this was some sort of woolly, feminine, emotional thing. This was a woman who had given birth and experienced all its emotional resonance. It's a human response to a human experience. I have this early memory of her coming into the bar and knocking back a drink and being just like the rest of us. And suddenly you had this non-smoking, teetotal anti-abortionist.'

The evidence, however, suggests that childbirth was just one of two factors which caused her to re-dedicate herself to the Catholic Church. The other factor preceded Emma's arrival. Something which began as a golden opportunity – only to plunge her into the most desolate period of life. Its name was Radio Telefís Éireann.

Her would-be saviour was a man called Muiris MacConghaíl. The former editor of RTÉ's most talked about current affairs programme, *Seven Days*, he was appointed Controller of Programmes in 1977, taking over the reins with a vision of intellectualising the State broadcaster. One of his first actions was to axe the nation's staple soap opera, the anodyne rural-based weekly drama, *The Riordans*, replacing it with the edgier *Bracken*, starring Gabriel Byrne, and James Plunkett's seamy *Strumpet City*. MacConghaíl's ambition was to elevate the current affairs department's level of erudition, creating a second generation of David Thornleys, the academic and politician who became one of RTÉ's most respected interviewers. By 1979, his vision was well in the process of implementation. Two promising young women lawyers had already been signed up. Susan Gageby, who would become the country's first woman Supreme Court judge, was then a researcher with *Seven Days*. The solicitor, Mary Redmond, who would found the Irish Hospice Foundation and become the first woman director of the Jefferson Smurfit Group and the Bank of Ireland, was on an RTÉ retainer while still a fellow at Cambridge University in England. Muiris MacConghaíl set out next to headhunt the young Reid Professor at Trinity College, scoring a hat-trick when she came on board the current affairs department as a reporter/presenter in March 1979. Now he had his dream team in place. And Mary McAleese had been gifted with an outlet for her pent up ambition, an outlet that might well have been the apogee of her career.

But that was not to be. In fact, it was all to go horribly wrong.

Two decades later, Muiris MacConghaíl admitted: 'I feel guilty that I had brought her in and was unable to fulfil what I had promised.'

# 6

# Outside the Pale

ANYONE WHO WORKED IN the television centre at Montrose was used to the din that emanated from Joe Mulholland's office most Friday mornings. It was nothing untoward. Just the usual intellectual oxygen of the station's flagship programme, *Today Tonight*. The A-team of two dozen producers, reporters and researchers would cram into the confined space of the editor's room at 10am every Friday to thrash out programme ideas. Sometimes they would be in there all day, arguing and expostulating. Poring tortuously over the nation's navel. The tempo of creative energy generated by the *crème de la crème* of Irish current affairs journalism.

This day, however, it sounded different. At first, there had been the usual cacophony of debate. Cut short by a lone female voice. Then a male voice, loud and angry. Followed by uproar. A door slamming. Footsteps hurrying away, down the corridor.

It was the month of May 1981, a week after the death of IRA hunger-striker Bobby Sands in the Maze Prison and RTÉ's current affairs department was tearing itself apart.

The woman who had spoken was Mary McAleese, a full-time staff reporter with *Today Tonight*. She was furious. Frustrated too. But, she felt, vindicated. The previous week, she had implored the editor to sanction extensive coverage of Sands' funeral, arguing that the hunger-strike was radicalising the nationalist community in the North and, therefore, it required to be taken seriously. Joe Mulholland had counter-argued that it would be a show funeral, nothing more than a staged media event where the mourners would be out-numbered by television camera crews. He refused to play ball with the Republicans' propaganda machine.

But Mary McAleese's forecast had proved accurate. Television teams had, indeed, flown in from around the world – from all over Europe, the United States, Japan and even Thailand. More significantly, nearly 100,000 people had lined the route from St Luke's Church to the Republican plot at Milltown Cemetery in Belfast for Bobby Sands' funeral on Thursday, May 7.

The US government issued a statement of 'deep regret', the Longshoremen's Union there announcing a 24-hour boycott of British ships. The New Jersey State legislature passed a motion honouring the dead hunger-striker's 'courage and commitment'. Irish bars in New York closed for two hours' mourning. The members of India's upper house stood in a minute's silence. The President of the Italian Senate, Amintore Fanfan, sent condolences to the Sands family. There were street protests in Milan, Paris and Oslo, where demonstrators spattered the Queen of England with ketchup. In the Soviet Union, *Pravda* recorded 'another tragic page in the grim chronicle of oppression and discrimination' in Ireland. *The Hong Kong Standard* denounced the failure of successive British governments 'to end the last of Europe's religious wars'. *The Hindustan Times* accused Margaret Thatcher of allowing a fellow member of parliament to 'die of starvation, an incident which has never before occurred in a civilised country'.

Now, six days later, Mary McAleese was letting loose in Joe Mulholland's office, berating the programme for failing to anticipate the full political implications of Sands' death. *Today Tonight* had lost the plot, she asserted. She knew. She was from Belfast. She was going up North nearly every weekend and witnessing for herself the groundswell of support for the hunger-strikers. *Today Tonight*, she charged, was so concerned with not being a pawn in the Provos' deadly stalemate, that it was actually achieving the opposite. Instead of alienating the people from the IRA, she claimed, it was alienating the people from RTÉ. The State broadcaster had become a joke where she came from.

Emotion was palpable in the room. A handful of her colleagues agreed with the Belfast lawyer, believing that the programme was wrongly downplaying the hunger-strike. The current affairs department had been engaged in its own bitter, internecine battle for minds since Sands started the hunger-strike on Sunday

February 29, with the team harshly dividing into two camps. It was the other, much bigger camp that held sway, mirroring the editor's own repugnance of the IRA.

Now, as Mary McAleese fulminated at the meeting in Mulholland's office, one of them exploded in a burst of temper, accusing her of losing her objectivity about the story because, after all, wasn't she herself 'a west Belfast Provo.' The insult caused pandemonium, the two sides shouting angrily at one another. A colleague demanded the remark be withdrawn but her accuser remained stubbornly tight-lipped. That was when she strode to the door, tears of rage and hurt glistening in her eyes – and stormed out.

'When she left the meeting that day, she went straight to a church,' revealed the same colleague who had leapt to her defence. 'She told me afterwards that that was when she had a rekindling with the Church.'

Just as she had 'turned her face away' from the violence in Belfast in 1969, it seems it was her faith that sustained her in RTÉ except now she would be unable to dredge up the mental resources she displayed then in supplanting her anger with a creed of compassion. Years later she would admit that she felt more traumatised by what happened to her in Donnybrook than by any of the violence visited on her family in the North.

Writing a guest column entitled 'Why I Am A Nationalist' in *The Belfast Telegraph* 15 years later, she recalled: 'In Dublin, I became very conscious that the language I spoke and what brought me there was not understood by the people I worked with. It wasn't their experience and they didn't really want it to be. I was almost as much an outsider there as here – maybe more.'

When she joined RTÉ in March 1979 the station was already in the painful throes of re-examining its role as the State broadcaster and the sole licensed broadcaster in the country. It had toed a line sympathetic to Northern Ireland nationalists since the outbreak of the Troubles, when Catholics were the underdogs and, most often, the victims. In the early 1970s, the RTÉ journalist, Kevin O'Kelly, had been hailed a hero when he went to jail for contempt of court rather than divulge the identity of an IRA man he had interviewed, believed to have been the chief-of-staff, Seán MacStiofán.

The political landscape had changed dramatically, however, with the emergence of the Provisional IRA and its chilling ability to mount high-casualty guerrilla attacks. In a single day in 1979, for instance, 18 soldiers had died in Warrenpoint, County Down – a five-minute drive from the Leneghan family home in Rostrevor – and the Earl of Mountbatten, godfather of the Prince of Wales, had lost his life in a bomb explosion while holidaying at Mullaghmore in County Sligo.

A row that broke out in Madigans pub in Donnybrook that evening captured the atmosphere of tortured self-analysis that prevailed in RTÉ. It erupted when a producer walked into the pub frequented by RTÉ staff and gave a clenched-fist salute of victory, provoking furious exchanges between producers, researchers and secretaries gathered randomly around the bar.

'RTÉ's response was overwhelmingly nationalist when the Troubles started, as was the rest of the media,' remembered senior station executive, Peter Feeney. 'There was a reaction against that in the '70s and it began a very painful process because it was re-evaluating the most important thing that was happening to the country at that time. It became very personal and bitter. There was no middle ground. It was an awful atmosphere.'

Twenty years later, the vestiges of that atmosphere were still evident in some people's fear of speaking about it publicly. 'There was always a feeling that if you talked about this it was felon-setting or McCarthyite,' said one of those who wished to remain anonymous.

Externally imposed factors contributed to the climate in RTÉ, like Section 31 of the Broadcasting Act, which prohibited interviews with members of proscribed organisations and was an enduring bone of contention between various governments and the National Union of Journalists. But the biggest outside influence was Conor Cruise O'Brien whose book, *States of Ireland*, was regarded as the progenitor of revisionist history. Back in the autumn of 1974, *Seven Days* had screened a two-part investigation of internment in Northern Ireland that was viewed by the Fine Gael-Labour administration as highly emotional in its treatment. Journalists covering the Labour Party Conference later that year memorably witnessed the Minister with responsibility for RTÉ, Conor Cruise

O'Brien, wagging his finger at the station's head of current affairs, Desmond Fisher, admonishing him over the programme on internment. It was the last exercise of that type, the Minister warned, that would be tolerated by his government.

At this stage, Mary McAleese was largely unaffected by the growing emotional conflict within the station. The once-a-week current affairs television programme, *Frontline*, had already been on the air for a full season before she joined it as a reporter/presenter. Though it was a tame, non-confrontational programme, failing to set any kind of news agenda, it was considered prestigious at a time when the station's current affairs output was otherwise limited to one hour on radio, five mornings a week. *Morning Ireland* and *The News At One* had yet to be conceived, leaving the gulf on the airwaves to be filled by television's current affairs department.

The Trinity professor, whose appointment to the station had been 'facilitated' by Muiris MacConghaíl when she formally applied for the job, turned out to be a natural television performer. She was relaxed and attractive, once a remedy was found to the shadows thrown across her face by her unruly mop of hair.

'We very quickly promoted her to studio presenter,' said Peter Feeney, her editor in *Frontline*.

This first year in RTÉ was a happy period for her, offering an escape from the staid world of academia and a chance to hone her obvious talent for communication. Issues of civil rights and social conditions were her forte, which she exercised most notably in an interview with Mary Robinson on the Diplock courts and in a documentary about Irish women travelling to England for abortions.

The researcher for the latter programme was another recent recruit to the station, the newsroom's future special correspondent, Charlie Bird. He recalled how he and Mary accompanied a young woman with an unwanted pregnancy, a patient of the pro-choice GP, Dr Paddy Leahy, on the boat to an abortion clinic in Liverpool. 'We had to make sure the woman wouldn't be recognised so I borrowed my wife's duffel coat to conceal her. I remember the weather was foul going over on the boat and I was sick.'

Mary McAleese told the *Irish Independent* in February 1984: 'I loved the experience of working on *Frontline*. Working as an academic can be very lonely and, in *Frontline*, we worked as a close-knit team. I was learning new skills and, most important, it gave me an insight to the workings of politics here. I knew very little of the political scene in the Republic when I came down here from the North first.'

It was nothing compared to the first-hand lesson she was about to receive in RTÉ's internal politics. Some people ascribe the first real shift in the corporation's overall ethos to the Pope's visit in September 1979, prompting a regression to orthodox anti-intellectualism in its programming. George Waters was appointed Director General that year, following the unexpected resignation of Oliver Moloney and sounding the death knell on Mary McAleese's honeymoon at the station. In less than a year her mentor, Muiris MacConghaíl, would no longer be Controller of Programmes and Peter Feeney would be replaced as her editor by a man as strong-willed as herself.

'Mary got stranded,' said Muiris MacConghaíl.

When Joe Mulholland was made editor of the new four-nights-a-week programme, *Today Tonight*, and inherited Mary McAleese as part of the package, it was a case of the irresistible force meeting the immovable object. Both straight-talking northerners with impressive academic portfolios and high ambitions, they could not, in fact, have been more dissimilar. It was their opinions that separated them and set them at loggerheads almost immediately.

In 1969, Mulholland had been toying with a job offer to teach French at Khartoum University in Sudan when he answered an advertisement seeking producers/directors at RTÉ. The eldest of five children from Ballybofey in County Donegal, he rose above his family's frugal circumstances by winning a scholarship to Finn College in Stranorlar and, later, acquiring a grant to Manchester Teacher Training College. Like his truck-driver father, who was forced to emigrate to England for work, the newly-qualified teacher left for France, where he met his wife, became fluent in the language and attained a doctorate in medieval theatre at the University of Nancy.

A man of dour countenance and formidable intelligence, he had made two award-winning documentaries for RTÉ by the time Mary McAleese became his subordinate. She survived his initial clear-out of the department when he was given *carte blanche* to recruit his own team. Joe Mulholland, an avowed workaholic destined to become television's managing director, brought a fresh energy to the current affairs department, making *Today Tonight* required viewing for the nation. It was avant-garde and broadly liberal and its editor had the clout to deliver extra resources and air time for his staff. Programmes on the Stardust nightclub fire, Fatima Mansions and Knock Airport won it acclaim for its fast response to breaking news stories. It was consistently in the top five of the TAM television ratings and formed the apex of every journalist's wish list. Its 10 producers and 10 reporters had the luxury of six to eight weeks working on a single programme, culminating in 52 minutes of painstakingly-researched film.

'It was mould breaking. A campaigning programme with a very young team,' remembered one of its producers. 'We were cutting our teeth on rattling the establishment.'

If Joe Mulholland brought verve and dynamism to the programme, however, he also brought a blind spot – Northern Ireland. A resolute pacifist, he abhorred the violence of the IRA and believed RTÉ had a bounden duty not to glamorise the Republican movement. He was passionate in his belief that the State broadcaster had a responsible role to play in shaping the national identity.

'The Irish public must decide,' he once declared at the MacGill Summer School in Glenties, 'that it wants and needs a public service broadcasting organisation which keeps it fully informed on developments in this society, which reflects our national identity in all its aspects and complexities, and which is a leading cultural force in the life of the nation.'

The result was that Northern Ireland tended to be side-lined by *Today Tonight*.

'We were very aware that RTÉ was anti-Provo at that time,' said Monsignor Denis Faul, the priest who ultimately brought the hunger-strike to an end and a fearless critic of the IRA. 'Fr Raymond Murray and I were working on highlighting the torture of prisoners and the cause of the Birmingham Six and we were seen as "Provo priests". I was barred from RTÉ, except the Irish language programmes. The Radio Éireann boys would come up to Belfast, drink in the bar and ring the RUC. That was our impression of their coverage of the North.'

At a seminar in Dublin nearly 15 years later, Mary McAleese confirmed the pariah status of the two clerics when she said: 'I remember so well the awful things said so confidently about two men whom I admire, I think, above all men on this island – Fr Denis Faul and Fr Raymond Murray – when they started their lonely battle. And I was in the room at times when things were said about them that were not just libellous, but unchristian to the nth degree.'

Monsignor Faul's impression of RTÉ's *modus operandi* is remarkably similar to one she expressed on *The Late Late Show* in 1993. 'RTÉ for me was a very, very difficult experience, even though I thoroughly enjoyed it and made some wonderful friends there,' she said. 'But working as I did during the hunger-strike here, I found it extraordinary. I hope my journalist colleagues won't be offended when I say this but I found an extraordinary degree of ignorance about what was going on in Northern Ireland. Absolutely extraordinary! There was I, somebody who had lived there and went back regularly at weekends, I'd be sitting there listening to these fellas. They'd be saying that coal lorries were going in and out of Andersonstown carrying arms. I said: "What!" They had it on good authority. You'd be saying to yourself: "Where did they get this from? Was it a barstool in the Europa Hotel?" – which invariably, I think, it was. You had that kind of curious attitude that the authenticity of your own experience was suspect.

'During that time,' she went on, 'if you were a Catholic from the North you were regarded as a Provo fellow traveller which was a disgraceful thing and a very silencing thing. I actually found that, in many ways, much more hurtful than having two machine guns emptied into the house by Protestants because I knew why they shot us. Because we were Catholics. It was that simple. But to feel that degree of silencing and of alienation here was very frightening. Quite traumatising.'

Her reading of the imperatives for RTÉ differed fundamentally from that of her boss. She believed that Northern nationalists were now being 'emasculated on two fronts: by revisionists saying nationalism is dead and gone, an out-moded nineteenth-century phenomenon; and the Provos saying we are super-nationalists, the true voice and the only voice'.

The new regime in RTÉ's current affairs, which she privately described as 'Kafkaesque', was, she feared, effectively gagging her own community. But she seldom won the toss when she spoke out at programme meetings. 'There used to be tears and tempers after the Friday meeting', remembered a like-minded colleague. 'Joe would lead the discussion and, to his credit, he could be very dispassionate about programmes. We lost discussion after discussion because four or five of the team regularly attacked our ideas. We would, all of us who were on the same side as Mary, so to speak, have felt somewhat beleaguered.'

A *Sunday Tribune* profile of Joe Mulholland quoted an anonymous source as saying: 'He is not very encouraging. If he doesn't like somebody's work he will be quite rude and blunt about it...,' The source depicted a boss who operated 'a divide and rule' policy, inviting staff to his office for drinks after work to test the political temperature within the station.

'I felt RTÉ's coverage of Northern Ireland nationalists was inadequate and they held us in contempt for that,' said Michael Heaney, a producer with *Today Tonight* whose family originally hailed from Bangor. 'That was my impression of how they felt because I went up there constantly and that is what they told me. I felt myself in a bond with Mary. She felt personally under challenge. It came from her pores.'

Distrusted as 'a crypto Provo' and, ergo, unsound on the national question, she was 'marginalised early on', admitted a producer loyal to Mulholland. 'There was something edgy about her,' said this producer. 'She was harsh. She didn't fit in. Joe was very curt with her. He didn't regard her as part of the team. She was always complaining. She was very intense and seemed to be laden with chips on her shoulder.'

In an interview with *The Irish Times* three years later, she complained: 'I was a Northern voice and I spent a lot of time there. Every weekend I was with friends and relations trying to find out what was happening in the North but I was not listened to. Whenever I tried to explain that more and more people were being drawn into the H-Block cause because of the failure of the British government to act, they wouldn't listen to me because they felt that anyone who was bringing that message into the programme had to be a Provo supporter. It was literally pillorying the messenger for bringing the message.'

On one particular assignment in Derry to cover the funeral of a teenage boy killed by a British Army rubber bullet, she was horrified by the insensitivity of a fellow crew member. Arriving late at the dead boy's home and finding the lid closed on the coffin in readiness for removal to the church, her colleague asked the boy's mother to open it again so that the corpse could be filmed. Mary McAleese was appalled and refused to work any further on the story.

On another occasion, she was working in RTÉ's Belfast studio on a programme about the H–Block hunger-strike, featuring the loyalist, Glen Barr, and the republican, Bernadette McAliskey. Barr had been invited on to give the Protestant community's reaction to the strike but, a short while into the programme, he started outlining the battle plans of the Ulster Defence Association, which was banned from the airwaves under Section 31. His repeated references to 'we' and the presence on the programme of McAliskey, who only months earlier had been shot seven times in a botched assassination attempt by the UDA, caused uproar back in Dublin. Joe Mulholland later apologised for the error but Mary McAleese remained convinced that she had been set up by some of her colleagues.

What was happening in RTÉ was replicated throughout the media as editors strove to balance the sensational human-interest aspects of the hunger-strike story with the more sinister motives of the IRA. In Britain, the Independent Broadcasting Authority demanded that Granada Television censor a programme on the hunger-strike on the grounds that 20 seconds' footage of another striker, Patsy O'Hara, in his coffin constituted Republican propaganda. Granada withdrew the programme entirely in protest.

When the Republican press office in Belfast embargoed a *Today Tonight* interview with Bobby Sands' sister, Marcella, it compounded the majority belief among the team that the 'ritual suicide' in the Maze was being exploited as a powerful publicity weapon. Conversely, when a reporter arrived back from Belfast only to be berated for interviewing Fr Des Wilson, a community activist in the city, it was felt that an unofficial black-list of interviewees was in operation.

Meanwhile, RTÉ was glorying in the success of *Today Tonight* and fêting its distinction in receiving an Emmy Award for a programme called *Victims Of Violence*. A powerful polemic on the long-term destructiveness of violence, it told, for the first time, the stories of Protestant victims in the North. Presented by Joe Little, who had started working in RTÉ on the same day as Mary McAleese, and screened at the height of the hunger-strike, it was viewed as a landmark in RTÉ's current affairs.

Despite its international success, some of the *Today Tonight* team felt uneasy about the programme, seeing it as a diversion from the on-going hunger-strike and evidence of another invidious influence within the station – the Workers Party. Though Joe Mulholland was never a member of any political party and, in fact, has threatened to disprove any such allegation in a court of law, his interpretation of events in the North tallied substantially with the ideology of the Workers Party. It was most openly debated at meetings of his trade union, the Workers Union of Ireland, which boasted the membership of the station's leading WP exponent, Eoghan Harris.

Though the Cork-born producer who joined RTÉ in 1966 never met Mary McAleese there, his influence was extensive. A recipient of three Jacobs Awards, he wrote a seminal pamphlet in 1976 entitled 'The Irish Industrial Revolution', repudiating nationalist claims on Northern Ireland, and had come to be regarded as the Workers Party's *éminence grise*.

'More than any other Irish institution, RTÉ was at that time the cockpit of that wider political struggle of conscience,' said Harris. 'During the 1970s, as the IRA began an ethnic cleansing campaign of Protestants in Fermanagh, and as the tide of Protestant blood began to creep under the door and into the conscience of the south, bitter battles broke out among RTÉ producers, in television and radio, about access to the air, about whether a revisionist like John A Murphy or a republican like Tim Pat Coogan would get star billing on a panel.'

This is borne out by the memory of a *Today Tonight* producer who witnessed a row at one of the Friday programme meetings about the composition of a studio panel. Mary objected vehemently to the inclusion of Gerry Fitt, arguing that the West Belfast MP had been discredited and no longer spoke for his nationalist constituents.

Mary's rubbishing of the former SDLP leader was taken as proof by her adversaries on the team that the Belfast woman was sympathetic to the hunger-strike. However, those who agreed with her saw it as a discomfiting Northern perspective intruding on a cosy Southern position.

'I remember talking to her in the Wellington Park Hotel in Belfast one day while she was waiting to meet her mother,' recalled Joe Little, who briefly lived in Andersonstown's Fruithill Park as a child. 'She told me she was very, very upset that people in RTÉ were calling her a Provo.'

Perhaps if she had allowed her own vulnerability to show in Montrose she would have won some understanding. Instead, she never let up haranguing the deficiencies she perceived. Even when she was called 'a west Belfast Provo' she questioned the geographical accuracy of the term, explaining sarcastically that Ardoyne was, in fact, located in north Belfast. She was a fashion victim in the atelier of ideology, wearing her knowledge, with her ambition, on her sleeve.

'Bright women with academic backgrounds found it difficult in RTÉ at that time,' said Muiris MacConghaíl. 'Sexism was certainly a factor in the problems Mary had.'

She, however, attributed her dilemma to the influence of the Workers Party.

'By and large, the newsroom of RTÉ was strongly nationalist,' said Eoghan Harris. 'In the programmes division, we balanced the books much better in those days. She met the "party" in the person of almost every second producer in television when it came to being critical of traditional nationalist attitudes to the North,' he added. 'In a certain sense, almost everybody she met in the Republic with a brain in their head was "Workers Party" when it came to the North.'

What many people in RTÉ were unaware of was that Mary McAleese had encountered the Workers Party at close range from the vantage of her father's pub back in Belfast. She told a friend it incensed her that members of the party were engaged in crime in the North and yet she had to listen to them preach about class politics in the South.

In a 1986 interview with the magazine, *In Dublin*, she fumed: 'Frankly, the Workers Party have nothing worth saying on the subject of Northern Ireland and I would not even glorify the Workers Party by entering into any analysis with them. I mean these are people who masquerade as a political party but who have strong known links with terrorists and with people who believe in the use of violence. I don't regard them as a legitimate political movement in any sense of the word. I think they have been guilty of an extreme con-trick on the population both North and South.'

She spoke about it again in 1993 for the book, *In Search of a State: Catholics in Northern Ireland*. 'I had a dreadful time with the Workers Party people who now hold very prominent positions in RTÉ – whose idea of coming to the North was to talk to Unionist politicians whom they cultivated in a really obsequious way, to talk to other Workers Party people, and then come back to Dublin and tell what was happening in the North.'

Inside *Today Tonight*, the ideological struggle was to lead to the most embarrassing near fiasco in the programme's lifetime. The IRA hunger-strike of 1981, following an aborted strike the previous year, was the end game of a prolonged 'Blanket Protest' at the Maze Prison. It had begun as a refusal to wear prison-issue clothing and a no-wash campaign in an attempt to secure political prisoner status from the British government and culminating in horrendous television footage of filthy bearded men incarcerated in cells that were smeared with human excrement. It was viewed with a jaundiced eye in RTÉ's climate of re-analysis, just as the hunger-strike itself was interpreted as emotional blackmail. When the Republican movement decided to field Bobby Sands as a candidate in the Fermanagh-South Tyrone by-election for Westminster in April 1981, it was greeted in RTÉ with the same deep cynicism. Joe Mulholland and his followers in *Today Tonight* were scornful of the hunger-striker's chances at the polling booth and failed to anticipate his historic victory by 1,446 votes.

Two of the programme's presenters, Olivia O'Leary and Barry Cowan, had felt professionally frustrated that they were prohibited from interviewing Sands or his election agent, Owen Carron, during the election campaign. Now they were appalled to realise that, even as *The Financial Times* was predicting Sands' win on the morning of the election, *Today Tonight* had not even sent a camera crew to cover the count. In a frantic eleventh-hour race to ameliorate the misjudgement, Joe Mulholland sent a crew to Enniskillen by helicopter but, in the flurry, the production assistant missed the flight, necessitating a costly taxi journey to catch up with the rest of the crew.

Years later, Mary McAleese confided to one of her colleagues on the programme that she had stayed back late at work that evening just to relish her boss's predicament.

But her own position on the programme had grown untenable. She was out of the loop. The pitches she made for stories at the weekly planning meetings invariably came to nought. She was floundering, with little work to do and a handful of friends within the station. During meal breaks, she was most likely to sit with the secretaries in the RTÉ canteen than with her professional peers.

Meanwhile, her husband had decided to pack in his job with 'Blueskies', which was frequently taking him away from home to places like Majorca, Sardinia, Lourdes and Greece. Martin, at the age of 30, had finally made up his mind to become a dentist, enrolling for four years as a full-time student at Trinity College that autumn. Now the sole breadwinner of the couple, Mary resolved to return to Trinity for a second tenure as Reid Professor. Little did she expect when she had left there for the allure of television that she would be so grateful to return.

The IRA hunger-strike continued to dominate the national headlines during that summer as the National H–Block Committee announced that four of the strikers would stand for the June 11 general election in the Republic. One of the four was Kieran Doherty, who had grown up near Mary's temporary home in Andersonstown. Aged 25, he was serving 22 years imprisonment for possession of firearms and explosives. Doherty was on the 22nd day of his hunger-strike when he was elected a TD for Cavan-Monaghan. When he died on August 2 after more than 70 days without food, the flags on government buildings in Dublin flew at half-mast.

Unknown to anyone in RTÉ, the dead IRA man had a connection with Mary McAleese. He had been the leader of a five-man gang arrested in August 1976 after a siege in the Malone area of

Belfast. When the gang's bombing mission was scuppered by security forces, they had run into a nearby house, threatening a gardener at the point of a machine gun. After several hours, a priest was brought in and he persuaded the gang to surrender. Among the five men later charged with causing an explosion and possession of explosives, firearms and ammunition, was Mary's first cousin, John Henry Pickering.

The son of her mother's older sister, Bridget, John Pickering was serving a further life sentence after being convicted in March 1978 of murdering a 77-year-old garage owner in Finaghy during a separate bombing raid. The trial judge said that Pickering, one of 12 children from Ramoan Gardens in Andersonstown, was probably the one who had shot Mr William Creighton dead. He and his accomplice, Terence Kirby, had blown up the garage and robbed the old man of £150.

John Pickering, known as 'Pickles' to his fellow inmates, was a model IRA prisoner, having already joined the Blanket Protest. When he volunteered to replace the tenth hunger-striker to die in September 1981 he fell ill almost immediately with a suspected stomach ulcer. But fate decided he would survive. The hunger-strike, which had claimed 10 lives and convulsed parliaments around the world, ended in October.

In Dublin, it brought the most wretched chapter of his cousin's life to a close. That time, she remembered, that 'created the syndrome of the apologetic nationalist'.

# 7

## It Happened on the
## Way to the Forum

'RTÉ'S ANTI-CLERICS GAVE me the boot', screamed the headline on the front page of *The Sunday Press* above a picture of Mary McAleese.

She was on the warpath. The object of her ire was the National Union of Journalists or, more specifically, its broadcasting branch, then composed exclusively of Montrose members. She may have quit the staff of RTÉ, but the epilogue to her brush with the Fourth Estate was still being written. The ink would take years to dry.

She had originally left Trinity College to escape the stuffiness of academia, gladly returning to its sanctuary three years later, emotionally scalded by her experience in the cut and thrust of broadcasting. The illustrious university islanded in the heart of the city, its cobblestones worn flat by the tread of generations, was the calm she sought after the storm. Trinity would be an anchor in her life for the next six years; a life that had listed and lurched ever since fleeing the family home in Belfast a decade before. Yet her sense of exclusion was to grow even deeper.

She took to jogging around the grassy college square with her friend, Yvonne Scannell, a lecturer in environmental and contract law and the only other woman on the permanent staff of the law school. At lunch-times, she would dash through the quadrangle for mass in the chapel, once arriving flushed and breathless, clutching the heel wrenched off a shoe in her haste across the cobbles. She was appointed registrar of the law school, putting in extra hours as an administrator and enhancing a curriculum vitae that would reward her handsomely in time to come. She embarked on a thesis for her masters degree on women in Irish prisons, and on a textbook on Irish criminal law. At the same time, she participated in a joint study comparing the conditions of child custody in Ireland, England, Wales and Scotland.

As Reid Professor of Criminal Law, she flexed her muscle with the Department of Justice, consulting with the civil service on the statistical reporting of the prison system, and wangling unprecedented visiting passes to Mountjoy jail for her students. 'She used to bring in psychologists and invite people from the Department to speak to the penology students,' recalled Dermot Cole, assistant secretary of the Justice Department. 'It was the first contact the Department had with them.'

Occasionally, she gave media interviews for stories relevant to her area of academic expertise. 'She was confident, clear and authoritative,' remembered Tom Savage who was working in RTÉ radio news features at the time. 'I would have thought of her as being in the radical *Irish Times* camp. She didn't wear her knowledge quietly. She had a reputation for being slightly aggressive. Not a wilting violet.

'But I saw another side to her. Because my wife, Terry, was working as well, I would sometimes bring our young son, Anton, with me on interviews. She had no problem with that. She neither seemed to resent it, as some people did, nor did she fuss over him. You could tell that she was well used to having children around.'

As yet, she had no children of her own. Though she suffered two miscarriages, she was not as traumatised by them as would a woman who was desperately yearning for a baby. 'To tell you the truth, I didn't regard them as traumatic at the time,' she told *The Irish Times* in 1984. 'I bounced over it but, after Emma was born, my mind was drawn back to those miscarriages. At the time they happened I had no fixed image in my mind of what they were or could have become. They were just a discomfort – a flow of blood – and also I was younger. There were all those years stretching ahead of me to have children.' When Emma was born in September 1983, she would wholeheartedly embrace the wonder of childbirth, giving vent to the full panoply of her maternal instincts. But for now, she was happy to live with her husband in the pastoral peace of Ratoath. It was the first time in her married life that Martin had been a constant presence. No more snatched weekends in Belfast, like the first year after their wedding when they had lived in two different cities. No more lonely nights in County Meath while her husband traipsed the holiday resorts of Europe keeping tabs on the travel business.

They were a full-time couple, at last. The proximity of their home to the border made it easier to visit their families in the North and for friends from there to drop in on their way to Dublin. Like her good friend, the Catholic Cardinal from Crossmaglen, Tomás O'Fiaich, who would, inadvertently, play a role in her showdown with the NUJ.

The McAleeses integrated into the community in Ratoath. She signed up for keep-fit classes and an evening course in German. They made lasting friends, including a young man who would, one day, be the catalyst for the most spectacular change in their life. His name was Harry Casey. One of 10 children from Longford, he was a teacher of religion and English at St Patrick's Classical School in Navan and, himself, a man of deep religious belief. It was Harry who introduced Mary and Martin to a local prayer group that met in each other's homes every Wednesday night for tea, sandwiches and scripture. They were an unlikely assortment – a local shop assistant, a school teacher, a mature student, a university lecturer, an elderly bachelor, and a priest who would later leave the clergy.

Life was as close to idyllic as ever it had been but, with Martin back in college as a full-time dentistry student, money was tight. Despite her ordeal in *Today Tonight*, Mary chose to return to RTÉ. This time, it was on her terms, as a freelance presenter cushioned by her day job in the university. When the television producer, Noel Smyth, invited her to co-present a new monthly programme with *Irish Times* journalist Conor Brady, she said yes to the offer and to the £65-a-month that came with it.

'She was excellent to work with,' Noel Smyth remembered, 'extremely organised and professional.'

The programme was *Europa*, a soft focus magazine-style voyage round the continent, dipping into the lifestyles of EEC capitals, with the odd foray to Scandinavia. One of her producers on *Today Tonight* described it disparagingly as 'like being transferred from Manchester United to Chesterfield', but whatever about its production credentials, the programme certainly improved her quality of life. The monthly format consisted of two filmed reports bought in from foreign stations and one 'home' produced story. With Conor Brady tied to Dublin because of his newspaper job, it fell to his co-presenter to record the overseas reports. For the duration of *Europa*, she travelled abroad about 15 times in all, leaving Trinity on a Friday evening to rendezvous with the television crew in any of a number of European cities on a Saturday morning. They usually returned to Dublin on Sunday night, ready to clock on for work on Monday morning.

It was an intensive routine, physically and mentally demanding. She once said that she used to come home from work with two things: 'my pay cheque, and exhaustion'.

Meanwhile, another RTÉ producer had spotted the Belfast woman's talent. 'If I see a resource that's being under-utilised I tend to work out a way to utilise it better,' explained Ed Mulhall. 'I was producing Pat Kenny's radio show and I was keen to do accessible court reports that were accurate. She was the ideal person to do them. She was an experienced broadcaster and a professor of law.'

Mary joined the show as a reporter, pushing back the boundaries of court reporting, a discipline rutted in a formula of antiseptic formality. Encouraged by Mulhall, she developed a style of 'colour' reporting, untried until then in Irish broadcasting, which brought an intimacy to the genre. Her coverage of the trial of Malcolm McArthur, the foppish murderer arrested in the Attorney General's apartment, set a new standard in RTÉ. When McArthur was jailed for life for bludgeoning a nurse, Bridie Gargan, to death in the Phoenix Park, the brutality of the murder provoked unprecedented scenes of public revulsion. It was an acutely sensitive story in political terms, having already led to the resignation of the Attorney General, Patrick Connolly, and destabilising Charles Haughey's Fianna Fáil government. Not everyone in RTÉ was happy with Mary McAleese's reports, particularly the station's legal advisers who saw it littered with potential banana skins.

Her critics in the station were gleeful therefore when the freelance reporter committed a glaring oversight. On July 18, 1983, the State prosecution announced it was dropping the second murder charge against McArthur, relating to the killing of a young farmer, Donal Dunne, with his own shotgun in Edenderry. By now, Mary was seven months pregnant with Emma and worried that she could be caught up in the angry scenes outside the Four Courts. The shouts of protest were menacingly audible in the courtroom. Using her legal contacts, she arranged safe passage for herself inside the building, thus missing the commotion outside the courthouse and the biggest story of the day.

'Commenting on ongoing court cases was controversial,' Ed Mulhall confirmed, 'and when she missed the mêlée certain critics of colour reporting were delighted.'

The incident made no dent in Mulhall's belief in Mary McAleese. When he was given charge of a new drive-time programme, she was his choice as one of its two presenters. *Studio 10* was a 90-minute mixed bag of news and current affairs and Irish radio's longest speech programme. A forerunner of *Today At Five*, it went out every Friday afternoon for six months, starting in November 1983.

It began with a baptism of fire, literally. Shortly into the programme on the first day, flames erupted in the control desk, necessitating the immediate evacuation of studio ten. Radio listeners were oblivious to the drama during a commercial break as the two presenters ripped off their headphones and ran helter-skelter down the corridor to resume broadcasting the show from studio five.

'She was a very consummate, confident performer,' said her *Studio 10* co-presenter, Colm Keane. 'Mary was incredibly bright, terribly diligent and professional. I remember doing a fairly hard-hitting interview with Brian Lenihan one day and, as he was walking up the studio steps after it, Mary looked over and gave me the thumbs up. A real, real pro. The rest of us used to go drinking after the programme but she never did. She was very thorough, almost blinkered.'

The programme, which featured regular contributions from the comedian, Dermot Morgan, and authors Colm Tóibín and Brendán O'hEithir, attracted critical acclaim. *The Irish Times* radio critic, Howard Kinley, tempered his positive review, however, with the assertion that Mary McAleese was more of 'an intellectual' than 'a communicator'. The basis of his thesis was that she had used the word 'correlation' rather than 'link' in an interview with the president of the Irish Astrological Society!

But the harmony of her new incarnation at RTÉ was about to hit a sour note. Once again, she would feel outside the pale in the city she regarded as her spiritual capital. The mystery lingers to this day as to what exactly precipitated her vitriolic quarrel with the National Union of Journalists. Fourteen years later, as President of Ireland, she would allude to it blithely at a media awards ceremony in the Berkeley Court Hotel and even then the massed ranks of the Fourth Estate would squirm with discomfiture.

She remained obdurate in her conviction that it all began on Thursday, February 9, 1984. The day she startled the nation by accompanying the Catholic bishops to the New Ireland Forum at the behest of her friend, Cardinal O'Fiaich. Her broadcasting colleagues, unaware of her involvement in Church politics, were stunned by her very public coming-out, which won her the nickname, the 'Episcopal Goldilocks'. Coming a year after the bitterly divisive referendum on abortion and at a time when the country was having paroxysms of conscience over unwanted teenage pregnancies, the general tenor of the media was to champion tolerance and liberalism. In such a climate, the Catholic Church, whose doctrine had dominated social legislation since the foundation of the State, was increasingly regarded as a negative force.

'I have a sneaking suspicion,' she said later, 'that if I had gone to the Forum with a Church of Ireland or a Jewish delegation there would not have been a word about it.'

In her mind, it was the trigger for what happened next. She was dropped from the union. At a special meeting of the NUJ's broadcasting branch in RTÉ, her membership was officially suspended and would, ultimately, be terminated two years later, in February 1986. The reason for her suspension was given as the union's pursuance of a policy to eradicate double jobbing in the sector. The establishment of a special committee was announced at the 1984 meeting to investigate the problem of members holding down jobs outside journalism. That committee never met.

Thirteen years after the episode's denouement, an extraordinary rash of amnesia still persisted in RTÉ about why precisely Mary McAleese was shown the door. Some people speculated that her suspension had been voluntary, a mechanism provided by the union to allow members take career breaks. That seems unlikely. She was in full flight as a programme presenter on both radio and television in a station that operated a closed shop. Others suggested that she might simply have stopped paying her union dues; another doubtful scenario as her income from RTÉ was precious. Her domestic arrangements in Ratoath had expanded to encompass a financially dependent husband, a six-month old baby and her 66-year-old father-in-law, Charlie, who had come to live with them after the unexpected death of his wife, Emma. In fact, Mary would tell friends afterwards that her £65 monthly cheque from *Europa* was essential to the household budget.

Adding to the mystery is the fact that the NUJ possesses no records whatsoever of Mary McAleese's membership of or departure from the union, either at its Irish office in Dublin's Liberty Hall or at head office in Acorn House, London.

'The broadcasting branch files in RTÉ up to 1991 were lost when they moved office,' confirmed the NUJ's Irish Secretary, Eoin Ronayne.

Undoubtedly, there were concerns about double jobbing in RTÉ at the time, as there were in other media organisations. Under the union's rules, members must earn two-thirds of their income from journalism. The broadcasting branch, made up solely of RTÉ in the years before independent radio and television licences were issued, guarded its territory as jealously as any other section of the media. 'The branch asked me about Mary McAleese's status. It was all done by word of mouth,' recalled Jim Eadie, who has since retired as Irish Secretary of the NUJ.

The woman at the centre of the affair, however, blamed a vindictive cabal of RTÉ journalists for her suspension. A news story in *The Irish Times* on February 10, 1986 recorded her belief that 'anti-Catholic prejudice had influenced some members of the NUJ'.

It went on: 'She said that one week after appearing at the Forum the branch spent a considerable time discussing her involvement with them. A special meeting took place in March 1984 to discuss her double jobbing. She was the only person named as engaging in it. She said there was a lengthy discussion at that meeting of her appearance with the bishops. It was argued that, like all members, she should derive most of her income from journalism and her membership was suspended.... In a letter she wrote to the branch, which was read at that meeting, she said she could understand the principle against double jobbing if it applied to everyone.'

The chairman of the broadcasting branch, Patrick Kinsella, dismissed McAleese's allegations as nonsensical. *The Irish Times* put it to him that the NUJ was being inconsistent as the *Today Tonight* presenter, Brian Farrell, was simultaneously an assistant professor of politics at UCD. 'Yes, there are anomalies,' Kinsella admitted.

There may, however, have been another causative factor in her sacking from the union. One that would have struck at the very heart of Irish journalism.

In a 'personality' interview published the same month as she appeared at the Forum, she told a newspaper reporter that RTÉ was little more than a distraction for her. 'At the moment I regard broadcasting as light relief,' she said. 'I don't play sport or have any other hobbies. I find you do need some kind of relief from law, so broadcasting has become my hobby.'

The comment was tactless and offensive. It smacked of intellectual superiority to those full-time journalists who prided themselves on their professionalism. Condemnation is a fact of life for anyone working in the media but, when a fellow practitioner denigrates the business as a mere 'hobby', fragile egos bruise easily.

Mary McAleese was acquiring a reputation for getting people's backs up. She had already ruffled some feathers in her profession of first choice. The previous year she had castigated the decision of the future Chief Justice and then a member of the High Court bench, Mr Justice Liam Hamilton. Writing in a law journal, the 31-year-old Reid Professor lambasted his judgment in the case of DPP v Vizzard and Carew, dealing with the offence of public nuisance, as 'stupid, lazy, plain wrong'. She forecast that the ruling made by the man who would swear her in as President of Ireland 14 years later was 'likely to give academic lawyers a case of the screaming abdabs.' The article went down like a lead balloon in legal circles, the judiciary's adverse reaction being duly communicated to the head of Trinity College's law department, Professor Robert Huston. 'He felt it was inelegant and going beyond the bounds of etiquette,' recalled a law lecturer in Trinity.

Mary McAleese was developing a habit of getting right under the establishment's skin. It was only a matter of time before the fingers of power would start to scratch.

# Holy Mary

THE WOMAN MADE HER pilgrimage every morning. She would leave her squat beehive cottage in the pitch dark, long before the lark had thought to stir. In the still of the sleeping countryside, she would walk the quarter-of-a-mile down the boreen to where it met the main road to Carrick-on-Shannon. Two miles further on, she would turn off onto the craggy slip road that led to the little church at Drumline, another mile away.

She was a tall woman, erect and proud. Her black belted coat, lace-up shoes and thick stockings barely visible in the early morning gloom. At the church, she would stoop low, retrieve the key left by the priest beneath a stone, and unlock the door. In the darkened chapel, she would light a candle, then follow the crudely crafted Stations of the Cross nailed to the walls in rapt prayer. When the priest arrived on the altar to prepare for eight o'clock mass, she would be there, kneeling in the flickering candlelight.

'In the winter we used to see her footprints in the snow,' remembered her neighbour, Seamus Butler.

Her name was Bridget Leneghan. She was a reserved gentlewoman, seldom leaving her humble cottage, except for her seven-mile trudge through the stony Roscommon landscape for mass every morning of her life. Her neighbours said she was a living saint. Her faith fortifying a life of disappointment as her children had scattered to the four winds. She never lived to know that she was the most enduring influence on the future president of her country.

'By the time I got to know her she had turned (so) consciously towards the task of going to morning mass that she rose earlier and earlier each day, until she established the custom of arriving at the church an hour early,' her grand-daughter remembered shortly before her inauguration as Uachtaráin na hÉireann.

'At first, I thought her strange,' Mary McAleese wrote in *Reconciled Being: Love In Chaos*. 'Later, I was grateful for her strangeness and for the gift of her teaching though, in fact, she never once explained to me what she was doing or why. But I knew even then that, in the stillness, there was a source which gave her courage and hope and meaning.'

In the Ireland of the 1950s, God-fearing devotion was chromosomal to the national identity. The Roman Catholic Church a dominant gene of the people's DNA.

'I...was nurtured on the rhetoric of the doctrine of transubstantiation, the smell of incense, the plaster statues, and apparitions ..', she wrote in 1997.

For the young Mary Leneghan, her religion dictated her identity and her destiny. The extreme devotion of her Granny Leneghan coupled with the victimisation of her fellow religious as she was growing up in Belfast would forge the motif of her life. As a Northern Catholic, her social status was sealed at birth. The word 'Taig' (Catholic) inscribed in the grooves of her fingerprints. Born into a ready-made tribe that clung together, stuck by the glue of their Church. Their isolation alleviated by the constancy of ritual and the exotica of its components. Like the black-robed Passionist priests in Holy Cross Monastery on the Crumlin Road. 'They dominated the landscape of my thinking and I loved them all,' she told a seminar in Dublin in 1995. 'And they dominated the spiritual landscape of my childhood. I owe them a debt that will never be repaid.'

When the Troubles began, she told Fionnuala O'Connor in her book, *In Search of a State: Catholics in Northern Ireland*, she had deliberately chosen not to be a revolutionary. 'And more important, (I) set out to try to find my way through the Church and through Christ. I struggled with that, couldn't sleep over it. But that was the decision I made – to go with the Christian view, not the way of violent revolution.'

She would rebel, of course. Like many teenagers, she would come to challenge the rules written with ancient authority. At the age of 18, the doubts that niggled inside her head stopped her in her tracks on her first day at Queens University. She had just enrolled as a law student and was strolling down the shady, verdant Elmwood Avenue, which housed the university's four chaplaincies. In the window of number 22, she spotted a poster inviting freshers to drop in for a cup of tea. She went in. There she met a man who would remain a friend for life.

Rev Cecil Kerr, one of four sons from a small farm outside Enniskillen, was the Church of Ireland chaplain to Queens. A soft-spoken holy man who would receive a 'People of the Year' award in Dublin in 1986 for his ecumenical work, he was her first encounter with the Anglican institution. She would return to number 22 Elmwood Avenue again and again, beginning a practice that would ignite the first controversy of her presidency by receiving Protestant communion.

But her rebellion would only serve to reinforce her faith. As she explained in a 1993 *Late Late Show* interview: 'I found that leaving mainstream Catholicism did not really satisfy me. I found it a very unhappy experience. I needed the mass as the centre of my life. So I re-committed myself to it.'

After the turmoil of RTÉ and, then, the birth of her first child, she became energetically reconciled with the institutional Catholic Church. In May 1983 she was a delegate to the annual Ecumenical Conference at Ballymascanlon Hotel outside Dundalk and became involved in Corrymeela, an inter-denominational peace group. Her bishop back in Belfast, Dr Cahal Daly of Down and Conor, rang her up when she was in RTÉ to see if she would work for the Church as a laywoman. She was introduced to bishops Dermot Herlihy and Jeremiah Newman of Limerick, the latter a powerful voice of orthodoxy in the hierarchy.

Her reunion with the Church coincided with her acceptance of its teachings on those moral issues she had 'struggled with'. The woman who had chaired a Pro-Choice meeting at Liberty Hall told the *Irish Independent* that she had voted for the constitutional ban on abortion in 1983. 'I'm an absolutist,' she explained. 'I'm very strongly opposed to abortion. I felt I had to make a forceful statement about it and voting "Yes" in the referendum was that for me.'

Having argued so trenchantly in favour of civil divorce at the Law Society debate in 1979, she now became a staunch opponent, a U-turn manoeuvred on the axis of her motto that 'there's no point in having a mind if you can't change it'. Her views on contraception were equally doctrinaire. Privately, she told a friend that 'the Pill was rammed down women's throats. It was a chemical experience on women's bodies.' Publicly, she made the unforgettable declaration that her husband had 'great self-control' in the planning of their family. She elaborated in a June 1994 interview with *The Irish Times*. 'I have a fear of tablets, pills and devices,' she admitted, 'and Martin and I are both very highly motivated and committed to each other so using the rhythm method is absolutely no problem, and it works – at least it's worked so far! I don't want to ram rhythm down people's throats. I think it's a deeply private matter....'

In early 1983 she was co-opted onto a working group of the Council for Social Welfare, an advisory body on social issues reporting to the Catholic Bishops Conference. During the Pope's address to the Irish bishops on his 1979 visit to the country, he had called on them to show special concern for prisoners. 'My dear brothers,' Pope John Paul urged them, 'do not neglect to provide for their material conditions and their families.'

The setting up of the working group, jointly by the Irish Commission for Justice and Peace and the Council for Social Welfare (which Mary McAleese joined fully in 1984) was a response to the Pope's appeal. Members of the group included Justice Sean Delap, Dr Maurice Hayes and the chaplains of Mountjoy Prison, Arbour Hill Prison and St Patrick's Institution for young offenders. Its report, 'The Prison System', was published in 1983 and called on the State to be moderate in its use of imprisonment.

'It is the Council's view that they should only be used to contain those whose offences are of such a serious nature that it is necessary to confine them in the interests of either society's protection or their own,' the report recommended.

By the time 'The Prison System' was published, Mary's star was in the ascendant of church affairs. She had shown herself to be willing and able, her legal expertise and her feel for humanitarian concerns combining to make her a sought-after committee worker.

'No matter where you were, when people were looking for advice her name always came up automatically,' said the Fianna Fail TD, Dick Roche, a former chairman of the Irish Commission for Justice and Peace. 'The thing to do was to ask Mary.'

So, when the Catholic bishops were planning their delegation to the New Ireland Forum, she was an obvious candidate. She was articulate, intrepid and, at the age of 32 with a face framed by a soft brush-back hairstyle, undeniably female among a phalanx of grey men. Cardinal O'Fiaich, who would ever after tease her as 'the bishops' woman', sounded her out. She said yes, telephoned her boss in *Studio 10* to warn him, and submerged herself in preparation.

She told the *Irish Independent* that, in the briefing before her appearance at Dublin Castle, she was not asked to present the bishops' point of view. It was patently unnecessary. 'I just heard what they had to say and found I could stand over everything they said. I share all the concerns they expressed,' she said.

The Forum had been set up by Garret FitzGerald, at the suggestion of SDLP leader John Hume, to re-examine the conflicting political positions on the island in an attempt to find stability and peace. Its agenda touched the very heart of Mary McAleese's own life as one who had directly suffered from the violence and volatility. She told a friend she believed the Forum was 'scraping away the barnacles of Irish history'. When she took her place in Dublin Castle at 11 o'clock on that February morning in 1984 her mind was focused on the imminent debate.

But the eyes of the most powerful man in that room were focused on her. She was still speaking to the Forum members when he had already resolved to give her life a daredevil spin on the merry-go-round.

# 9

# Rejection

HE WATCHED HER WITH those famously hooded eyes. Appraising her performance. Scrutinising her attractive, mobile face for any telltale signs of weakness. Cheering inwardly whenever she scored a point. Her sensible suit and sober blouse disguising an exciting mind. She was stealing the show from the four princes of the Church who flanked her.

'The sad thing,' she was saying, 'is that the only people in Northern Ireland, in the eyes of many – unfortunately, particularly many of the young and unemployed – who seem to be able to get things done are those who have guns in their hands. That is a factor that we must worry about because, as I've said, many people who put their vote in the box for Sinn Féin would not give their vote to violence but give it out of a sense of frustration of the small person against the big system by which he is oppressed. A way of telling people: "I am fed up. Do something for me." I wonder how far off is the day when these same people's ambivalence about violence may be resolved fully in favour of violence, which it most certainly will be if the Forum, for example, is not successful, if constitutional politics are not successful'.

He liked what he was seeing. Composure. Fluency. Intelligence. And that rare appetite for confrontation – a quality abundantly present in his own psychological armoury. When the Labour Party's representative, the redoubtable Senator Mary Robinson, lobbed the inevitable grenade at the bishops, he tensed, waiting to see how she would handle it. The atmosphere bristled with the ideological conflict between the two women lawyers from Trinity College, sitting on opposite sides of the magnificent conference room, poles apart politically. The missile Mary Robinson launched was the controversial question of integrated education and why the bishops were so hell-bent on blocking it.

'The notion that consensus comes from contact or even that understanding comes from contact is wrong,' the Senator's academic junior responded with implacable belief. 'It is a dubious and simplistic notion. It would be nice if it were right. There are very many levels of contact in Northern Ireland between people which do not demand honesty in relationships.

'I myself lived in an area which is often described as a flash point area, known as Ardoyne,' she went on, easing into her characteristic first-person narrative. 'It was a mixed area as I was growing up. I had tremendous contact with Protestant neighbours, played with them. They were in and out of my home but it did not stop one of them from becoming a member of the UDA and now doing a life sentence for killing five Catholics.

'Consensus does not always come from contact. It is worth noting in this context that Catholic education in Northern Ireland – I do not think anyone would deny, first of all, the right of parents to decide what kind of education is best for their children – that Catholic education arises in the context, not of a desire to create a sectarian education system, but out of a genuine desire to extend the human vision, the vision of a Catholic way, the way of life simply to the school.'

She had delivered the *coup de grâce*. It was enough for him. The audition was over.

'I want this woman as a candidate,' Charles J Haughey told his party's general secretary, Frank Wall. 'Find a constituency for her,' he ordered.

Of all the men in Ireland, Charles Haughey was the most loved, the most despised, the most feared, the most distrusted and the most intriguing. As a government minister in 1970, he had been sensationally charged with conspiring to import arms for use in Northern Ireland. Though he had been acquitted, the son-in-law of former Taoiseach Seán Lemass spent the next seven years in the political wilderness. His rehabilitation, when it came, was swift. Within 30 months of his prodigal return to the cabinet, he had fought off George Colley to assume the leadership of Fianna Fáil from Jack Lynch in December 1979.

By the time of the Forum he had already spearheaded Fianna Fáil in three bitter general elections and staved off as many internal party putsches against his leadership. He was determined to stamp his authority on both Fianna Fáil and the country at the next general election. And, in Mary McAleese, he saw a means to that end.

Though she was not a party member when Bishop Cahal Daly led her into the Forum as part of the Irish Episcopal Conference delegation, she was already active in Fianna Fáil. One of less than 20 members of the party's Women's Committee, set up by Haughey in 1981, she was involved in formulating policy designed to attract more women to the organisation. Her contribution to a position paper on divorce, teasing out the jurisdiction implications of the growing phenomenon in Ireland of the foreign decree nisi, did not jar with the no-divorce stance of either the Church or the party.

'Fianna Fáil had been terribly male-orientated up to that point,' Charles Haughey recalled. 'In my time in Fianna Fáil, particularly in the Dublin organisation, the rank and file were mainly women. A large proportion of the ordinary cumann membership would be women but they weren't prominent. The Women's Committee became very active in drawing up policy to attract new candidates.'

The role of women in Fianna Fáil, in fact, was akin to the flower arrangers and priests' housekeepers in the Catholic Church, largely relegated to the duties of sandwich-making and envelope-licking. A handful of women, like Maire Geoghegan-Quinn from Galway, had made it into national politics at Leinster House where she chaired the All-Party Oireachtas Committee on Women's Rights. She and the other women from the Fianna Fáil parliamentary party made up the bulk of the Women's Committee, along with a number of key officials, like Frank Wall's secretary, Catherine Byrne. Another was a 23-year-old public relations executive called Eileen Gleeson, who would play a significant part in Mary McAleese's life.

The Women's Committee usually met in Leinster House or at the party's headquarters in Upper Mount Street. By the time Mary came on board, it was in the throes of organising its inaugural annual conference, under the chairmanship of another woman who would play a pivotal role in her campaign for the presidency, Mary

O'Rourke. 'She was very gregarious,' the latter recalled. 'She didn't talk to us much about what happened to her family in the North. It was as if she consciously didn't want to be making a scene about it.'

Charles James Haughey and Mary Patricia McAleese had much in common. Both ardent nationalists who refused to kowtow to England, 'the old enemy', both harbouring great personal ambitions, they were a pair of street-wise straight-talkers who formed something of a mutual admiration society. 'I thought he was lovely,' she said many years later. 'I thought that, as a politician, he was one of the colourful stars.' Haughey had an empathy with Northern Catholics like herself that she recognised as a type of political fire-proofing. In 1986 he would begin the secret dialogue with a Redemptorist priest, Fr Alex Reid, which would eventually result in the peace process. It is recorded in *The Fight For Peace* by Eamonn Mallie and David McKittrick as the moment when 'Father Reid's venerable Volkswagen Polo first arrived at Charles Haughey's grand mansion at Kinsealy, north of Dublin.'

Mary told Caroline Walsh of *The Irish Times*, in June 1984: 'I have a very deep admiration for anyone whom the British government fears and I'm very sure they fear Charlie.' At the time of the New Ireland Forum, Haughey boasted a grand total of 52 first cousins in Northern Ireland. They included Carmel McGuinness, the wife of the SDLP's first Lord Mayor of Belfast, Alban McGuinness, and a future leader of the Women's Coalition, Monica McWilliams, the daughter of his favourite uncle.

'She (Mary McAleese) was very impressive at the Forum,' Charles Haughey recalled 15 years later. 'I wasn't terribly surprised that she was with the bishops. The bishops would have been very anxious to get somebody articulate and with a legal background. They had a very sticky wicket on the question of whether a separate education system was contributing to the divisions in the North. They wanted to hold onto their traditional role and, indeed, so did the Protestants. In the context of the Forum, it was a difficult one to cope with.'

Three months after her fateful Forum appearance, Mary McAleese addressed the first Fianna Fáil women's conference at Jurys Hotel in Dublin where she described Eamon de Valera as 'Ireland's greatest visionary' and where Charles Haughey described her as 'just out on her own'. Among the 400 delegates to the conference was a young

Fianna Fáil back-bencher who called for the promotion of women from within the party's own ranks. 'But we are always willing to have able, willing women from outside, like Mary McAleese,' she added. The back-bencher's name was Mary Harney.

*The Irish Times'* report of the conference the next day appeared under the headline, 'FF in Raptures at the Courtship of Mary'. The Mary in question was, of course, Mary McAleese.

She joined the Peadar Macken/Constance Markievicz cumann in 1985 – chosen because of its proximity to Trinity College in the constituency of Dublin South East – where she replaced her proposer, Tom Cosgrove, a highly-prized factotum in the Mount Street headquarters, as cumann secretary.

She had found a safe haven, an oasis where she felt comfortable, in a city that had harshly disappointed her expectations so far. 'She used to regale us with stories of RTÉ, the in-fighting, the cliques and the scheming,' said Charles Haughey. 'She was quite cynically amusing about it. She was bright, lively, humorous, very well informed. Any down side to her? Talkative! No, she was a quite articulate person with very strong views.'

There had been some speculation that she might contest the local elections in 1985 but it was never really a runner. In May of that year, the McAleese family practically doubled with the birth, at Daisy Hill Hospital in Newry, of the twins, Saramai and the boy, Justin, whom she named in honour of Fr Coyne, 16 years after his sudden death at Holy Cross Monastery. Martin, by now, had graduated from Trinity College and was commuting daily from Ratoath to work at a dental practice in the border town of Bessbrook run by Des Casey, a dentist originally from Bray, County Wicklow. In 1987, Martin would buy into the practice, displaying his business acumen with a decision to expand with a second surgery in Crossmaglen.

Mary, meanwhile, was stretching her amazing energy to the limit, and growing ever more politicised. As a full member of the hierarchy's Council for Social Welfare, she worked on a number of publications, dealing with public health policy, the travelling community, the penal system, and the Status of Children Bill. The Council also issued four booklets based on Pope John Paul's encyclical, *Laboren Exercens* (On Human Work).

At the same time, she was publicly ventilating her feminist ideology, announcing her intention to stand for election to the board of the Bank of Ireland, an exclusive male preserve for more than two centuries. Perhaps it was her knack of never applying for a job she was uncertain of securing (a track record that would be spectacularly ruptured within three years) that made her withdraw her name before the annual general meeting in July. In the event, the Bank of Ireland voted by 120 votes to 50 against appointing a woman director, 51-year-old Patsy Lawlor of Kildare County Council with whom Mary had initially planned to storm the bastion.

But she had plenty other irons in the fire. In 1985, when she joined the Fianna Fáil cumann in Westland Row, she was appointed a founding member of the Irish Commission for Prisoners Overseas, a sub-section of the bishops' Commission for Emigrants. The Prisoners Commission, which lobbied for redress of the injustices perpetrated in the landmark cases of the Birmingham Six, the Guildford Four and the Maguire Seven, held its first public meeting in the Republic that winter. It was held in the Oak Room of the Lord Mayor's residence, the Mansion House in Dublin, and was attended by Seán MacBride, the English historian Robert Kee, Annie Maguire, a grandmother who had been wrongly convicted on bomb charges in the English law courts, Commission member Dr Eamon Casey, the Bishop of Galway, and Mary McAleese.

'What was so good about her was her willingness not to unquestioningly accept information that was put out,' said Nuala Kelly of the Irish Commission for Prisoners Overseas. 'There are so many vested interests when an injustice happens that you need somebody with integrity to ask the questions.'

Her reputation as a powerful advocate of human rights was gaining circulation. While committed to such voluntary organisations as Focus Point, Victim Support and the Rape Crisis Centre, she was also engaging in the discourse that touched the very core of her being – Northern Ireland. In February 1985, she addressed an anti-strip search conference at Trinity College with the psychologist, Professor Ivor Browne, and the campaigning priest, Fr Raymond Murray. Three hundred people heard her that night condemning 'the continual excuses emanating from the Northern Ireland Office' as 'a sham'.

Her political credentials were impeccable. A university lecturer and a television journalist with a household face and a name bylined on a weekly column she had started to write for *The Sunday Tribune*. On paper, she was a dream electoral candidate. Theory, however, fell flat on its face when she contested an early selection convention for Fianna Fáil in Dublin South East on January 26, 1986. She came last, with a paltry seven votes. 'She was shafted,' Haughey believed. Sitting TD Gerry Brady and Councillor Michael Donnelly, a former Lord Mayor of Dublin, were chosen. The other candidate, Eoin Ryan, whose father, an elder statesman of the party, had publicly denounced Charles Haughey as 'an electoral liability', came in ahead of her, in third place.

The selection convention was a temporary set-back. Nothing more. She was, after all, the heir hand-picked by the leader himself. Assurances were given that she would be on the starting line when the election was called. In the interim, she would not be idle. It was the year of the first divorce referendum, a major plank of Dr Garret FitzGerald's constitutional crusade to make the Republic a more hospitable place to Northern unionists. To Mary McAleese, it was a monstrous proposition.

She had been working sporadically for Veritas Video Productions, an off-shoot of the Catholic Communications Centre in Booterstown. Now she was commissioned to make a documentary-style video on divorce, featuring a number of interviews, including one with her fellow Trinity lawyer, Professor William Binchy. The end product caused a furore, drawing the wrath of the Labour Lawyers Group who slammed it as 'bare-faced, anti-divorce propaganda and below the objective standard people expect from the legal profession.' The group singled out the 'loaded anti-divorce questions' put by Professor McAleese to Professor Binchy for special criticism.

She was not deterred in her resistance to the referendum proposal to allow divorce, despite her persuasive argument in its favour seven years earlier in Galway. In June 1986, she accepted an invitation to launch a book entitled *The Facilitators,* published by a Glenageary pro-life/anti-divorce activist, Nick Lowry. She used the occasion to launch a stinging attack on the Taoiseach, Dr Garret FitzGerald, and, by default, the media.

'First, wives will be better off after divorce, said Garret – clearly thinking that now he was capable of walking on water,' she ridiculed, 'he was equally capable of multiplying the loaves and fishes: making one salary, which had formerly provided for one family, now do the work of two. Not a whisper of dissent from the press.

'He claimed Northern Unionists would be sweetened by divorce,' she continued her withering assault. 'God help his wit and ours that have to listen to him! The North, it seems, is full of well-meaning pluralists on the Unionist side just waiting for some sign in the heavens that pluralism and democracy are at last on the horizon in the 26 Counties – and then we'll be marching over the border in droves. These are the well-known liberals and pluralists who conceded divorce over 30 years before they conceded one-man-one-vote. Divorce, we are told, will make us liberal, democratic, tolerant, pluralist. Terrific! We can proudly join the other liberal democracies of the world – Russia, South Africa, Poland, Northern Ireland.'

A month later, in a caustic review of a book by the religious affairs journalist, John Cooney, she wrote in the *Irish Independent* of the social exclusion which blighted her own public life. 'Those who favour divorce, limited (of course) abortion, etc., are courageous, brilliant, expert, etc. – all remarkably nice words. Those who do not (i.e. the vast majority of the citizenry) are characterised as clergy-ridden, scapular-soused, sectarian thicks, incapable of independent, profound thought who piggy-back ride on the croziers of bishops.'

It was the sort of colourful, fearless prose admired by the Fianna Fáil faithful, and true to the party's conservative policy on the so-called moral agenda. When the divorce referendum was resoundingly defeated on June 26 by a two-thirds majority, it was a mortal blow to the coalition government.

Mary was now twinned in spirit with Fianna Fáil. They were at one on two fronts: constitutional morality and Northern Ireland. Garret FitzGerald and Margaret Thatcher had signed the historic Anglo-Irish Agreement at Hillsborough Castle in November the previous year. It allowed for the setting up of an inter-governmental conference to be jointly chaired by the Northern Ireland Secretary of State and the Republic's Minister for Foreign Affairs and serviced by a secretariat of British and Irish civil servants based at Maryfield on the eastern outskirts of Belfast. The Agreement stipulated that any change in Northern Ireland's status could only come about with the consent of a majority of its people, obliterating any prospect of a united Ireland in the short term. Unionists in the North responded with a raging protest of No Surrender. In the South, Mary McAleese deemed it 'an awful fudge of a document'. Charles Haughey was of the same mind, putting down a failed motion of amendment in Dáil Eireann.

On October 12, 1986, as Garret FitzGerald's government was starting to wobble, Charles Haughey announced at the annual Wolfe Tone commemoration in Bodenstown, County Kildare that Fianna Fáil would seek to renegotiate the Agreement when the party returned to power.

In the same month, Mary McAleese travelled to Warrenpoint, Rostrevor's neighbouring town, to address the local SDLP branch. She told them she hoped any strains that had arisen between Fianna Fáil and the SDLP since the signing of the Anglo-Irish Agreement could be overcome. Her fealty to Fianna Fáil, the Republican Party, did not go unnoticed.

Five days before President Patrick Hillery dissolved the 24th Dáil on January 31, 1987, she finally secured her place on the Fianna Fáil ticket. Exercising its discretionary powers, the party's National Executive appended the names of both Mary McAleese and Eoin Ryan to the running order in Dublin South East.

'I was actively involved in securing her as a candidate,' Charles Haughey confirmed. 'There was no great mystery about it. If the leader of a party wanted a candidate there would be nothing unusual about getting it done. It was a weak panel (in Dublin South East) and it needed strengthening. She didn't take much persuading. She was always a politically conscious person.'

The auguries were rosy. The outgoing Fine Gael/Labour administration had presided over an economy that teetered on the brink of Armageddon. The budget deficit had risen inexorably to £1.39 billion, prompting swingeing cuts of £300 million in public spending. Unemployment stood at a record 250,178. The people were battle-weary from the divisive abortion and divorce referendums. The haemorrhage of emigration was bleeding the country dry of its young and the fall-out from the Troubles continued to spill over the border. Three months before the election, the newspaper opinion polls had shown 53 per cent support for Fianna Fáil, more than enough to realise that elusive dream – a majority government.

When Charles Haughey launched his party's campaign in Jurys Hotel to the strains of Beethoven's 'Emperor Symphony', the majestic grace notes sounded as much like an omen as a crescendo of vanity.

If anything, it was the klaxon of disaster. Beethoven was chosen to underscore the statesmanlike theme Haughey had dictated for the party's campaign. He wanted to run a positive, dignified campaign. The outgoing coalition, one of the most disliked ever, would be spared the expected onslaught. There would be no 'going for the jugular', the Fianna Fáil leader decreed. It was a spectacular mistake.

It took no account, for instance, of the Progressive Democrats, the fledgling party founded by Des O'Malley and Mary Harney, destined to take 14 seats in the new Dáil. Formed primarily by a rump of disaffected Fianna Fáilers who had despaired of Haughey's leadership, the party fielded a formidable line-up of high-profile candidates. Like the respected print journalist, Geraldine Kennedy, who chose to stand for the PDs in Dun Laoghaire, after the Lord Mayor of Dublin, Bertie Ahern, had approached her to run for Fianna Fáil in Dublin West.

In Dublin South East, the PDs had another impressive candidate in Michael McDowell, a barrister and former Fine Gael chairman in the constituency. His appearance in the line-up shifted the scales which had hitherto leaned in Fianna Fáil's favour, Dublin South East being the stomping ground of three outgoing coalition members – the Taoiseach, Garret FitzGerald, his running mate, Joe Doyle, and the Minister for Labour, Ruairi Quinn.

Fianna Fáil had held two seats here in the June 1981 election, and the party wanted the second one back. The plan was that Mary McAleese would liberate the hijacked seat from Fine Gael. She set about her task with gusto and the omnipresence of her husband at the hustings. It was Martin's name that appeared, in tiny print, at the bottom of her election literature and posters as the official publisher. The couple's friend and periodic babysitter in Ratoath, Harry Casey, joined them as Mary's election agent. Though she would later describe it as 'a very collegial experience', they worked in virtual isolation, the internal rivalry in the local Fianna Fáil organisation feeding the electoral dilettantes to the jaws of real politik.

One day, they were spotted by a bemused party member canvassing in the up-market Merrion Shopping Centre, oblivious to the fact that it lay outside the constituency boundary. Nobody had told them.

Dublin South East accommodates some of the richest and the poorest people in the country. The aura of affluence hangs over the elegant addresses of Ailesbury Road and Herbert Park. But, in places like Ringsend, Irishtown, Marrowbone Lane and the Basin Street flats, voters were struggling to keep their heads above the economic recession. Many of them had been affected by the closure of the Irish Sweepstakes and Irish Shipping. The government's health policy had also led to the closure of Sir Patrick Dun's and Mercer's hospitals in the constituency. It was in these places that Mary McAleese thrived, happily dissecting the problems in public housing, cuts in the health service and the creaking social welfare system.

In the wealthy suburbs, which lend their postal code to 'Dublin Four' liberalism, she got a rude awakening. Dublin South East revelled in the distinction of being the most liberal constituency in the country, having returned the biggest votes against the abortion amendment and for divorce in the referendums. Here she encountered an underlying antipathy to her conservative Northern identity, seen as a blow-in and a puppet of the hierarchy. Her posters vaunted the woman in the frilly blouse as 'A Fresh Start', but the voters were not buying it.

In a letter to each household, she enumerated her qualifications for a Dáil seat. 'I am an academic lawyer, housewife and mother of three children,' she wrote. 'I am the eldest of a family of nine, born in Belfast's Ardoyne. We lost our home and business in "The Troubles", but kept our sense of humour, and faith in the value of human life, constitutional politics and forgiveness. I practised as a barrister in Belfast before joining the staff of Trinity College in 1975. I worked as a current affairs journalist with RTÉ; I was a member of the Roman Catholic Episcopal delegation to the New Ireland Forum and for many years I have been politically active in a wide range of organisations concerned with social justice.' As a job application, it was probably the most ill-considered of her career, only serving to emphasise the very reasons why she was being greeted with such suspicion.

'It looked like we were grabbing the Church's nominee,' remembered Seamus Brennan, a member of Fianna Fáil's national election committee in 1987. 'She was known to have a lot of conservative views that could have got us into trouble. She was a dreadful candidate. She was very intense, engaging in philosophical debate on the doorsteps. She probably felt it was all these views that got her selected but the fact is it was purely because she was a high-profile candidate. There was an arrogance there at that stage. There's a difference between knowing it all and being seen to know it all. She was a bit over the top.'

The feedback from her canvass was negative. 'She has mellowed since but, at that stage, she seemed to be very uptight and angry,' recalled her running mate, Eoin Ryan. 'Cumann members were saying: "This woman ain't doing it." She was quite dogmatic.'

Across the country, the dull four-week election campaign was threatening to expire from boredom. Fianna Fáil had spent £2 million in its quest for the 84 Dáil seats that would give it a working majority in government. But its rating in the opinion polls had started to slide.

When the polls opened on Tuesday February 17 they were marked by voter apathy in Dublin South East, recording the lowest turnout in the country, at just 65 per cent of its 69,800 voters. It was an unpropitious omen for Fianna Fáil, and for Mary McAleese who had promised that, if elected, she would resign as Reid Professor at Trinity to be a full-time public representative. In her final letter to the electorate, she had written: 'It would be much easier for me to stay out of politics and to join in the familiar patter of criticism and contempt which usually accompanies talk about politicians. But good governments can bring more than prosperity to a country. They can bring self-confidence, pride, stability, dignity and respect, qualities that no economist can measure but which are a vital part of a nation's lifeblood nonetheless.' She had signed off with the valediction: 'I love this country and its people'. The signs were that her love would go unrequited.

She went to the theatre that night to see John B Keane's play, *The Field*, with Martin and Harry Casey. Before the curtain rose, she got talking to the people sitting beside her. They were from the North. They had recognised her and lavished her with well wishes. It was a surreal interlude on the day her political fate was sealed in the Republic's ballot boxes. It must have struck her in that darkened theatre as she watched the Bull McCabe threaten the stranger in town: 'No foreign cock with hair oil and a tie-pin is goin' to do me out o' my rights.'

As they were leaving the Abbey after the play, Harry asked her: 'Will you be disappointed tomorrow?'

'No,' she said.

But the extent of her loss was immeasurable. Victory would have launched her on the ladder of ministerial power. 'I would almost certainly have made her a junior minister,' Charles Haughey confirmed. Instead, with only 2,243 first preference votes and more than 5,000 short of the quota, she was facing rejection once again.

It was a creditable performance, elimination coming on the eleventh count with Fianna Fáil increasing its vote by 1.6 per cent in the constituency. At the count centre in the RDS, Garret FitzGerald, Ruairi Quinn and Gerry Brady had already been declared elected when it was announced that Michael McDowell had finally reached the quota.

Mary McAleese did not hear the announcement by the returning officer. She had already left.

# 10

# The Last Straw

'I'VE DONE WITH POLITICS,' she told Gay Byrne on *The Late Late Show*. 'I was talked into it and I talked myself into it.'

Politics, however, was not finished with Mary McAleese. Hardly had the ballot boxes been stored away after the 1987 general election than she became embroiled in a fierce battle of wills with her erstwhile political soulmate, Charles Haughey. The ties that held them together unravelling in a welter of recrimination. The man they called 'The Boss' had not earned his reputation as a political Houdini for nothing. Time and again he had survived when all the indications had been that his career was about to be buried. He had mastered the art of expediency, elevating the political U-turn to the level of high art. She might have believed there was no point in having a mind if she could not change it. He, on the other hand, seemed to think it was a prerequisite of ownership.

Fianna Fáil had returned to the Dáil with 81 seats, two short of a clear majority but still the only party with any hope of forming a government. Haughey was elected Taoiseach in a day of pure drama when the Ceann Comhairle's casting vote tipped the balance of a House deadlocked at 82 votes for him and 82 against. He had survived once more.

But the estrangement from his former protègè was already looming. It began with something so monotonous the rest of the country nearly fell asleep. The Single European Act (SEA) was one of those tedious treaties spewed out by the European Community every so often. Achingly worthy, with far-reaching consequences, it was written in the sort of eurocratic gobbledegook best applied to kindling the home fires. Its terms had already been hammered out and agreed by the Community's governments and now only needed their imprimatur to make it effective. It was routine. Hardly the stuff of epic political drama. At least, not until Mary McAleese's legal antennae started to twitch.

The SEA was, basically, a charter for cross-Community commerce, abolishing tariff barriers to trade at the member states' frontiers. Garret FitzGerald's coalition had planned to ratify it in the Dáil, despite Fianna Fáil's disgruntlement over perceived implications for Ireland's neutrality and the fear that a single market could wipe out what remained of Ireland's indigenous industries. On December 9, 1986, Charles Haughey had bullishly warned the House: 'It is dishonest and misleading for the Taoiseach, government ministers and anyone else to attempt to put the ratification of this Single European Act across as something of great benefit to the people of this country because that is not, in fact, the case.'

The seeds of revolt, meanwhile, were taking root a few hundred yards from Leinster House, in the genteel environs of Trinity College where a small coterie of academics had resolved to impede the passage of the SEA. Though brought together by various and divergent concerns about the legislation, they were united in their determination to knock it on the head. Two of the prime agitators were Anthony Coghlan, a senior lecturer in sociology at Trinity, and Raymond Crotty, an agriculture economist and a part-time lecturer in statistics at the university. They believed the SEA was designed to extend the powers and competence of the European Community beyond its legitimate brief. Crotty, in particular, feared that the free movement of capital would pose a threat to Ireland's sovereignty. In his autobiography, *A Radical's Response*, he wrote of the SEA ushering in 'a growing dependence of a former capitalist colony on former imperial powers'.

The group decided to contest parliament's ratification of the treaty in the Irish courts with Raymond Crotty as the plaintiff. In November 1986, The Constitutional Rights Committee was established to raise awareness and, more importantly, funds for the battle ahead. That was when Mary McAleese joined the fray. Her motivation differed fundamentally from the ideals of the others. She foresaw the SEA opening the floodgates to legalised abortion in

Ireland. Article 118a of the Act provided for the free movement of services within the EEC, which, she predicted, would include the surgical termination of pregnancies. Yet, Senator Des Hanafin, Fianna Fáil's conscience on the abortion debate, who was to create a political crisis by insisting on a protocol safeguarding against abortion in the later Maastricht Treaty, envisaged no such threat.

Anthony Coghlan approached the Reid Professor in Trinity to sound her out about joining the Constitutional Rights Committee. She readily consented to become its co-president with John Carroll, head of the Irish Transport and General Workers Union.

'Work was in progress to mobilise persons more closely identified with the centre of Irish politics,' Raymond Crotty recounted in his autobiography. 'This became the Constitutional Rights Campaign, under the joint chairmanship of Professor Mary McAleese and Mr John Carroll. Mary McAleese is a Professor of Law at Trinity College Dublin and had been associated with Family Solidarity in the divorce referendum.'

She assumed the mantle long before the general election, when Fianna Fáil, in opposition, was vociferating against the SEA. Her stance was symbiotic with that of a party frothing over the shibboleth of neutrality, a family jewel they flaunted as Dev's special legacy. On November 10, 1986 she was one of 15 lawyers who wrote a letter to the national newspapers outlining their concerns about the constitutionality of ratification. The letter, featuring the signatures of her friends, Seán MacBride and Kadar Asmal, was published in the *Irish Press*, Dev's own paper.

The Committee rented offices in Molesworth Street, within a stone's throw of Leinster House. As the Dáil's December deadline for ratification drew nearer (the SEA was due to come into operation throughout the EC on January 1), the campaign liaised with a similar outfit in Cork, led by husband-and-wife solicitors Joe Noonan and Mary Linehan. The couple, both stalwarts of the Campaign for Nuclear Disarmament and worried that Ireland's neutrality could be compromised by the SEA, had their own band of activists in the Munster capital called 'People First – Meitheal'. Among them was a young CND supporter named Adi Roche, who worked voluntarily in the office, sometimes delivering documents to the Dublin committee in Molesworth Street.

In another portent of the presidential election that lay 11 years off, Raymond Crotty initially engaged a Dublin solicitor to brief counsel in the case. The solicitor was TCG O'Mahony, who, more than a decade later, would claim credit for Dana's candidacy in the presidential election. In his 1988 autobiography, Crotty described O'Mahony's involvement in the campaign as follows. 'A most able, trenchant opponent of the SEA, who had been largely instrumental in creating an awareness of the possibility of challenging it in the courts, Mr O'Mahony had strong religious views which he did not hesitate to express. While not necessarily dissenting from Mr O'Mahony's views, nor of course questioning his right to express them, it seemed to me as the case developed that it would be prudent, given its highly political nature, to change to a solicitor of less pronounced views, less forcefully expressed.'

Before he departed the campaign, TCG O'Mahony briefed the senior counsel, Paul Callan, on its application to the High Court for an injunction preventing the ratification of the Single European Act.

At five o'clock on Christmas Eve, as the citizens of the capital raced to complete their festive shopping, Mr Justice Donal Barrington sat in special session to consider the application. The courts were in holiday recess and eerily empty, but for a couple of peeved guards and the troupe of Crotty's supporters hanging onto the judge's every word. Their whoops of triumph echoed through the black bowels of the Four Courts when Judge Barrington announced that he was granting the injunction. The Taoiseach, Garret FitzGerald, went to bed in south Dublin that night with a crisis on his hands. And on Christmas morning, more than 300 million Europeans awoke to the news that the treaty's implementation was being stalled by Ireland.

Mary McAleese was preoccupied with electioneering when, in February, the High Court threw out the campaign's argument that the SEA could not be endorsed by the Dáil but warranted a vote by all the people. In the lacuna between the general election and the formation of the new Fianna Fáil government, Charles Haughey had undergone a Pauline conversion at a meeting with the president of the European Commission, Jacques Delors. The threat of Ireland's isolation in the Community and the tantalising carrot of munificent structural funds were dangled before the Taoiseach-in-waiting. He returned to Leinster House convinced that the SEA was, after all, a very good thing for the country.

The Constitutional Rights Committee, however, refused to go away. Once granted leave to appeal the High Court decision, the campaign moved up a gear, collecting almost £16,000 in donations to fight the case. The Committee began to attract broad support, some from the most unlikely quarters. One day, a young woman strolled into the office in Molesworth Street and offered to help. She explained that she had her own public relations firm, that she was a friend of the Haughey family and that she was utterly disillusioned with the Taoiseach's volte-face. Her name, she said, was Veronica Guerin.

'We thought at first she was a spy and we had a bit of debate about that,' Anthony Coghlan remembered. 'She knew the Haugheys. She'd even been to Innisvickilaun. But it turned out that she really was disillusioned with Haughey and she was worried about the neutrality aspect. We made her our publicity officer.'

Ten years before she was shockingly murdered for her work as an investigative journalist, Veronica Guerin stepped innocently onto the landmine of Mary McAleese's rancorous relationship with RTÉ. When the Supreme Court ruled in April that the government was, in fact, constitutionally obliged to hold a referendum on the SEA and a date was set for the plebiscite the following month, the state broadcaster devoted substantial airtime to examining its ramifications. Mary's former colleagues in RTÉ were planning two programmes on the issue and the anti-SEA campaign was anxious to participate. Mary was their obvious spokesperson. Personable, articulate and a professional broadcaster, she was, even more strategically, associated in the public's mind with Fianna Fáil. The campaign's publicity officer went to Montrose to make the pitch.

'I remember Veronica coming back from RTÉ looking very glum,' said Anthony Coghlan. 'She said she'd been told we could have anyone we wanted on the programme – but not Mary McAleese.'

RTÉ had slammed the door shut in her face. Now Charles Haughey was to do the same. After the Supreme Court ruling, he told the Dáil: 'We have a responsibility to our partners in the

Community to take expeditious steps to enable the Single Act to come into force.'

Mary McAleese saw Haughey's about-face as a betrayal. He saw the campaign she was part of as troublesome and somewhat embarrassing. 'I had to phone all the other heads of state to explain that we had this constitutional tradition which meant we couldn't sign up for the SEA immediately,' he remembered. 'I told them we were going to have a referendum and we'd almost certainly carry it.'

At a press conference in April, Mary McAleese questioned whether a united Europe was even desirable if it meant the country had to relinquish its core values for the payback of economic largesse.

As he left Leinster House that evening, a reporter asked the Taoiseach how he felt about the maverick line being taken by a prominent member of his party.

'Did you say prominent?' he replied tartly.

But the lady was not for turning, despite a *Sunday Tribune* report on May 24 that dissidents would be severely disciplined by the party after the referendum. She embarked on a series of public rallies around the country, defying her leader's vexation. At a meeting in Arklow, County Wicklow she showed the steel of her mettle when she refused to lie down, declaring: 'I'll stay in the shagging party, even if he throws me out!'

But the outcome was to prove unworthy of such self-sacrifice. The government won the referendum handsomely, by 70 per cent of the vote. It was Mary McAleese's second defeat at the polls in the space of three months.

It was not the end of her battle with Charles Haughey, however. While the tussle over the SEA had been a scintillating public duel, much of it was innocuous posturing. In her way, Mary McAleese was every bit as pragmatic as Haughey and she recognised artful politicking when she saw it. She had taken off on a kamikaze mission that nose-dived. The exercise could be chalked up to experience. The crux of their next confrontation, though, went to their very souls. It would leave the Belfast woman dejected and hurt, and feeling as let down as ever she had been.

The contentious issue of extradition had been a burgeoning one since before Haughey took office. The notion of handing Irish suspects over to the British authorities rankled in a country still nursing its wounds after centuries of occupation by its bigger neighbour. It ran counter to every republican cell in the Fianna Fáil leader's body and Mary McAleese had felt comforted by that knowledge.

Having witnessed the introduction of internment in Belfast in 1971 and the arbitrary 'lifting' of Catholic men in Ardoyne, the very idea of extradition repulsed her. She harboured a deep-seated distrust of the administration of justice in Britain, and in Northern Ireland where it was rubber-stamped by the Diplock courts. She had argued against the system on November 30, 1986 in a regular column she had started to write for *The Sunday Tribune*. 'Whether the Diplock courts have one judge or three, whether those judges are from Northern Ireland or Timbuktu, the court will still operate the same rules of evidence and of admissibility of confession statements, which in reality are the things which most truly mark the Diplock courts out from the "ordinary courts". 'Good old Lord Diplock,' she wrote, 'did away with that because, quite simply, it was making life too tough for the prosecution. So, in the Diplock courts it is the accused person who must establish that the statement was forced out of him.'

She possessed an instinctive compassion for prisoners that she had channelled into much of her academic work as a penology lecturer. Just as she had wept listening to Eddie Cahill's harrowing account of prison life at the Milltown hearings seven years earlier, tears would course down her cheeks when she shared a television programme with Hugh Callaghan of the Birmingham Six. Under the auspices of the Irish Commission for Prisoners Overseas, she chaired a public meeting in 1987 on the topic of prisoner transfers from England. Her impression of the British jurisdiction was that it was 'clearly incapable of filtering hysterical racist prejudice out of its police, its juries and its judges'.

Though the Commission had no official position on extradition, it did make representations to the government to withhold its support until measures were adopted to redress the injustices in cases like the Birmingham Six.

In her newspaper column of December 14, 1986, Mary McAleese had warned Garret FitzGerald about Britain's track record in its treatment of Irish suspects. 'He ought to be reminded,' she wrote, 'that among the issues which jaundice Northern nationalists' attitude to British justice are the spectre of Giuseppe Conlon who died in prison for something he did not do, Annie Maguire, her family, the Guildford Four, the Birmingham Six – all jailed for being Irish, Catholic and in Britain at the wrong time.'

When Haughey took power, he pursued a policy of non-co-operation. That changed, however, when the gardaí finally hunted down the notorious Armagh terrorist, Dessie O'Hare, after his gang had kidnapped a Dublin dentist, John O'Grady. On the day O'Hare was apprehended, the Taoiseach revealed his new attitude to the Dáil. 'The recent combination of events – the seizure of a massive shipment of arms by the French authorities (on board *The Eksund*), the kidnapping of John O'Grady and the slaughter at Enniskillen – bring the whole question of subversive threats to the security of this state into a new and urgent focus. We are not soft on terrorism, domestic or international, and we must give a clear and unequivocal signal to that effect.'

His revised position on extradition was a natural progression of Haughey's recent acceptance of the Anglo-Irish Agreement, which he had opposed so vehemently a year before. Mary McAleese's low opinion of the pact oozed from a *Sunday Tribune* column she penned in November 1986, exactly a year after the Agreement was signed. 'Reconciliation between the two ambitions of full membership of Great Britain and a sovereign united Ireland is simply impossible,' she argued. 'They are, as Unionists keep telling us, mutually exclusive. If that is so, and if our politicians still believe, as they purport to, that Ireland's future is best served within the framework of a sovereign independent state, then why participate in a violent and ineffective charade which still postpones indefinitely the search for a full and final settlement of the Northern crisis?'

Her opposition to the Anglo-Irish Agreement lumped her into a bizarre alliance, with Ian Paisley bellowing 'No surrender' on one side and, on the other, Senator Mary Robinson parting company with the Labour Party on the principle that the pact ill-served the unionist community.

The test of time has since shown the value of both extradition and the Anglo-Irish Agreement as building blocks for the peace process of the 1990s. Speaking to the Belfast journalist, Fionnuala O'Connor, in 1993, Mary McAleese conceded as much in relation to the Agreement. 'I thought at first that the Anglo-Irish Agreement was an awful fudge of a document,' she admitted, 'but it's what people think it says that matters, and it did grow. The Agreement and direct rule – between them, they've offered people a way of life.'

Her reading of events, however, contains an implicit refusal to make a full capitulation. What she is saying is not so much that the Agreement *per se* was well judged but that the way it was interpreted proved fruitful. That it was somehow saved by others' erroneous understanding of it.

The Anglo-Irish Agreement did, in fact, take on a life of its own, breathing some of its vitality into Charles Haughey's political career. And extinguishing the last embers of Mary McAleese's burning desire to find peace of mind in the Republic.

# 11

# Packing Up

HER LIFE IN THE Republic changed Mary McAleese in ways she never expected. She grew more circumspect; less romantic in her attachment to the South.

There had been a time when she regarded Dublin as the caring motherland reaching out to cuddle her in folds of tender love. The capital had beckoned to her as a young adult in north Belfast yearning to escape the nightmare of death and hatred. She had thought she was coming home to a family waiting to clasp her to its bosom. But there had been no blazing fires, no yellow ribbons fluttering for the prodigal daughter.

'One thing I had in common with a lot of Protestants was my image of the Republic,' she confessed. 'I thought it was full of Gaelic-speaking Catholics who dropped to their knees at the ring of an angelus bell, and who were champing at the bit to get their hands on the wee North, paint it green and, in a move of blinding triumphalism, install the Pope in Stormont.'

She did not know these people who turned a deaf ear to her story, whose eyes narrowed in wariness at the inflections of her words. They were strangers who spoke in forked, foreign tongues.

The sense of belonging that had always greeted her on the family holidays in Roscommon was a mirage that soon evaporated in Dublin. She was alone, an outsider. Dispossessed of her place among a people she had always thought of as her own. 'I met this coldness and: "Don't tell me. Your story is the story of a Provo." Merciful God!' she told Fionnuala O'Connor. She did not recognise the faces: the coalface of RTÉ, the spurning face of the NUJ, the face of suspicion in Dublin Four that frowned on her Catholic, Northern nationalist identity. Only in Trinity College, with its learned tradition of tolerance, did she feel at ease. 'I sensed she was disenchanted with the Republic in a big way,' said her fellow law lecturer, Gerard Hogan. 'I think she felt that Northern nationalists were not quite accepted here.'

Gradually, she began to curtail the telling of her story, alerted by the glazed eyes of an unwilling audience. It went against her nature, that impulse to recount the life experiences that informed her opinions. A confessional trademark too of feminist oratory which, in the Dublin of the 1970s, was dismissed as seditious stuff and nonsense.

'Her statements came from experienced reality. They would be quite personal,' David Norris recalled. 'That has the strength of emotional charge but it can also make you vulnerable by betraying too much about yourself. Actually, I never heard her moan. She never whinged about Belfast. She never milked her experiences for sympathy.'

To her, Dublin was not Ireland. It was a different country, riddled with complexities and straining at the leash of its conservative past. Stories of dead newborn babies and tragic teenage mothers filtered up from the mists of its rural hinterland, to be clinically dissected in the city's chattering salons, there to expose the entrails of Ireland's repressive culture. Dublin had gone on ahead. And Mary McAleese rushed to catch up. She would make her mark on its march.

She did not lack personal ambition. It was what led her to this juncture in her life: the first of her family to attain a university degree; the irresistible lure of a nominal professorship at the age of 24. But she had other motivations too. The need to assimilate into a country she doggedly refused to disown. Maybe even, a craving for enough power to influence its destiny, from the perch of the establishment – Fianna Fáil, RTÉ, the Roman Catholic Church and Trinity College.

She had been rejected at almost every turn: RTÉ, the NUJ, the voters of Dublin South East. Haughey had not included her among the Taoiseach's eleven nominees to Seanad Éireann. After 10 years as Reid Professor, there was no major *œuvre* that might have merited a fellowship of Trinity. Even her warnings about the Single European Act had gone unheeded.

Throughout it all, she had never surrendered her integrity. She could still laugh. She could still cry. She prayed hard, she haggled for tickets to Croke Park whenever Down were playing, she knitted intricate sweaters for herself, she read books, invited friends home for dinner and thanked God for Martin's father, Charlie, the pivot of her home without whom, she said, 'our lives couldn't exist'. Nor was her compassion diminished. Quietly and anonymously, she tried to make life more comfortable for others. Friends in Ratoath tell of how she used to pass on parcels of baby clothes, through a third party, if she heard a family was struggling. On one occasion, she had a domestic oil tank replenished with fuel for the winter, never telling that family she was their benefactor.

Dublin's greatest gift to her had been the support structure in her private life that would allow her to chase her dreams. Martin, the man she might never have married had not the city undermined her promise to marry another. He was her rock. Gentle and serious with a way of poking fun at his wife, dampening her ardour whenever it threatened to combust. An atmospheric life force that she knew to be elemental; vital. She had stood by him when he went back to college to study dentistry at the age of 30, the sole provider in those four years when their three children were born. He, when the need arose, would return the favour tenfold.

The first time he had seen her, that night in St Dominics Convent when they were both only 17 and she had tossed her hair with impatient energy, he had recognised something in her. A quality that fascinated him, a dynamism that would peter out at her peril. So he gave her space. Gave her the quiet support and the freedom, even tranches of his own career path, to nurture that energy.

Martin too had been jolted by Dublin. Like his wife, he had suffered the viciousness of Belfast, his family burnt out and his brother's arm sliced in a sectarian assault. Yet, he was sheltered from the harsher realities Mary encountered in their adopted city, protected by the apolitical atmospherics of the travel business, the disciplined life of a mature student and, at the end, daily commuting to the North. But he saw how it was tearing his wife apart. It was he who decided they should go back home.

'I would have been happy to remain in Dublin but (I) was dragged screaming by Martin,' Mary once revealed.

She told Fionnuala O'Connor: 'Martin, my husband, and I felt, looking back, that our living in Dublin had been a shocking experience. We had left Northern Ireland because of the bigotry here: both our families had been victims of that. We both have a phenomenal love for the Republic. However, Dublin isn't the Republic and revisionism isn't Ireland.'

They found a house in Rostrevor, a comfortable family home occluded by tall, perfumed shrubbery. It was named 'Kairos', the Greek word for 'opportunity'. They could see the tranquil, softly rippling waters of Carlingford Lough from every window. 'Kairos' fit snug into the heart of the village, beside the butcher's shop in Bridge Street, near her parents' home. In the first week of August 1987, they took out a mortgage in their joint names with the Ulster Bank. They put Emma's name down for her first day at school in St Louis, telephoned their friends to say they were coming home, and loaded up the car with their worldly goods for the 100-minute drive to a new life.

# 12

# Bringing Home the Baggage

SHE HIT BELFAST LIKE a rocket. Shrapnel of outraged indignation exploding in a tornado of political controversy. It ricocheted off the solid, civilised portals of Queens University to crash-land spectacularly, across the Irish Sea, in the lap of the House of Commons. In one of the most ironic twists of her life, her return would directly contribute to the momentous events yet to unfold in Northern Ireland's modern history.

And all because Mary McAleese got a new job.

She had come back to her alma mater, The Queens University Belfast founded in 1845, which had been the beacon of her early adult life. She officially began work in January 1988, as Director of the Institute of Professional Legal Studies, once her contract with Trinity College had expired, three months into the academic year. It was a prestigious position, the kingpin in the North's elite legal firmament, grooming the solicitors and barristers of the future for the courtrooms she herself had found so intimidating. The Institute was something of a novice, only established 12 years earlier and still unsteady on its feet. It needed somebody at the helm with energy, imagination and inspirational self-confidence.

What it did not need, in the horror-filled eyes of the establishment, was a woman, a Catholic and a Fianna Fáil has-been. The unholy trinity of Mary McAleese who had been blaspheming from south of the border for years. Her activities and aspersions had winged their way from Dublin, reverberating round the predominantly unionist fraternity of the North's legal establishment. They knew her as someone who had sought election to Eire's parliament for an organisation that styled itself The Republican

Party, led by a man who doubled as a voodoo doll in the loyalist clubs of the Shankill.

Moreover, she had taken every opportunity of her 12-year sojourn in the South to ridicule the criminal justice system that operated in Northern Ireland, describing it as 'the archetypal police state'. Strip-searching, the RUC, the Diplock Courts and their judges – she had lambasted them all, never sparing her stridency. She had urged against extradition from the Republic, warning that British justice could not be trusted, and complained that the Divis area of Belfast was subject to 'the harassment of its people by successive waves of British regiments'. Now here she was, ensconced in one of the most influential positions of that self-same system she had hounded so relentlessly. In Dublin, she had boldly declared her vision of 'a nation state' and self-determination for the island. In one of her most provocative pronouncements, she had verbally bulldozed the cornerstone of unionist and loyalist hostility to the Republic.

In an interview with *In Dublin* magazine, 18 months before her return to Belfast, she had laid into the cosy relationship between religion and politics inherent to a brand of unionism that liked to sneer at the popery of the South. 'I think there are Northern unionists who use the Rome jibe too easily and too maliciously and when the finger is pointed at the Republic of Ireland as a sectarian state,' she railed. 'Let me tell you something, I have lived in both states and, for a confessional state and a sectarian state, there is nothing on the map to beat Northern Ireland in Western Europe. There are politicians who are ministers, ministers who are politicians and the influence of religious rhetoric in politics in Northern Ireland is infinitely stronger that anything in the Republic.

'I wouldn't deny,' she went on, 'that you would also find that rhetoric in the Republic. It's hardly surprising that you would in a country with an overwhelmingly Catholic population. But to accept that jibe from people who deliberately created a Protestant state for a Protestant people and who make no secret of the fact that they want to get back to that situation, I simply refuse to enter into debate with them. I refuse to justify the credentials of this state (the Republic), whose credentials are accepted world-wide, against the cheap allegations from people whose past history in terms of sectarian politics speaks for itself.'

In a normal society, such forthrightness is tolerated as an exercise of free speech. Admired even, for its stark absence of obfuscation and political pussy-footing. But Northern Ireland was no normal society. It was a fragile goldfish bowl awash with the hurts of unguarded language – and she had dived in headlong with a tankful of oxygen. To say she was not welcome back in Belfast is an understatement. The scarlet jezebel of Rome would have got a warmer reception. But there was one other aspect to her appointment at Queens University that nailed the coffin of her welcome. The career ambitions of her old law lecturer, David Trimble. Since her graduation in 1973, he had been promoted to the level of senior lecturer and was regarded as a potential vice-chancellor. David Trimble personified the Protestant middle-class culture that prevailed in the university. Known as a militant unionist, he had been William Craig's deputy in the hard-line Vanguard when Craig talked of 'liquidating the enemy' at a mass rally in Ormeau Park. A gauche, bespectacled academic, David Trimble was a member of the Ulster Unionist Party by 1988, and chairman of the Lagan Valley Unionist Association.

More critically, he too had applied for the job as Director of the Institute of Professional Legal Studies.

The position had initially been advertised in *The Belfast Telegraph* on April 9 1987, setting May 7 as the closing date for applications. The text of the advertisement read:

> The Queen's University of Belfast
> Director of Institute of Professional Legal Studies
> The Institute of Professional Legal Studies was established in 1976 by the University (in co-operation with the Inn of Court and Incorporated Law Society of Northern Ireland) to provide a full-time vocational year course of professional legal training for law graduates intending to practise as solicitors or barristers in Northern Ireland...
> Applicants for the Directorship, which will be held for a period of five years in the first instance, subject to renewal by mutual agreement, should preferably be barristers or solicitors, with experience in professional practice, but not necessarily holding qualifications to practise in Northern Ireland. Experience in law teaching would be desirable but not essential. The salary of the Director is negotiable and

will be comparable to that applicable to posts in the public
service outside private practice...

The Institute was designed to fill the gap between law graduates'
academic qualifications and the practical experience of full-time
work, giving them a grinding in negotiation skills, advocacy,
drafting and client care. The new Northern Ireland jurisdiction, set
up in 1920, had left a vacuum in the area of professional training.
Unlike England, there was no chambers system and no rule of
pupillage. The *ad hoc* custom was for newly-called barristers to work
with an experienced junior counsel for six months. A committee set
up to examine the weaknesses in the system recommended in the
1976 Armitage Report that a new structure be implemented.

Clause 39 of the Report stated: 'It is clear to us from the evidence
submitted that the successful completion of existing courses of
professional training provides no guarantee as to the competence or the
quality – beyond academic quality – of a candidate for either branch of
the profession. We are satisfied that the case for change is overwhelming.'

The Report proposed the establishment of an institute to bridge
the gap, to be headed up by a director 'with wide experience in
successful practice'. Clause 101 stated: 'Such person could expect to
command a salary as a practitioner above the maximum professorial
salary paid by Queen's University. We therefore recommend that
the salary should be fixed at the maximum professorial salary of the
University and we would expect this amount to be supplemented by
limited private practice or other outside sources.'

There had been two directors since the Institute was founded;
both men, both Protestants, and both solicitors. The inaugural
director, James Elliott, had been Belfast City coroner. The second
incumbent, James Russell, had been a senior partner of the firm JW
Russell & Sons for more than 20 years. Their appointments had
been consistent with the political climate in the university where, in
the early 1980s, as few as 20 per cent of the staff in some departments
were Catholics and 100 of the 104 professors were Protestants. The
Institute of Professional Legal Studies was governed by the Council
of Legal Education, including representatives of Queens, the Law
Society and the Bar Council, chaired by the Lord Chief Justice.

In the summer of 1987, the Council set up an interview panel to
fill the vacancy created by James Russell's retirement. There must

have been a dearth of interested talent, however, as none of the candidates was considered suitable. The job was re-advertised and individual members of the interview board began privately canvassing potential candidates by word of mouth. It finally came down to just two: David Trimble, who had devoted his entire career to teaching law at Queens since graduating with a first-class honours degree in 1968; and Mary McAleese, who had taught criminal law, criminology and penology at Trinity for nine years.

It was a short list with an even shorter fuse. By September, word had leaked out that Mary McAleese had got the job – the first Catholic, the first woman and the first barrister to fill the position. It was met with disbelief, quickly followed by fury. David Trimble, whose wife, Daphne, was working as a solicitor, was stunned. He had invested his whole professional life in the university, only to be passed over for a parvenu who had flitted between academia, journalism and party politics in a foreign country. He was deeply resentful. It was cold comfort to him that his colleagues in legal circles and in politics were fulminating about his rival, the usurper they depicted as a cynical careerist and a Roman Catholic zealot with no interest in teaching law. A token Taig in a skirt.

At the Institute office in Upper Crescent, the news was received with a mixture of bafflement and apprehension. Primarily, it met a wall of silence.

'She was probably an unknown quantity to some members of the profession and a known quantity to other members of the profession,' recalled Anne Fenton, a lecturer at the Institute who would work with Mary McAleese for the next decade. 'There was a wariness of what she would be doing for the Institute. There were some hostile vibrations from the profession.'

The vice-chancellor of Queens, Professor Gordon Beveridge, tried to dampen the protests by insisting that Mary McAleese had been the most suitable applicant for the job. But the protesters only scoffed at his effort to mollify them. The cacophony of unionist voices grew all the louder asserting that, for the single year she had practised as a barrister, her name never even featured in any cases documented by the Northern Ireland Reports. She had been called to the Bar of the Republic in 1978 and had never practised there at all. She patently failed to fill the criterion of legal practice specified by Armitage, they clamoured, ignoring the fact that their own favourite, David Trimble, was burdened with the same handicap. The only reason Mary McAleese had got the job, her critics darkly surmised, was as some kind of political sop bestowed by the Anglo-Irish Agreement, engineered by her political mentor in Dublin, Charles Haughey.

More than a decade later, the retired Fianna Fáil leader rubbished the allegation. 'I'd love to be able to claim it but it is absolutely not true,' Charles Haughey said. 'Anyone with any knowledge of the political and academic realities would know any such suggestion is absurd.'

But her detractors were determined to make an issue of the appointment they characterised as the parachuting in of a nonentity from a foreign jurisdiction. 'There is a certain type of Unionist who simply cannot bear the thought of any Catholic getting anywhere on their own merits,' she retorted to no avail.

In December, four Unionist MPs tabled a motion in the House of Commons, calling for a full debate. It was an 'early day motion'; an instrument of parliament regularly employed to either condemn government policies or to record such historic events as an MP's home football club winning the FA Cup. Early day motions are seldom debated, most often vanishing into the ether of Westminster's records. The motion proposed by the Northern Ireland quartet contained 10 questions and read as follows:

> That this House, believing in the principles of merit, equal opportunity and fair employment, shares the concern among members of the legal profession and others regarding the appointment of Mary McAleese as Director of the Institute of Professional Legal Studies at Queens University, Belfast; and calls for an early debate, to establish, if the post was advertised for a semi-retired or retired practitioner of several years standing; if Mary McAleese has practical legal experience; if on graduating from Queens University, Belfast, she went to live and work in another jurisdiction, namely the Republic of Ireland; if she has ever practised in the jurisdiction of the United Kingdom; if she now spends two days per week on average in Belfast and still lectures in Dublin; the level of salary afforded to the Director of the Institute of Professional Legal Studies at Queens University, Belfast; the number of lectures given by Mary McAleese since her

appointment at Queens University, Belfast, to date; whether there is validity in the speculation that Mary McAleese was nominated by the Premier of the Republic of Ireland, Charles Haughey, and appointed for political reasons rather than merit; and the number of applications made for the position of the Director of the Institute of Professional Legal Studies at Queens University, Belfast, and the qualifications of each applicant.

The four signatories to the Commons motion, Roy Beggs, Clifford Forsythe, Cecil Walker and John Taylor, were all leading members of the Ulster Unionist Party. Less than eight years later, John Taylor would become deputy leader of the UUP on the resignation of James Molyneaux and upon the succession of a new leader, one David Trimble.

He had looked like the rank outsider in the leadership stakes. Swotty and socially ill at ease, the Bangor grammar boy was firmly aligned with the more reactionary flank of the party. Furthermore, he had spent most of his career in the relatively non-contentious world of Queens, happily engrossed in deciphering complex legal papers. But, when David Trimble, the Orangeman, marched triumphally down the Garvaghy Road in 1995, hand-in-hand with Ian Paisley, his ratings shot upwards within the party. That was the year the Drumcree parade sprouted as an ugly metaphor for the wider divisions in the North and Trimble's surprisingly exuberant defiance won him precious brownie points with the Orange Order.

The month before his election to the leadership, he had appeared on a quirky UTV television programme, entitled *If I Should Die*, presented by the former Moderator of the Presbyterian Church, Rev John Dunlop. The programme was a somewhat macabre piece of whimsy, predicated on the participants' fascination with their own obituaries. When Mary McAleese was the featured guest in August 1995, it sounded distinctly more macabre than whimsical as David Trimble repeated the old accusation that she had only landed the Queens job because of political pressure from Dublin.

She faced him down on the air. 'There were two candidates short-listed for the Institute,' she replied acidly. 'I was one and he was the other. I leave it to people to make up their own minds about that, except to say that within a week of my appointment as Director in

1987 there were 10 questions tabled at Westminster by a member of his party about my appointment.'

In private, she told friends she was convinced the parliamentary motion had been tabled at Trimble's behest.

The bitterness endured between the two of them until one of the worst atrocities perpetrated in 30 years of violence forged a public reconciliation. It was in the aftermath of the Omagh bomb, which killed 29 people in August 1998, sending shock waves round the world. She, as President of the Republic, had travelled from her grandparents' old home in Roscommon to attend the funerals of three little boys from Buncrana who died in the explosion. And it was there, in the midst of unbearable grief wrought by vicious intransigence, that she shook the hand of her old enemy, the man who was now First Minister designate of Northern Ireland.

Watched by an unwitting world media, it must have struck them both, as they followed a child's coffin into a sobbing country churchyard, how the tangling of their own lives had led to this poignant settling of their differences. For the people of the two parts of their island might never have been united in such revulsion and heartache had not Mary McAleese got that job in Queens 10 years before. Because, had she not, then David Trimble might never have flung himself into full-time politics as an antidote to his disappointment, winning the Upper Bann by-election in 1990 and subsequently, as the Ulster Unionists leader, steering his constituency towards approval of the historic Good Friday Agreement.

When she returned to Northern Ireland a decade before, the place had been convulsed with grotesque terrorist outrages, tit-for-tat killings and poisonous hatred. While she had been away, the IRA had become the most expert civilian death force in the world, singling out what it termed 'legitimate targets' for assassination, like the 11 Protestant people killed by 40lbs of IRA gelignite in Enniskillen on Remembrance Day, November 8 1987. In response, the loyalist terrorists of the UDA and the UVF had inflicted a reign of terror on the Catholic population with random executions of victims whose only crime was to live in nationalist areas.

Mary McAleese had every reason to fear that she too would become the telescopic focus of loyalist guns.

# 13

# The Death Threat

EVEN ROSTREVOR HAD NOT escaped the Troubles. The sleepy village lapped by lake water, garlanded with tumbling petunias and forsythia. Where a fat tabby cat dozed in the midday sun. At the bend on the hill, the grey stone church pealing its bells of praise in the shadow of the towering Mournes. The five pubs in the crook of the hamlet where villagers slaked their thirst and swapped life's philosophies. And the rambling old house by the shore where people came from as far as New Zealand to pray for peace.

Even here in this peaceful oasis, man's inhumanity to man respected no boundary. Splintering the serenity with the death cries of two policemen slaughtered outside the post office. A father and son ambushed in their lorry, the younger man powerless to save the one who had given him life from the murderous bullet. A man returning from his brother's funeral, clinically picked out by the gunman's rifle-sight. Nearly 30 people brutally cut down between the first roundabout outside the village and the house where people prayed for it to end; an area of 10 sparsely-populated square miles.

By the time the McAleese family came to live here, the South Down brigade of the IRA had become one of the most active and pernicious. Tranquillity was but an illusion. In the neighbouring seaside town of Warrenpoint, the lethal division was daubed in red, white and blue on the footpaths. Out in the hinterland, where cattle grazed and birds sang, unseen hands had painted rough country roads with the spine-chilling warning, 'Taigs Beware'.

There was no escape. Life was a lottery. Those kissed by fortune breathing deep guilt-edged sighs of relief when it was not their number that came up. In the wider expanse of Northern Ireland, her return coincided with one of the most volatile phases of the Troubles. The shooting dead of three IRA members by the SAS in Gibraltar sparked off a frenzy of retributive killings. A lone loyalist terrorist, Michael Stone, calmly approached the burial obsequies for one of the three in Milltown Cemetery on March 16 1988, killing three mourners in a terrifying gun and grenade attack. Three days later and against the backdrop of loyalist graffiti trumpeting 'Three Taigs With One Stone', two soldiers newly arrived in Northern Ireland inadvertently drove onto Andersonstown Road during the funeral of one of Stone's victims. They were set upon by an angry mob, beaten, shot and their ragged bodies dumped in the GAA grounds of Casement Park.

Mary McAleese came back to this place, and wrestled with it. Though she told a Dublin newspaper that she had 'no regrets' about leaving the South, she later confided to a friend that she found it hard to fit back into the North. 'She felt she had grown apart from it,' said the friend. 'That she had become very Southern.'

She had been hurt, insulted, caricatured and alienated in Dublin, but she had not gone to bed at night fearing the balaclaved intruder and his cold muzzle of steel. Nor had she driven to work in the morning, flagged down by armed soldiers in combat fatigues, passing police stations crouched behind mountains of sandbags and barbed wire.

She was the mother of three children under the age of five. Three little lives, fragrant with promise, whispering their bedtime love pledges, impervious to anything scarier than the bogeyman. Every day, her husband made the 40-mile round trip into the minefield of South Armagh, to drill and fill his patients' teeth in Bessbrook and Crossmaglen, where the British Army's hidden road-spikes burst suddenly out of the ground to slash the tyres of his car. And where foreign television crews would come to film the grisly road sign that cautioned, 'Sniper At Work'.

It was because of his eldest daughter that Paddy Leneghan had brought his children here in 1973 when her friend, the former Church of Ireland chaplain at Queens, Cecil Kerr, told her about the pub that was for sale in the village. Cecil and his wife, Myrtle, had moved to Rostrevor, making themselves objects of odium by opening the Christian Renewal Centre on the Shore Road where people from all over the world came to stay and to pray. One of the most frequent visitors to the ecumenical house was the young Derry singer, Dana, the pretty gap-toothed winner of the Eurovision Song Contest in 1970. She and the distinguished looking Anglican churchman became good friends and, when she married Damien Scallon at Newry Cathedral, she asked Cecil to read one of the liturgical lessons at her wedding mass.

Mary McAleese's father had sold The Corner House pub in the village square in November 1978, preferring to work part time in the Old Killowen Inn across the street. He and Claire lived a contented life, happy to see some of their children return, bringing the grandchildren with them. Kate, the second eldest daughter, who was married to a pilot, lived nearby with their two children. Claire was a nurse in Newry. John, a bachelor, had his own hair salon in the village. Nora, single also, returned from Dublin to a small Victorian terrace tucked away behind the Shore Road. Now Mary was back with Martin, Emma, Saramai and Justin.

But there were still some loose ends she needed to tie up in Dublin. Bits and bobs she believed were a matter of life and death. In the past, particularly in RTÉ and in her public pronouncements, she had got into trouble by flexing the dictum of never being pigeonholed that she had devised for herself as a girl in Belfast. It had made her an outsider in the Republic, adrift from what she saw as the liberal bandwagon speeding away from its abandoned history. In the North, it had gifted her detractors with enough ammunition to attack her bona fides as a guardian of the law. Strangely, though, it was one of those characteristic throwaway lines that she fed to the lions every so often, the seemingly harmless excesses of a loquacious tongue, that put her life on the line.

In a final interview with *The Irish Times* before her move back to Rostrevor, she declared somewhat facetiously that the only thing she would be taking up in the North was her knitting. Her extra-mural activities had proven unfulfilling, she explained, and her family life was what she cherished.

The knitting allusion was picked up by the biggest circulation newspaper in the country, the *Sunday Independent*, on October 4, 1987 in a headline stretched across the bottom of the front page. 'Home Rules – So Mary Returns To Her Knitting', it proclaimed.

The article beneath the headline dredged up the old hostilities in RTÉ where, it was reported, she had been dubbed 'that Provo lady', adding that the NUJ had 'given (her) the boot for double-jobbing'. The first line of the article read: 'So farewell then Mary McAleese, publican's daughter, self-publicist, professor and conscience of the "set menu" rather than à la carte Catholics.'

She was incensed by the personalised tone of the story, written in the style of correspondence addressed directly to her. Moreover, she worried that the depiction of her as an IRA sympathiser would single her out as a target back in the North. She instructed her solicitors, Eugene F Collins & Co. who were also, coincidentally, RTÉ's legal advisers, to sue the paper for damages in the two jurisdictions of Northern Ireland and the Republic. In her statement of claim, she contended that the newspaper had endangered her life and the lives of her family by wrongly associating her with the IRA.

A measure of how seriously she was treating the action was to be found in the calibre of her legal team, the future president of the High Court, Fred Morris, and Garrett Cooney, probably the most feared defamation law practitioner in the country. The litigation was shaping up to be a sensational, emotion–charged confrontation. Martin McAleese prepared to give evidence on his wife's behalf. Also waiting to take the stand as character witnesses were two of her former bosses at RTÉ, her *Frontline* editor, Peter Feeney, and her radio producer from the *Studio 10* days, Ed Mulhall.

As the trial grew closer, it threatened to descend into an ugly regurgitation of that bleak period in RTÉ, old adversaries at Montrose eyeballing one another under the legal privilege of a courtroom. Observers predicted it would be a lengthy trial, hanging the state broadcaster's dirty linen out for public inspection and potentially damaging the career aspirations of some of the station's brightest talent. Nerves began to jangle.

The case was listed for hearing on November 17, 1988 in the Dublin High Court. When the day dawned, Mary and Martin drove to the Four Courts to wait with her lawyers for the case to be called. As they waited, a message came from the other side of the round hall that the defendants were prepared to save them all several days in court, and deprive an expectant audience of a public spat. Intensive negotiations ensued at the door of the courtroom, resulting in a generous settlement in conclusion of the separate actions in the two jurisdictions. One of the terms of the agreement was that an approved apology would be published by the *Sunday Independent* that weekend.

It appeared prominently, as had the offending article, on the bottom of the front page, beside a picture which, the lawyers for the two sides had agreed, would be supplied by the plaintiff. The apology, considered 'grovelling' by the defendants, stated that the editor accepted the contents of the original story had been entirely without foundation and had caused her great distress. It added that 'a substantial sum' in damages had been paid in respect of the proceedings in Belfast and Dublin. The payment, in fact, amounted to £47,500 – a huge sum by the standards of the time – plus £20,000 in legal fees.

If humour had been the trigger for the offending 'Knitting Mary' headline, the stress of the legal action had not managed to quench her spark of mischievous wit.

Nine months after the case was settled she and Martin took out a mortgage, again with the Ulster Bank, on a mews apartment at the back of Merrion Road, opposite the RDS in Dublin. They invited their friends to come and see their new Dublin pad in the capital's most desirable location, cheerfully attributing the purchase to the proceeds of the libel action. Thereafter, the apartment was jocosely known among the McAleese circle as 'Independent House' in honour of the *Sunday Independent's* Middle Abbey Street office.

Unfortunately, the case was not settled in time to deter another periodical from publishing a similarly libellous story in Northern Ireland. Over two pages in its August/September edition in 1988, *A Belfast Magazine* carried an extensive account of her time in the Republic as fodder for the political attack on her appointment to Queens. The article, headlined 'The Knitting Professor', portrayed her as 'a passionate supporter' of 'reactionary Catholic theology' who had been 'shunted out of RTÉ' and had 'committed political suicide in 1987' by campaigning against the Single European Act. It repeated the allegation made in the House of Commons that she had only got the job as Director of the Institute of Professional Legal Studies on foot of 'a political move generated by the Anglo–Irish process', claiming that her experience as a barrister had been 'limited in the extreme'.

Once again, she took action to vindicate her reputation. This time she instructed the Belfast firm of L'Estrange & Brett to issue writs against Brendan Clifford, the magazine's editor and publisher, and Eason & Son (Northern Ireland) Limited, the distributors. The leading Queen's Counsel, Donal Deeney, was briefed and summonses were issued on January 26, 1989. In her statement of claim, she asserted that the article was false and malicious, enumerating 19 grounds for defamation. Among others, she contended that the natural and ordinary meaning of the defendants' words were that she was unfit for her job at the Institute, that she was a bigot, that she held the Institute in contempt, that she was idle, lazy and unfit to be a barrister-at-law.

'By reason of the publication of the said article,' the statement claimed, 'the plaintiff has been greatly injured in her credit, character and reputation and in the way of her chosen profession and in her standing in public life and has been brought into hatred, ridicule, odium, public scandal and contempt'.

Once again, the case never reached the courtroom. It was settled on September 30, 1990 on undisclosed terms. *A Belfast Magazine*, printed in a cheap A-4 format when it first appeared in the mid-1980s, did not have the same recourse to funds as the *Sunday Independent*. Though Brendan Clifford was, and continued to be, one of the North's most prolific publishers, he produced *A Belfast Magazine* on a shoestring budget out of his Athol Street office.

But Mary McAleese's fears that the pejorative publicity could endanger her life were no fanciful flights of self-aggrandisement. 'There were threats to her when she went back to Queens,' confirmed her friend and 1987 election agent, Harry Casey. 'Key Catholics in public positions were being targeted.'

Anywhere else her life as an academic might have been impenetrable, secure within the fortress of the ivory tower. But even Queens University was not immune to the Troubles, as evidenced in 1983 when the 29-year-old law lecturer and Young Unionists chairman, Edgar Graham, was fatally shot in the head by the IRA in its vicinity. His colleague and best friend, David Trimble, had taken to carrying a revolver for his personal protection after the murder.

Neither were members of the legal profession considered out of bounds. Several members of the judiciary had already been targeted. One of them, Judge William Staunton, dying from a single bullet at the gates of Mary's old school, St Dominics on the Falls Road, as he was dropping his children off to their lessons. In the late 1980s, the RUC warned 12 Catholic lawyers that their names featured on a UFF hit list. Solicitors like Paddy McGrory who acted for the families of the three IRA members shot dead by the SAS in Gibraltar. And Pat Finucane, Bobby Sands' lawyer during the hunger-strike, who died in a hail of bullets in front of his wife and children at his north Belfast home in February 1989.

Another name on the UFF death-list was that of Mary McAleese. She was visited by the RUC late in 1989 and advised on various measures to safeguard herself and her family but she declined an offer of police protection on her home in Rostrevor.

Twenty years after that defining moment in the kitchen of number 657 Crumlin Road, when she had consciously rejected the call to armed revolution, she now learned that faceless strangers wanted to kill her. She has told her friends since that she harbours no fear of death but the terrifying consequences for her husband and children engulfed her in anxiety. Whatever twisted rationale was used to single her out – her provocative denouncements of the system, her political activities in the South, her nationalist espousal of a united Ireland – Martin and the three children were the innocent victims. That must have been the hardest burden to bear.

Perhaps it explains the new softly-softly image of Mary McAleese that unfolded in Queens University. And why some Catholic students were nonplussed by her reputation as the outspoken, non-compromising daughter of the ghetto.

# A Woman of Many Parts

THERE IS NO ONE Mary McAleese. No definitive persona in which all the parts are choreographed in a single snapshot. She has an amoebic capacity to reshape herself, virtually at will.

'There are at least three or four Mary McAleeses,' according to the Dungannon priest, Monsignor Denis Faul.

'Mary has a great capacity for repositioning herself,' agreed the political commentator and former Northern Ireland Ombudsman, Senator Maurice Hayes.

A woman who projects herself as an uncomplicated, down-to-earth extrovert, she is the sum of her multifarious and conflicting incarnations. There is the feisty, defiant Belfast nationalist. The warm, compassionate chatterbox. The barrister with a sharp tongue. The prayerful spirit. The wife and mother, the daughter, sister and friend. The feminist who pours molten scorn on male fortresses. The quintessential homemaker, knitting geansies and baking buns for her family. The high achiever toughened by having made it against the odds. The indomitable opponent propelled by a wellspring of implacable self-belief.

If the staff and students of Queens University thought they knew Mary McAleese, the high-octane thorn in the establishment's side portrayed by the headlines, they were unprepared for yet another manifestation. There entered The Diplomat. Avoiding controversy, courting her colleagues instead of the spotlight, keeping her bib clean and her head buried in her work.

She even looked different. In grainy newspaper photographs before she came back from Dublin, her hair had been modishly short, haloing her face with an elfin softness. Now she wore big roundy spectacles and her hair had grown long, severely held back with a practical Alice band. Her clothes were a functional uniform of tweed jackets and plain blouses, the ensemble of a woman not wishing to attract attention.

One of the first things she did when she arrived at the Institute of Professional Legal Studies was to invite the staff down to Rostrevor for dinner. In the conviviality of the family home, her apprehensive underlings watched the ogress they had heard about metamorphose into an unthreatening, even charming, human being. And they began to relax. Many of them, in fact, would come to sing her praises. This was her period of rehabilitation in the city that had formed her, rejected her, and grudgingly took her back. She worked hard at proving she merited the job, that she was more than just the token woman Catholic. Streamlining the organisation of the Institute, putting to good use the administrative experience she had gained as a registrar in Trinity College.

'Mary had a different vision for the Institute,' recalled her deputy, Anne Fenton. 'Skills training was one of her big concerns. She was extremely intelligent with a very quick grasp of things and a terrific memory.'

Teaching law graduates the essentials of client care was less than cutting-edge education but it was necessary and she attacked it with gusto. In one of her most progressive initiatives, she brought in the Institute for the Deaf and devised the first module in Europe teaching the lawyers of the future how to communicate with aurally impaired clients. It was a technique she had mastered long ago in endless conversations signing with her brother, John.

She had been disenchanted with the physical conditions of the job when she arrived at the dingy offices in Upper Crescent that housed the Institute. She considered the place unfit for staff and students alike and resolved to get the whole operation transplanted. To that end, she launched an unremitting charm offensive that culminated in a visit to the university by the Solicitor General, Sir Nicholas Lyle. She spotted her opportunity as the distinguished guest was being given the grand tour by Queens' vice-chancellor, Sir Gordon Beveridge. The Solicitor General, on a flying visit from London, must have been taken aback when, on being introduced to the Director of the Institute, he was firmly taken by the elbow. She steered him determinedly across creaking floorboards, past cracked, peeling walls and ceilings, refusing to release him until he had even got a bird's eye view of the musty old attic.

The following Christmas, the Institute opened for business at number 10 Lennoxvale, a solid detached house shaded by a canopy of beech trees off the Malone Road, less than half-a-mile south of the university campus. The Director's ground floor office was large and airy with a stuccoed ceiling and a window onto the garden.

In the meantime, she had started studying Spanish at Queens, attaining a diploma after three years and membership of the Institute of Linguistics. She told her colleagues her interest in the language was prompted by her lineage, which had been traced back to a family of Sephardic Jews who fled mainland Europe during the Spanish Inquisition.

Outside of the university, she kept a low profile. After her 'unfulfilling' experiences in Dublin and, probably, in pursuit of self-preservation and the safety of her family, she remained aloof from party politics, devoting herself to the three priorities in her life: 'My husband, my children and God.' Her domestic routine revolved around helping the children with their homework, cooking meals, playing cards at the kitchen table and having friends round for dinner. Martin, a teetotal non-smoker determined to keep fit after quitting football, would go for a 10-mile run up the Fairy Glen in the evenings after work. They became pillars of the 2,000-strong village community.

Rostrevor was the birthplace of TK Whittaker, the legendary retailer, Ben Dunne Senior, and the wealthy businessman, Edward Haughey of Norbrook Laboratories, one of Albert Reynolds' nominees to the Seanad in Dublin. The village had a reputation as something of an artists' colony, counting among its residents the singer Kieran Goss, the Sands family of traditional musicians and the historical novelist, Siobhán Ní Dubhain, whose daughter sang for President Bill Clinton in the White House. The village held a festival every year commemorating a local United Irishman and organised by the Cultural Institute, which Mary helped found. She joined the village drama society, attending rehearsals for the Christmas pantomime, cast as a health inspector opposite Tommy Sands' 'Ratcatcher' in the romantic lead. Most Monday evenings she walked down to Cecil Kerr's house on the Shore Road for the weekly 'Praise and Prayer' meeting for Christian renewal.

Despite the sulphurous attacks on her Queens appointment and the shadow of the loyalist death threat, this was a calm interlude in her life. She seemed determined not to lift her head above the parapet, at least not until she had proven her credentials for the job. If nationalists in the university thought the arrival of an outspoken Catholic woman in the upper echelons was a godsend to their cause, they were going to have to think again.

She was not about to plunge straight into the argy-bargy of campus conflict so soon after her recent battles. 'She was very good at academic politics,' Maurice Hayes remarked. 'And she had a way of bucking institutional pomposity.'

The dreaming spires of Queens were beset, however, by something far more insidious than mere donnish affectations. The university was, in fact, one of the most sectarian employers in Northern Ireland, an institution guilty of wholesale ethnic imbalances. When it was investigated by the Fair Employment Commission in 1989, Queens was bluntly told to put its house in order. A group of independent consultants was commissioned to conduct a fair employment audit, resulting in a 1992 report containing more than 90 separate recommendations designed to create a neutral working environment.

Under legislation enacted in 1989, several members of Queens' 3,500 staff had brought claims of discrimination to the Fair Employment Tribunal. By 1995, the compensation payout amounted to £350,000, attracting atrocious international press. But it was a case initiated in 1992 that finally blew the problem of endemic discrimination wide open, jolting the authorities into remedial action.

Joe Copeland was the third most senior employee in the bursar's office when the job a grade above his became vacant. He duly applied for the promotion, but his application was not considered. Less experienced applicants from the University of Ulster were called for interviews and the position was filled. Joe Copeland took his complaint of discrimination to the Tribunal, where it was settled on the doorstep. Despite a confidentiality clause in the settlement, the details of the Copeland case were soon made public by zealous student activists, seriously embarrassing the university and forcing it to confront the issue.

Up to then the nationalist-dominated Students Union had made most of the running in the equality campaign. As more and more young Protestants left for universities in England and Scotland, the student populace of 12,000 compromised almost equal proportions of both communities – with a ceiling of 700 on its intake from the Republic. However, it was the nationalist students, many of them living in flats in the city, who had controlled the highly politicised and polarised union ever since 1969.

In 1991, the Students Union decided to contest four seats in the Senate, the university's governing body, on a manifesto of equal representation. At the annual Convocation of the graduate body they succeeded in having three of their candidates elected to Senate. They were the Irish-speaking Protestant surgeon, John Robb, a former senator in the Oireachtas; Philip Mateer, a Protestant barrister; and Tim Attwood, a Catholic and SDLP official, brother of the party's future Assembly member, Alex Attwood. The result was hailed as a symbolic and effective victory for the campaign against discrimination, providing a platform in the policy-making Senate with its 60-strong membership of Northern Ireland's great and good.

Throughout it all, Mary McAleese maintained a low profile, as did most of the senior nationalists on the academic staff. Only Professor Simon Lee from the law school, who later transferred to Hope College in England, publicly supported the students.

'The silence from senior nationalists in Queens was deafening,' recalled one of the union activists.

Tim Attwood had been president of the Students Union in 1988 when Mary McAleese took up her position in the Institute of Professional Legal Studies. He was singularly unimpressed with the new Director when he led a campaign to reverse a recently imposed rule requiring law graduates to undergo psychological tests before they qualified for admission to the Institute. The move had arisen from the Bromley Report, a review study that had been initiated in 1985. The report recommended a number of curricular changes at the Institute, which were subsequently negotiated by the Law Society, the Bar Council and the Institute itself. The students opposed the psychological tests on the grounds that law graduates had already completed four years' study and that the proposed tests had not been professionally validated. They sought a meeting with the Director to make their case.

Tim Attwood, who would go on to become the SDLP's director of development at the party's headquarters on the Ormeau Road, led the student delegation at an arranged meeting in the Director's office. But, if they were expecting affinity and acquiescence, they were sorely disappointed. She stoutly refused to recommend that the rule be abolished, vigorously contesting the case they made. 'We nearly walked out of the meeting because she was so offensive,' one of the student delegates recalled. 'She lacked sympathy.'

The students, who included the daughter of Sir Oliver Napier, the former leader of the Alliance Party, decided to take their complaint to a higher authority. They considered seeking a judicial review in the High Court. When, however, they discovered that the university's royal charter provided for appeals to be heard by the Queen of England, in the guise of the Board of Visitors, they took that route. And, ultimately, lost their case. The board, chaired by Lord Scarman, the peer famous for having investigated the outbreak of the Troubles in 1969, upheld the rule requiring psychological tests for entry to the Institute.

The episode had soured the relationship between the Students Union and Mary McAleese but it had been a significant litmus test of her independence as Director. She had come through it with flying colours, proving to those still wary of her nationalist baggage that she had not brought partisanship to the job. She reaped the rewards of her quiet diligence in June 1994 when she was made the most junior of the university's three pro vice-chancellors. The first woman and only the second Catholic to fill the position, her new status was comparable in the corporate sector to that of a deputy managing director. While retaining the directorship of the Institute for Professional Legal Studies, she now dealt exclusively with its policy matters, the newly appointed Associate Director, Anne Fenton, taking over its day-to-day running. In the staff common room, she earned the appellation, 'Mother Mary'.

As pro vice-chancellor, with responsibility for Queens' external affairs, she was hugely empowered to influence the university's business. Queens was labouring under a severe shortage of funding and low morale. It had grown defensive over the controversy sparked by its track record as a sectarian employer with more than 25 cases still pending before the tribunal. It limped along in a permanent mode of crisis management. Despite the scarcity of money, Mary McAleese almost immediately got the go-ahead to realise a dream she had long held – to establish outreach campuses in both Omagh and Armagh.

'She got the Armagh programme up and running in about a year,' remembered an impressed Monsignor Denis Faul.

When she commandeered the site of the old City Hospital in Armagh's Abbey Street, providing facilities for masters degree courses and undergraduate studies, it won her kudos and some unlikely admirers. The hilltop home of the Strangford MP, John Taylor was an imposing edifice in the cathedral city. On the day the campus opened with 120 students in September 1995, the Unionist politician was among those who came to praise her, nearly eight years after condemning her in the House of Commons. Having survived an assassination attempt by the IRA, John Taylor was seen by nationalists as one of the most hard-line of his party. His regard for Mary McAleese, a so-called 'tribal nationalist', was one of the most ironic quirks of her new manifestation. In private, Taylor told friends that, while he did not agree with the woman's opinions, he had to admire the forceful way she expressed them.

After her promotion, she became increasingly integrated into the mainstream functioning of Queens. She travelled to China with her husband to sign an agreement with the Communist Minister for Education entitling students of the University of Beijing to study in Belfast. During the trip, Martin McAleese made a favourable impression on their hosts at dinner in a restaurant one evening. Adroitly picking up some peanuts with his chopsticks – first with his right hand, then with his left – his ambidexterity helped ease the formality of the occasion.

Mary travelled to Minneapolis to address the William Mitchell Law School and to Paris to speak at the International School. She became a course consultant to Nottingham Law School and the University of Wales, making guest lecture appearances at Bristol University and the Institute of Advocacy in Oxford. Back in Queens, she served on a number of university bodies, like the Academic Council, the Equal Opportunities Group and the Staffing Committee.

She emerged as an able administrator. Her external affairs committee commissioned Drury Communications, a Dublin public relations firm with an office in Belfast, to tackle Queens' negative image. Its brief was to assess the effectiveness of both internal communication with staff and the external image of the university transmitted by the media. Even though the project had been put out to public tender, allegations of a Catholic cartel followed when Drury Communications, who had conducted a similar review for University College Dublin, was awarded the contract in November 1995. It was grist to the unionist rumour mill that the managing director of Drury Communications (NI) Ltd was a nationalist called Tom Kelly, a former vice-chairman of the SDLP. Kelly had formerly worked as parliamentary assistant to the party's deputy leader, Seamus Mallon, and as an election agent for the party's West Belfast MP, Joe Hendron. Accusations of jobs-for-the-boys and preferential treatment for Catholics rumbled though the establishment, despite the fact that a unionist, Dr Jonathan Rose, wrote the initial draft report. The consultants' damning 64-page strategy document, 'Communicating Excellence', bewailed the lack of leadership shown by senior management and described the university's 'head in the sand approach to problem-solving'. Unionists were outraged. Queens graduate, Ian Paisley Junior, scion of the DUP leader, saw it as 'the continuation of the nationalist onslaught against Queens University.' He added: 'I understand the erstwhile Fianna Fáil candidate, Mary McAleese, is favoured by many nationalists to replace Sir Gordon.'

The predominantly Unionist daily paper, *The News Letter* of June 29, 1996 fuelled the controversy when it darkly hinted at a nationalist conspiracy to transfer more power to pro vice-chancellor Mary McAleese. 'There is an agenda to promote her,' the paper quoted an anonymous source after the vice-chancellor, Sir Gordon Beveridge, announced his intention to quit the position he had held for 11 years. The Scottish academic denied rumours that he had been pressurised into early retirement. 'I have not felt under pressure to step down,' Sir Gordon insisted. *The News Letter* was forced to climb down with a mealy-mouthed apology on November 12 after a flurry of legal correspondence on behalf of Mary McAleese.

'It has been pointed out to us that the article may have been interpreted as suggesting that Professor Mary McAleese abused her position as pro vice-chancellor in order to promote herself within the university,' stated the single-column page-three retraction. 'It was never our intention that this suggestion should be made. While we still do not accept that this suggestion is expressed in the article, we take this opportunity to clarify that at no time in the said article was it our intention or design to make the aforementioned suggestion relating to Professor McAleese and we accept that Professor McAleese at all times acted in a manner appropriate to her position.'

Tom Kelly would, henceforth, play a significant role in Mary McAleese's career. Resident in Newry, he even became a dental patient of Martin's.

'Mary is a very warm individual and we very quickly developed a rapport, not only as individuals but also as two families,' Kelly recalled. 'They were very interested in politics and religion. She was certainly an ambitious person – no more than any others I know in business and politics. Yet, as a trait in a woman it always seems frowned upon. They were a remarkably close couple.'

It was Tom Kelly who introduced Mary McAleese to Martin Naughton, a businessman from the Republic with an estimated wealth of £500 million who had started his multi-million-pound domestic appliances empire, Glen Dimplex, in Newry. Her external affairs committee was actively seeking funding from private sources and Kelly was hoping to persuade him to sponsor the newly established School of Management, in line with his record as a successful entrepreneur. After that first meeting, Martin Naughton invited Mary and Martin McAleese to dinner at his home, Stackallen House outside Navan, ultimately agreeing to contribute approximately £250,000 to the university. He had one request, however – that he be given an outline of how the money would be spent.

But, when she apprised the Executive Council at Queens of its benefactor's largess and his wish for an indication of its expenditure, she found herself accused of trying to set pre-conditions. If that were the case, she was huffily told, the university would be better off without the money. In the end, the donation was accepted and Queens bestowed an honorary degree on Martin Naughton in 1997.

But the incident reinforced Mary McAleese's belief that the university still operated an unofficial two-class policy.

Despite her ability to avoid confrontation as Director of the Institute, she began to grow vocal again after her 1994 promotion, believing that the institution continued to be inherently sectarian in its dealings and that the senior management of Queens was populated with 'deadwood'. As a pro vice-chancellor she was automatically made a member of the governing body, the Senate, where she shed her reticence to speak out against sectarianism. One Senate member recalled a particularly stormy meeting where she became exercised on the topic of the powerful lay-Catholic business organisation, the Knights of Columbanus. The Senate had been asked to deliver a policy ruling on a row over the use of university rooms by the graduates' branch of the Freemasons, an exclusively male Protestant organisation. Masonic functions had not been held in the university since the mid-1980s when they were adjudged contrary to Queens' equal opportunities policy. The thrust of the debate at the Senate meeting was that the Masonic Lodge was entitled to meet there as long as the Knights of Columbanus enjoyed the facilities. A furious Mary McAleese cut in, objecting to the equating of the Knights with the Masons and insisting that the Catholic organisation was, in fact, a non-denominational one.

'If Mary felt there was a wrong, she couldn't let it lie,' said Anne Fenton. 'She couldn't pass something by and take the easy option. She had tremendous courage and a great sense of herself.'

On another occasion, she rounded on a colleague at a meeting where she was the only Catholic present. She had been delayed at the funeral of a Belfast woman, the mother of a student, who had been shot dead at her front door during a spate of random sectarian killings. The dead woman, who had four daughters aged from 22 down to five, had been married to a Peruvian man. When Mary McAleese arrived at the meeting, she apologised for being late, vaguely explaining that she had been at a funeral.

'There's a lot of talk about these murders being sectarian but I don't know,' one of the men at the table piped up. 'There was one of them there and the family was Peruvian. I think that had something to do with those Shining Path guerrillas. I think that man was mixed up in something.'

'Do you?' she responded icily, struggling to quell the anger which, she said later, she could feel rising up from her toes. 'I have just come from that woman's funeral and she wouldn't have known a Shining Path guerrilla if one had walked up the street and sat down beside her. She was shot simply because she was a Catholic, because of hatred. Because an awful lot of people in this country hate Catholics. And an awful lot of people in this country hate policemen. And, as long as people like you say things like that, it will go on.'

Her barely concealed fury startled the man who had spoken. 'I'm sorry,' he apologised. 'I'd forgotten you were a Catholic.'

'That's obvious,' she snapped.

The fact that her colleague had indeed forgotten she was a Catholic is telling. It is a measure of the low profile she had maintained in the wider political conflict of the North since arriving at Queens. As pro vice-chancellor, however, she threw off the shackles of reticence and became fully engaged in the on-going tug-of-war between the traditional unionist ethos and the increasingly assertive nationalist identity on campus. She did not duck, for instance, when a cacophony of accusations erupted over the Senate's decision in December 1994 to end the RUC band's customary rendition of the British national anthem at graduation ceremonies. So emotive was the issue that it generated the biggest campaign of letters-to-the-editor in the history of *The Belfast Telegraph*. The Unionist Graduate Association sent a protest letter to vice-chancellor Sir Gordon Beveridge, predicting that the ban would turn the university into 'a sectarian ghetto'. *The News Letter* reported that the letter specifically targeted Professor Mary McAleese. The proposed compromise rendition of the European anthem, Beethoven's 'Ode To Joy', provoked jeers of derision. The dispute was intrinsic to the prolonged debate over the general display of flags and emblems on campus and Irish-language signs in the Students Union office. It had the effect of shifting the balance yet again in the see-saw of Mary McAleese's public image, drawing hostile allegations from unionists that she was working to a nationalist agenda at Queens.

It redeemed her, however, in the eyes of those students who had earlier been disillusioned by her lack of support for their cause. 'She became an advocate after she was made pro vice-chancellor,' one of them recalled. 'The proposal to drop the anthem was part of the drive to create a neutral environment in Queens. Graduation day used to be very difficult for some students. The night before you'd be in a panic over whether to sit or stand when the RUC started playing "God Save The Queen". A lot of people decided to stand because they didn't want to spoil the day for their parents. But some people would stay sitting down and it caused a lot of tension. A friend of mine was hit by another graduate because he didn't stand up.'

In her private life, Mary was cushioned by the security of a substantial income. Several directorship fees for service on company boards considerably boosted her generous stipend from Queens. Her promotion to pro vice-chancellor had swollen her salary, paid in sterling, by about £15,000, bringing it up to £70,000. Martin's earnings were also more than adequate. His surgeries in Crossmaglen and Bessbrook were flourishing, with four dentists employed full time. It meant the couple no longer had to worry about money. Their lifestyle was not lavish, but it was a long way from the time, less than a decade earlier, when she was reliant on her extracurricular £65-a-month cheque from RTÉ for *Europa*. Their two-car family consisted of Martin's Volvo and Mary's Peugeot, frequent entertaining at home and annual skiing holidays in Austria and France. Though they had the house in Rostrevor, and the valuable apartment in Dublin, they did not flaunt their wealth. Instead, they invested it wisely, probably conditioned by the fragility of their parents' circumstances two decades earlier when both their families had lost their homes in the blink of an eye.

It was not generally known but, by the early 1990s, Mary McAleese had acquired yet another persona: that of landlady. It was an incarnation that would leave five students at Queens with bitter memories. All five of the young men were in their second year at the university: four studying chemical engineering, and the fifth a medical student. Two were brothers from Waterford, one from Dublin, one from Belfast and one from Ballycastle in north Antrim. In September 1992 they became tenants of the Director of the Institute of Professional Legal Studies when they began renting a four-bedroom house in Stranmillis Gardens, located just a stroll from Lennoxvale. It was a 12-month letting with a rent of £650 paid by direct debit every month to her bank account.

'She wasn't the nicest landlady,' according to one of the students.

One aspect of the arrangement they disliked was that Mary's father, Paddy, retained a key to the house and had a habit of dropping in without warning. 'We'd come downstairs in the morning and find him walking around the house,' one of them remembered. The other aspect that bothered them was that they never received a copy of the lease. They were unaware that under the law pertaining to Northern Ireland no lease was required for a letting of one year or less. When they decided to vacate the house eight months into the 12-month letting, they erroneously believed the absence of a lease freed them from any legal obligation to see the letting through. They wrote to their landlady in May 1993 giving 28 days' notice of their intention to leave as the five of them were dispersing for the summer.

She replied in person. The students guessed it must have been the morning she received their letter that she arrived at the house, furious and demanding they leave immediately. 'She was red in the face, fuming and shouting. There was no arguing with her,' one of them recalled. 'She brought a locksmith with her and he started changing the locks. She even threatened to call the police.'

The students, four of whom were due to sit their second-year chemical engineering exams the following morning, dossed down in friends' flats that night.

'She was so angry. Her face was all red and blotchy with temper,' said one of the students, since qualified as a hospital doctor. 'OK, we were students and we were all pretty scruffy and what not, but we'd never caused any trouble. We never even had a single party in that house. Considering her position in the University, it was strange how she handled five students.'

The saga over the house in Stranmillis Gardens illustrates the extent of Mary McAleese's complexity. The apparent lack of sympathy in her dealings with her student tenants jars, for instance, with the inherent compassion she exhibited for prisoners and her strongly-held Catholic beliefs. Yet it resonates with another incident years earlier when a County Meath schoolboy with aspirations of a career in law visited her at home in Ratoath. The boy had gone to seek advice on becoming a lawyer but came away with the distinct impression that the professor had little sympathy for him. She had made it clear that, in her time, the choice was stark: either join the IRA or knuckle down and make your own way as a lawyer.

She had been proving herself all her life, as a woman, a Catholic nationalist and a highly politicised academic. No matter how valiantly she tried to rise above the glib name-calling and lazy stereotyping, there had always been someone there to put her back in a neatly labelled box. That defiance of the political identikit became not only the credo of her life but also a motto of her parenting. She tried to inculcate a sense of individuality in her children, teaching Emma, Justin and Saramai to question the easily learned catchphrases handed down by generations. Her friend, Harry Casey, remembered being in the McAleese house one night when Queen Elizabeth appeared on the television screen. When one of the children made a derisory comment about the British monarch, their mother reprimanded them. 'That lady has never done us any harm,' she scolded.

In yet another intriguing twist to her life, she was to find her private precept of fair play being reciprocated by none other than the Queen herself.

The two women first met in October 1995 at a reception in St James's Palace, London, to celebrate the 150th anniversary of Queens, University College Cork and University College Galway. It was a glittering affair attended by more than 600 guests drawn from academia, politics and business. The Belfast Catholic and advocate of a united Ireland must have made a deep impression on the head of the House of Windsor and the Church of England because, early in 1996, she received an invitation to lunch privately at Buckingham Palace.

Mary McAleese was surprised to get the phone call from Sir Simon Cooper, head of the Queen's household, inviting her to dine at the palace. 'But why?' she asked Sir Simon. Because, he explained, Her Majesty wished to hear more about her background and the place she came from.

Twenty-four years after being terrorised out of her home, the woman who had been denounced in the Queen's parliament, found herself being ushered inside the most famous royal edifice in the world. As Queen Elizabeth II listened to her subject tell the story of her life, little did she imagine that her guest would, one day, hope to return the compliment – on an equal footing.

# Church Politics

SHE HAD BEEN IN the world a mere 11 days when her identity was sealed for life. As the priest scooped water from the stone baptismal font in Holy Cross Monastery on July 8 1951, letting the cold droplets dribble onto the infant's head, he anointed her arrival into a world apart. The ceremonial rite of passage to a life of predestined culture, ethnicity, social status, political position and religious affiliation. Her christening conferred both her name and her place, branding her forever in the inflexible caste system of Northern Ireland.

For most Roman Catholics of her generation in the North, the Church was their anchor; a refuge of comforting, familiar ritual supervised by quasi-politicians who squared up to the other tribe. Mother Church, consoler and protector. It percolated through their veins, infusing their lives. For Mary McAleese it was, at once, a rock and a marker, measuring the distance between it and a hard place.

Her faith was not blind and neither was her allegiance to the institution. She had questioned both as a young adult, scrabbling at the warts of dogma, struggling with the dichotomy of authoritarian rules and a well-informed conscience. Her voyage to acceptance had been biblical. The life-defining call beckoning thrice: in August 1969 when she searched for missiles to throw at the B Specials; in November 1972 when she had wanted her brother's attackers 'lynched'; in May 1981 when she fled to a church from the verbal abuse in RTÉ. But it had only ever been a conditional acceptance. That was to be her Calvary.

The apparent inconsistency of her à la carte Catholicism is the most perplexing aspect of Mary McAleese. On the one hand, she has championed gay rights and the cause of women priests. On the other, she has opposed contraception, divorce and abortion under all circumstances. Where other, secularised Catholics choose the most palatable dishes from the menu, she has painstakingly contrived her own pottage. The key to understanding her is to remember the touchstone of her life denying anyone the luxury of labelling her. To critics of the Catholic Church, she is the acceptable face of a bunch of regressive, out-of-touch old bishops. To traditionalist adherents of the Vatican's teachings, she is a dangerous, mutinous blasphemer.

Somewhere between the two impressions lies the real Mary McAleese, the one whose public willingness to parade her beliefs has made her an exile both outside and inside the Church. 'The only infallibility she believes in is the infallibility of Mary McAleese,' according to a lay commentator on Roman Catholic affairs.

One of the most remarkable characteristics of her life is the preponderance of priests, nuns and bishops in her social circle. In any list of her friends, at least half of them would bear a religious prefix to their names. It began with the priests of Holy Cross and the nuns of St Dominics. There was the late Cardinal Tomás O'Fiaich, then Cardinal Cahal Daly, followed by the Bishop of Down and Conor, Dr Patrick Walsh, who was the Roman Catholic chaplain when she was a student at Queens. Her personal friendships with those three doyens of the Irish Church lent her a powerful ear and an entrée to the hierarchy.

Against that background, she built up a reputation as one of the most active and influential lay Catholics in the country. Even before her dramatic appearance at the New Ireland Forum as part of the episcopal delegation in 1984, her credentials had been well established. She had been attending the Ballymascanlon inter-church conference since the late 1970s, she was a member of the bishops' Commission on Social Welfare, she was a prolific contributor to religious magazines, and her freelance work for the Church-owned Veritas Video Productions cemented her image as a voice of the institution.

In one such video on human fertility, produced by the Catholic Communications Centre in Dublin, she interviewed an Australian Anglican priest, Fr John Fleming, a trenchant opponent of *in vitro* fertilisation. Visibly pregnant with the twins at the time, she provocatively stated that there was a big difference between the 'mechanics' of producing a child through IVF and 'creating a baby as a result of a loving, happy relationship'. The video was deeply hurtful to infertile couples and offensive to women. In the course of the interview, Fr Fleming claimed that 90 per cent of those women who used IVF because of damaged Fallopian tubes had caused their own problems, through abortion, sexually transmitted disease and use of the intrauterine contraceptive device. To her eternal discredit, Mary McAleese never challenged his assertion.

She told *The Irish Times*, on June 15, 1984, that she saw no need for abortion after rape, adding: 'It seems to me to be a rather primitive act of revenge or retribution, vented on a foetus.' In her *Sunday Tribune* column of December 7, 1986, she penned a robust defence of 'the much maligned' Opus Dei, the secretive right-wing Catholic organisation. A photograph of her and Martin on pilgrimage with the three children at Clonmacnoise graced the cover of *Pilgrims*, the first of three religious text-books written by her friend, Harry Casey, whose brother was Cardinal Daly's private secretary. The third book, *In The Beginning*, featured a chapter entitled 'Walking in the Garden that is the Catholic Church', which she wrote.

Gradually, she became the flavour of the rank and file clergy, receiving a raft of invitations to preach in their churches. She delivered novenas at the Knock shrine in Mayo, Mount Argus church in Dublin, Holy Cross on the Crumlin Road and the Redemptorists' Clonard Monastery on the Falls Road. In her book, *Reconciled Being: Love in Chaos*, she recollected her debut on the altar of Dublin's Pro-Cathedral. 'I was to be the first woman to mount that forbidding pulpit who did not have a yellow duster and a tin of Mr Sheen furniture polish in her hand,' she wrote.

God was central to her private life. She read St Thomas Aquinas' 'Summa Theologica' in the original, read the lessons at Sunday mass and the bible in her home, prayed daily, joined the parish committee, and observed her Lenten penance. 'She used to give up coffee and tea for Lent because she enjoyed them,' remembered her Queens colleague, Anne Fenton. 'It was never chocolate, for instance, because that had a benefit – you lost weight – and therefore it wasn't pure sacrifice.'

She became a convert to the form of meditation espoused by the Benedictine monk, John Main, a professor of international law at Trinity College in the 1950s. It required her to set an hour aside each day, to empty her mind and succumb wholly to her spirituality by silently repeating the mantra, 'Maranatha'. At the international John Main seminar in Maynooth, which she addressed in the footsteps of the Dalai Lama, she described an amusing session of meditation she shared with Emma, when her eldest daughter was five years old. 'Sit up straight,' her mother instructed the child, explaining about the mantra and the need for absolute silence.

'Five minutes into my meditation,' she recalled, 'the little voice interrupted me: "Excuse me mammy, but is God talking to you?"

"Yes," I replied rashly.

"Right!" she said. "Will you please tell him that, when he's finished with you, I'm still waiting".'

In Dublin she reproached the 'rampant' anti-clericalism she witnessed in the capital. She once declared that the division between nationalists and unionists in the North was 'no more bitter, no more real than the gulf between Catholic and anti-cleric in Dublin'. She developed a special devotion to the Blessed Sacrament, wrote a book about 17 Irish martyrs from the sixteenth and seventeenth centuries and came to admire obscure saints like Catherine of Sienna and Julian of Norwich.

And all the while, her star shone ever brighter in the firmament of Church politics. In the early 1990s, she accepted an unprecedented invitation from Cardinal Daly to speak to the bishops behind closed doors. The meeting took place at the college in Armagh and was also attended by another leading lay Catholic, Jim Fitzpatrick, proprietor of *The Irish News* and a former Redemptorist seminarian in Galway. The thrust of his thesis to the hierarchy was that they should more usefully exploit the parish unit. Mary McAleese's submission, however, did not make easy listening. She criticised the Church for failing to listen to its people, she berated it for excluding women and rapped the bishops' collective knuckles for acting as 'an alternative political party'. She told the Cardinal and his fellow brothers in Christ that they should preach forgiveness to the IRA, not ostracise them as 'scum' and 'maniacs' in the language of political condemnation.

She expanded on this theme in her interview with Fionnuala O'Connor for the book, *In Search of a State: Catholics in Northern Ireland*. 'I think the Church should have dialogue with the Provos,' she argued. 'They are the people who are literally keeping hell going in this community...The very fact that almost all of them are ethnic Catholics means that somewhere along the line they were baptised in the faith...it's work of evangelisation, work for clergymen that Christ sent them on this earth to do. The people in the churches are irrelevant. They're in the bag. They should concentrate on the ones who came like little shining beacons at Confirmation – what the hell happened?'

Others were beginning to ask the same question about Mary McAleese. What the hell had happened to 'the bishops' woman'? That was what Cardinal O'Fiaich had called her after the Forum when she went on to oppose abortion and militate against civil divorce in a referendum campaign that likened divorced women to second-hand cars. She had upbraided Dublin Four liberals for being anti-Catholic, claiming that her association with the Church had caused her to be ousted from the National Union of Journalists.

Now, suddenly it seemed, she had started lashing the bishops with the serrated whip of her tongue.

'She's culturally a Catholic, no doubt – but a "devout" or "fervent" one?' questioned the reactionary Catholic magazine, *The Brandsma Review*, edited by her old ally, Nick Lowry.

She began to criticise the hierarchy in public for their 'very old, rather seigniorial, magisterial ways of dealing with problems'. She electrified the clergy when she appeared on *The Late Late Show* in 1993 and lambasted some of the Pope's views as 'having a touch of woodworm about them'. The following year, at a conference in Cecil Kerr's Christian Renewal Centre in Rostrevor she cavilled at the anachronism of the Church, where the colours of men's socks 'denominate their places in terms of where they are in the hierarchical system'.

After the Catholic priest, Fr Brendan Smyth, was jailed for repeated and depraved sexual attacks on children, she again rounded on the leaders of the Church. Her comments in no way softened by the fact that the notorious priest was legally represented by her good friend, Denis Moloney, a lay theologian and senior partner in the

Belfast law practice of Donnelly & Wall. 'I listened to the Cardinal say there would be no hiding place for people like Brendan Smyth, but the truth of the matter is that he's still saying mass in prison,' she said. 'I find that deeply offensive – that on one level there is a hiding place within the Church.'

But it was her stance on the ordination of women that most infuriated her clerical critics. They saw her as a feminist, a harpy and a loose cannon promulgating perfidy and sedition.

'She has a Messiah complex,' believed Monsignor Denis Faul, an arch critic of her feminist philosophy. 'She wants to be a liberator of women.'

It began with a private letter. The correspondent was Soline Vatinel, a gentle Frenchwoman living in Blackrock, County Dublin with her husband, her children – and a lifelong vocation to the Roman Catholic priesthood. In 1994, she wrote to Mary McAleese, informing her of a new organisation she had co-founded with her husband and a clergyman for the promotion of women priests. It was called BASIC, an acronym for Brothers and Sisters in Christ. Soline enclosed a membership form and mailed the letter to Queens University in Belfast.

She had a reply within days. The letter was encouraging, but what accompanied it was even more so: the creased membership form, now with the blank spaces neatly filled in.

'I was very surprised because we were unknown,' said the woman who arrived in Dublin to study history at Trinity College in 1973, and stayed. 'None of our members was a prominent figure. She had a high profile and contacts in the Church. I remember thinking she was taking a big risk. We could have been just a bunch of crackpots for all she knew.'

Mary McAleese has told friends that she does not have a vocation, but she has long resented the exclusion of women from the priesthood. She has written in *Reconciled Being: Love in Chaos* about the years when she choked back that resentment. 'To challenge the awesome authority of the hierarchy seemed to open up an aptly named Pandora's box of things which might be difficult to swallow,' she explained. 'If the Church was wrong on an issue on which it spoke with a chilling clarity and certainty, then how many other errors might lie buried in that theology. There was a comfort in burying myself inside the group consciousness and putting my hands over my ears so that I could not hear the doubts that were running about in my head. To pit myself against the group meant challenging mother, father, family, parish, community and to live with some form of exclusion which, whether mild rebuke or subtle shunning, would inevitably follow.'

On March 25, 1995, the Feast of the Annunciation, BASIC held an inaugural day-long seminar at the Jesuit Conference Centre in Milltown Park, Dublin, addressed by Mary McAleese and President Robinson's chaplain, Fr Enda McDonagh, professor of moral theology at St Patrick's College in Maynooth. Less than 300 people attended. Others who might have come were frightened off by the Pope's stern rebuke of the campaign and a threat by the Vatican's Prefect of the Congregation of the Faith, Cardinal Ratzinger, that those who continued it would effectively excommunicate themselves from the Church. There was the further complication of a petition boasting more than 20,000 signatures, calling for 'all ministries and offices in the church to be open equally to both women and men, and for all sexist structures and regulations to be abolished'. Cardinal Daly had refused to receive the petition on behalf of the Church. Soline Vatinel had repeatedly written to him in Armagh, seeking a meeting. When, after nine months and in desperation, she sent him a Valentine card, he consented to meet. They talked for two hours but the Cardinal never wavered. He said the Pope had spoken and, in conscience, he could not receive the petition, which bore, among the lists of names, the signature of his friend, Mary McAleese. As a woman, she believed she was at the bottom of the Church pyramid and that the ban on female ordinations was little more than an implement of gender bias.

'It was a steel wall,' Soline recalled. 'I came out of that meeting and I was fit for nothing.'

Mary was 'incensed' when Soline told her what the Cardinal had said, and pointedly referred to it in her address to the seminar at Milltown. 'There is no official forum that I know of that you or I can submit feedback for transmission upwards through the system' she complained. 'In fact, it is very interesting that, when Soline tried to send the petition in favour of the ordination of women to the Cardinal, his Eminence felt unable to receive it.

Mary with her godmother,
Auntie Una, in Ardoyne.

Making her First Communion.

Mary Leneghan on her father Paddy's lap, and her
younger sister Nora, seated on her mother Claire's lap.

*Irish Independent*

Taking her seat between her husband and the Taoiseach for the press conference following her sensational nomination by Fianna Fáil for the presidential election.

*Donal Doherty, Irish Independent*

Mary and Martin in Dublin, 1985.

The many faces of Mary McAleese.

Fr Alex Reid, the Redemptorist priest who first mooted her candidacy for the presidential election to Martin Manseragh.

The Belfast solicitor, Denis Moloney, a key figure in the Friends of Mary McAleese.

Mary McAleese at Trinity College in 1984.

The picture that appeared beside the
*Sunday Independent* apology.

Side by side with Bertie Ahern
at the launch of her campaign
for the presidential election.

Mary McAleese addressing a Fianna Fáil conference,
with her political soulmate, Charles Haughey.

*Eamonn Farrell, Photocall Ireland*

The two Marys – Robinson and McAleese leaving Dublin Castle after their
battle of intellects at the New Ireland Forum.

*Pacemaker Press International Ltd*

On the terrace of her home in
Rostrevor after her appointment
as pro-vice chancellor of Queens
University in 1994.

*The Longford Leader*

Harry Casey with Mary McAleese.

*Maxwell*

The candidate and her husband enjoying a light moment during the presidential election campaign with their children, Emma, Saramai and Justin.

*Tony O'Shea*

Mary McAleese newly nominated as Fianna Fáil Presidential candidate, September 1997.

*Michael Hogan, Doyle's Photo Agency*

Emma McAleese.

*Michael Hogan, Doyle's Photo Agency*

The McAleese twins, Saramai and Justin.

*Robert Doyle, Doyle's Photo Agency*

Mary McAleese with Maureen Potter.

Tony O'Shea

Victor and vanquished: Albert Reynolds takes his place at the press conference in Buswells, announcing the nomination by Fianna Fáil of Mary McAleese.

Tony O'Shea

After being selected as Fianna Fáil candidate for the Presidential Election, Bertie Ahern emerges with Mary McAleese from Leinster House.

*Maxwell*

The Outsider within: The inauguration watched by a cast of players in her life, including Mary Robinson, John Bruton, Bertie Ahern, John O'Donoghue and Chief Justice Liam Hamilton.

*Tony O'Shea*

With Bertie Ahern on Grafton Street. October 1997.

Mary McAleese. October 1997.

After her victory in the Presidential election. October 1997.

Dick Roche with Mary's mother, Claire Leneghan.

*Tony O'Shea*

With the Taoiseach, Bertie Ahern, and Táinaiste,
Mary Harney, after her inauguration.

© *Kim Haughton*

A jubilant Mary arriving at the Ballsbridge
apartment on the day of the election count.

*Tony O'Shea*

President McAleese greeting schoolchildren
after her inauguration in Dublin Castle.

*Maxwell*

Inauguration day. November 1997.

Rory McShane.

The president-elect with her family.

Mary McAleese, Inauguration day.

Celebrating with her parents, Paddy and Claire Leneghan.

'I love the Church. I love the bones of it; I love the stones of it,' she told her audience. In a flippant aside, she emphasised her equality with the Pontiff in the eyes of God. 'In fairness to his Holiness, the Pope,' she said, 'I have to say that he has always accepted and acknowledged my private correspondence on (this) subject. He does not agree with me, you will be interested to know, but he has, on a number of occasions, offered to pray for me. I reciprocate.'

Eight months after the seminar, the Vatican declared that its teaching on a male-only priesthood was infallible.

'Mary immediately accepted the invitation to speak at the seminar,' said Soline Vatinel. 'We didn't have to twist her arm or anything. And she wouldn't take any payment. She returned it by post and said the group needed the money. She's a very loyal Roman Catholic, a woman of prayer. First and foremost she would see herself as a Christian. There would be pain in coming to that realisation. To stay within is painful but she is a great believer in conscience. People in other countries have lost their jobs and have been blacklisted because of their involvement in the campaign. In Australia a woman was refused communion by her bishop.'

Mary McAleese has often echoed that sentiment. Speaking at the Clonard Novena in Belfast on June 25, 1996, she admitted that 'being so far at odds with Church teaching is a very uncomfortable place for a believer who is also a mother and who wants her greatest gift to her children to be the gift of faith'. Two years later, when, as President, she addressed the Charismatic Renewal Leaders Conference, she said: 'If you are too comfortable, there is something wrong.'

When the papers delivered at the Milltown seminar were compiled in book form, the Dominican nun and historian, Sr Margaret McCurtain, officially launched it at a reception in Stauntons Hotel on St Stephen's Green in Dublin. Later, in an event that presaged her own career, Mary McAleese joined a BASIC delegation to the Phoenix Park in November 1995 to present President Robinson with a copy of the book.

Mary McAleese is a natural maverick. It is a tendency she shared with Tomás O'Fiaich, the cardinal who believed there was no reason in dogmatic theology or in biblical studies why women could not be ordained. She bridled at the accepted sexism of St Paul and Thomas Aquinas but above all, at the contemporary Church of Rome. Privately, she disparaged Pope John Paul's pamphlet on contraception, Love and Responsibility, as 'a work of sheer intellectual pygmyism'. Her favourite popes had been John XXIII and Paul VI who both believed that the Church should confront its 2000 year history of women's subordination.

'I don't know where this conservative view of her came from because she was always regarded as very radical in Church circles,' said the Fianna Fáil TD, Dick Roche, who first met her when he chaired the Irish Commission for Justice and Peace in the early 1980s. 'She always was a person who prodded the princes of the Church.'

Despite her uppermost contacts and prodigious lay work, Mary McAleese's view of the Church was never the roseate one perceived in Dublin. She certainly bemoaned the growing secularism south of the border where the Catholic Church was suspiciously regarded as an institution of repression. Coming from a place where religion dictated life, and often death, it was unsurprising that she would feel tied to it by 'a spiritual umbilical cord'. But it was never a passive relationship, her brash can-do self-confidence ringing early alarm bells in the more traditional cloisters.

Tom Kelly, the public relations executive who worked with her at Queens, saw her as 'an ecumenist, politically and religiously, rather than some sort of orthodox Catholic nationalist'.

Her refusal to be silenced is reminiscent of the Irish martyrs whose lives and deaths she chronicled in a slim published volume. It comes from the same preparedness to suffer for religious beliefs. The seeds of rebellion sown when she was just 18 and occasionally received communion at the Anglican mass in Queens University. When she publicly flouted her own Church's ban on inter-communion within a month of becoming President, one of her sharpest critics was the Archbishop of Dublin, Dr Desmond Connell. Unknown to the public, however, the pair had parted ideological ways long before then.

Its genesis was the 1992 abortion referendum. In February that year, when Albert Reynolds succeeded Charles Haughey as Taoiseach, the celebrated X-Case erupted in a blaze of controversy.

It concerned a 14-year-old rape victim who had been impregnated by her attacker. When the Attorney General, Harry Whelehan, discovered that the girl's parents were planning to accompany her to England for an abortion, he referred the matter to the High Court under the eighth amendment to the constitution, the legacy of the 1983 abortion referendum.

The High Court held that the victim should see the pregnancy through but, on appeal, the Supreme Court ruled that she was at risk of suicide and, therefore, was entitled to have the pregnancy terminated. In delivering its verdict, the judges of the land's highest court gave the Oireachtas a humiliating dressing down for failing to legislate on the substantive issue of abortion.

The country was gripped with hysteria. Anti-abortion activists condemned the State for sanctioning what it called 'the murder of an innocent baby'. The pro-choice lobby lashed out at the moral police who were prepared to deny the fundamental right to travel in an Ayatollah-style regime. To quell the unrest, Albert Reynolds proposed another referendum on three concomitant issues – freedom of travel, the dissemination of abortion information, and the limited circumstances in which abortion may be necessary. He warned that, if the amendment was not approved, his government would introduce legislation permitting abortion in the more liberal circumstances allowed by the Supreme Court judgment.

The referendum wording on the substantive issue read: 'It shall be unlawful to terminate the life of an unborn unless such termination is necessary to save the life, as distinct from the health, of the mother'. It was a compromise that fell between two stools, satisfying neither side in the debate and sparking one of the most vituperative referendum campaigns in the history of the constitution.

Mary McAleese, who had virtually vanished off the Republic's radar screen since her return to Belfast, believed it was the best compromise the anti-abortion lobby could secure from the government. As legal adviser to the Cardinal, she urged Dr Daly to accept it as a reversal of the Supreme Court judgment. But her advice flew in the face of the Pro-Life Campaign's tactic of calling for a 'no' vote and resuming the battle for yet another referendum to comprehensively outlaw abortion once and for all.

'Ireland would have been the first country in the world to put abortion into its constitution,' claimed Monsignor Denis Faul.

She adopted a high-profile role in the effort to have the referendum passed. On October 25, 1992, a letter appeared in *The Sunday Tribune*, signed by Mary McAleese, Director of the Institute of Professional Legal Studies at Queens University Belfast; Patricia Casey, professor of psychiatry at UCD and the Mater Hospital; and Cornelius O'Leary, Emeritus professor of political science at Queens.

'We welcome and support the forthcoming referendum on the substantive law of abortion,' it read. 'We hope that all those who are pro-life will feel as we do and will vote "yes"... No wording is perfect, but we believe the wording offered by the Government is pro-woman and pro-unborn. It is an opportunity to reaffirm the State's commitment to both the unborn and expectant mothers. This chance is not likely to be given again.'

The letter, also published by *The Irish Press* two days later, caused consternation in the offices of the Pro-Life Campaign where its founder, John O'Reilly, who had dedicated his life to rolling back the moral agenda, expressed grave concern about Mary McAleese's influence on the Cardinal. The appearance of Cornelius O'Leary's signature at the foot of the letter was the first public fissure in what, up to then, had been an impenetrable united front. O'Leary had earlier served as vice-chairman of the Pro-Life Amendment Campaign, which had steered through the 1983 amendment.

When the Catholic Bishops Conference issued a statement on November 5, advising the faithful to vote according to their own judgment, the Pro-Life Campaign was furious. In their eyes, Mary McAleese was the bête noire bending the Cardinal's ear.

'In my opinion she had little experience of the subject and, in the opinion of myself and the Pro-Life Campaign, her advice, as manifested in the letter, was misinformed,' recalled the Fianna Fáil senator, Des Hanafin, a papal knight and chairman of the Pro-Life Campaign. 'She got it hideously wrong and probably helped steer the hierarchy on the same course.'

The episcopacy's statement was designed to walk the tightrope between its hard-line and pragmatic wings but it could not sustain the balance. The rift inside the hierarchy became glaringly obvious nearly two weeks before the plebiscite when the Archbishop of Dublin issued a pastoral letter at all masses on November 15 in which he announced he would be voting 'no' on all three questions in the referendum. In private, Mary McAleese fumed that Dr Connell had broken ranks from an agreed position by the hierarchy. But he was joined by the influential Bishop of Cloyne, Dr John Magee, the Pope's former secretary at the Vatican, who also wrote a pastoral letter calling for a three-way 'no' vote. In all, five bishops stepped out of line, the clearly visible dissent in the episcopal conference only adding to the bewilderment of the electorate.

Behind the scenes, the divisions had so alarmed the Papal Nuncio, Dr Emanuele Gerada, that he attempted to reconcile the two sides. The diminutive and diplomatic Maltese ambassador from the Vatican invited Cardinal Daly to a meeting at his residence, number 183 on the Navan Road, to discuss the problem with the Pro-Life Campaign's eminent legal advisor, Professor William Binchy.

Meanwhile, Senator Des Hanafin decided not to wait for divine intervention. Instead, he boarded a plane bound for Rome with his wife, Mona, and told the Pope, face to face, that the indecisiveness of the bishops back home was threatening to pave the way for abortion. He pleaded for pontifical intervention. The Cardinal, the recipient of Mary McAleese's legal advice, was duly summoned.

'It was very nasty,' Senator Hanfin remembered. 'I got into a lot of trouble for going over their heads.'

Mary McAleese remained undeterred, however. In a *Late Late Show* abortion special the weekend before the referendum, she appeared as one of three advocates for the proposal. The television studio assumed the trappings of a mock courtroom, presided over by the retired president of the Circuit Court, Mr Justice Peter O'Malley. Two future judges, Nial Fennelly and Fidelma Macken, represented the case for the referendum. Acting for the bizarre coalition of pro-lifers and pro-choicers opposing the referendum, were the criminal law barrister, Felix McEnroy, and Mary's senior counsel in her *Sunday Independent* libel action, Garrett Cooney.

Wearing a demure black velvet dress and a string of pearls, a thick sheaf of hair falling to her shoulders, she appeared as a witness for the referendum. 'I see the X-case as permitting liberal abortion,' she argued.

Though the referendum on the substantive issue was ultimately rejected by a bruised and bamboozled electorate, that *Late Late Show* was a significant event in the life and times of Mary McAleese. That was the night she first met Professor Patricia Casey, her co-signatory to the newspaper letter and a woman who would help clear the way to Áras an Uachtaráin.

# 16

# A Woman of Substance

*Hate follows hate in a hard and bitter circle – our hate,*
*The hate I give, the hate I am given:*
*We should have used Pity and Grace to break the circle.*

EVEN AS THOSE WORDS were being transcribed from John Hewitt's *The Bloody Brae* to précis an interdenominational report on sectarianism, Northern Ireland was busy burying its dead. The year was 1993, when the early morning radio bulletins brought almost daily news of yet more murders; more funerals. A tense, hellish year of random killings, culminating in the multiple fatalities of an IRA bomb explosion on the Shankill Road and a loyalist reprisal massacre in Greysteel, County Derry.

Horror rained from the clouds that hung low over Belfast's Black Mountain. In the ghettos nestling in its shadow, terrified householders reinforced their front doors with sheets of metal and serried shooting bolts. They stayed inside their makeshift fortresses, knowing that the bric-à-brac of their lifestyles marked them out as sectarian targets – the streets they walked, the pubs they frequented, the newspapers they read, the cigarettes they smoked. The houses where they lived. The names they were given as new-born infants.

When the dissident Catholic theologian, Hanz Küng, visited Belfast he described it as a city where the hatred was palpable. The 'hard and bitter circle' of Hewitt's poetry. The same vicious circle that 17 men and women had spent two years trying to undo, almost breaking themselves apart in the process.

At the routine Irish Inter-Church meeting in 1987, the leaders of the Church of Ireland and Roman Catholicism, Archbishop Robin

Eames and Cardinal Tomás O'Fiaich, had agreed to commission a report on sectarianism. Four years later, in February 1991 and a year after Cardinal O'Fiaich's death, the 17-strong working party met for the first time in a small room beside Newry Cathedral. The committee spanned the religious gamut of Roman Catholic, Church of Ireland, Presbyterian, Methodist, Quaker and Mennonite. It was jointly chaired by John Lampen, a community worker in Belfast, and Mary McAleese. Their brief was to find a way towards reconciliation in a community riven by religion-fuelled hatred, but the immediate imperative was to maintain peace within the group itself.

'I was certain there would either be 17 minority reports or no report at all,' Mary McAleese admitted later. On another occasion, she confessed: 'Being part of the group was not easy. Discussions were frank. Sometimes we were cut to the quick. Sometimes we heard things and said things that offended. Many times I felt like leaving.'

At the outset, the group brainstormed over a definition of sectarianism, ultimately agreeing on a formula of words. 'Sectarianism is a complex of attitudes, beliefs, behaviours and structures in which religion is a significant component, and which (i) directly, or indirectly, infringes the rights of individuals or groups, and/or (ii) influences or causes situations of destructive conflict.'

Their own heated debates – mostly conducted at the Inter-Church Centre on Belfast's Elmwood Avenue after the initial meeting in Newry – were an object lesson in the corrosiveness of sectarianism.

'We all knew sectarianism was a problem but we didn't realise how deeply it bit,' recalled Rev Sam Burch, a Methodist minister and founder of 'Cornerstone', an ecumenical organisation on Springfield Road working to eradicate tribalism. 'I remember Mary saying that this thing begins when you are born. You take it in with your mother's milk. She said that, whenever there was a news flash on television saying someone had been shot, the first thing people thought was who did it and who's the victim. She impressed me. She's quick and intelligent and committed.'

Monsignor Denis Faul was another member of the committee. Though an outspoken critic of Mary's McAleese's stance on women priests, he admired the control she exerted over the committee. 'I liked her very well. She was quiet spoken at the meetings. She's very good on committees, when she's with her peers and she has to keep her head.'

The crisis point was reached when one of the committee, Dr Joe Leichty, an American Mennonite, an expert on Irish evangelism and a history lecturer in Maynooth, produced a document on the role of religion in Irish history. It caused ructions. The thrust of the document reflected the revisionist history that prevailed in the Republic and it infuriated the Northern Catholics on the committee.

'He was lit upon,' Mary McAleese told a conference in Rostrevor a year later. 'Eaten, savaged and spat out by a bunch of very well meaning Christians. I left him to the station and his relief when he saw the train pull into the station was palpable.' She also recalled that day in her book, *Reconciled Being: Love in Chaos*. 'The group members heaped abuse on each other and on him...' she wrote. 'Joe went back to Maynooth on the train, happy to have escaped with his life but otherwise in shock.'

In the end, they never did reach a consensus interpretation of Irish history and Joe Leichty's document was published as a separate, personal account entitled 'Roots of Sectarianism'.

Those two years, however, left a lasting impression on Mary McAleese. The report that flowed from the working party, 'Sectarianism: A Discussion Document', makes several references to 'bridge-building', the slogan she would adopt four years later as the theme of her presidency. Among the report's recommendations were the introduction of a bill of rights, official condemnation of illegal actions by the security forces, public investigations into major disputed killings, and that priority be given to community harmony over the right to march. The report, however, upheld the divisive core principle of segregated education and, on the contentious issue of mixed marriage, it merely suggested that Catholics needed to acknowledge how the supersedence of their Church in such unions hurt Protestants.

Its single paragraph on the Republic of Ireland stated: 'In the context of the protection of minorities generally we believe that a review of the inadequacies and gaps in constitutional and legislative provision is now required. In particular, religious discrimination, other than by the State, is nowhere explicitly outlawed in the Constitution. We believe that it would now be appropriate for the Republic to make some specific provision for the outlawing of religious discrimination more generally. Such legislation would be an important symbol of an open and non-discriminatory society.'

Since she left Dublin at the end of 1987, 'dragged screaming by Martin' back to the North, Mary McAleese's life had undergone a gradual transformation. From the upstart Catholic woman arraigned on the altar of Westminster, she had ascended to the elite ranks of the establishment. A beneficiary of the socio-demographic revolution in Northern Ireland that created a rising Catholic middle class. Her diary contained the private unlisted phone numbers of some of the most influential people in Ireland, Britain and the US, where two of her sisters had worked as child-minders for the former congressman, Joe Kennedy, son of the assassinated attorney general. Once a refugee within a sectarian state, she could now afford to accompany her children on school skiing holidays in continental Europe and to send Emma to summer camp in Eton to play sport with the sons and daughters of the realm. Her home life was contented and comfortable. Her annual New Year's Eve parties in Rostrevor were a growing legend for their eclectic guest lists.

Less than two years after her return, she joined the BBC Broadcasting Council for Northern Ireland, resigning in June 1992 to become a director of Channel 4 television. She remained unflappable whenever anyone tackled her, a deeply religious, moral woman, over the brash young station's sometimes lewd programming. As a guest on *The Late Late Show* in March 1993, she joked about a controversial new talk show on Channel 4 where none of the participants wore clothes. 'An omnibus edition of *Songs of Praise* would do more for your sex life,' she dismissed it with a laugh. 'When we discussed the all-nude chat show at home my father said it was a cure for bad thoughts.'

In August 1991 she was appointed by the Economy Minister, Richard Needham, to the nine-member board of Northern Ireland Electricity (NIE), which was about to be privatised. Chaired by Sir Desmond Lorimer, NIE was one of Belfast's three pillars of corporate men-only Protestantism, along with Shorts and Harland & Wolff. A fellow non-executive director remembered her constantly challenging perceptions at board meetings, chipping away until there was a climate conducive to appointing the company's first Catholic chief executive, Patrick Haren from Fermanagh.

Meanwhile, she had also been nominated by the Minister for Health to the Royal Group of Hospitals Trust for acute health care. The trust supervised three of the city's biggest hospitals as well as the dental hospital and Queens University's medical school. During her three-year tenure, when another efficacious trustee was the former Unionist Lord Mayor of Belfast, John Carson, the Trust sanctioned a £50 million redevelopment scheme for the Royal Victoria Hospital.

Between the three company boards, she was earning nearly £25,000 a year in director's fees on top of her £70,000 Queens salary. In addition to £35,000 worth of shares she held in NIE, she and Martin had the house in Rostrevor, the apartment in Dublin and her father's homestead in Croghan, County Roscommon. Her income and her public profile were further boosted by occasional freelance journalism, like a Radio Four series she made on Protestantism in 1995 and her frequent contributions to *Thoughts of the Day* for the BBC.

Her workload and her stamina were breathtaking. She co-founded the Belfast Women's Aid refuge with Patricia Montgomery, a solicitor in the Northern Ireland Office, chaired the Royal Victoria Hospital's complaints board, and sat on the Strategy for Sport steering group. She joined Through The Glass Ceiling, an organisation working for the advancement of women in business, and was the Northern Ireland rapporteur for the International Bar Association. She travelled to Washington as a delegate to the White House conference on trade and investment in Ireland in 1995, and to Pittsburgh for the follow up conference the year after.

The plethora of hats she wore included:
- honorary president of Newry & Mourne Royal College of Midwives Association;
- chairwoman of Northern Ireland Electricity's remuneration committee;
- honorary president of the Northern Ireland Housing Rights Association;

- member of the National Institute of Trial Advocacy in the UK and Northern Ireland;
- member of the British and Irish Legal Technology Association;
- member of the Society of Public Teachers of Law;
- member of the European Bar Association;
- member of the Institute of Advanced Legal Studies.

By the mid-1990s, Mary McAleese was a woman with bags of clout. One of the three most senior academics at Queens, a leading light of the Roman Catholic Church, a top academic lawyer, and a boardroom influence on the North's commercial environment. When she spoke, people listened. And when she went back to north Belfast in the first weekend of October 1994 to chair a community conference on policing, organised by the Ardoyne Association, she returned to her homeplace as a woman of substance.

The conference was held over two days in the Golden Thread Theatre, part of the self-sufficient Flax Trust set up by her old friend, Fr Myles Kavanagh of Holy Cross Monastery. David Cook, chairman of the Police Authority, and Jim Grew, chairman of the Independent Commission of Police Complaints, addressed an audience that included the SDLP's Alex Attwood and Sinn Féin's Joe Austin. Another Sinn Féin official present was Martin Meehan, the former IRA leader in Ardoyne who had been the last Republican suspect released from Long Kesh when internment ended in 1975.

At the end of the first day, the chairwoman summed up the various submissions. 'Everyone agreed on the need for order within our community,' Mary McAleese summarised. 'Systematically, the acceptability of the RUC was examined by conference participants and it was concluded that the RUC as an organisation carries with it an historical image and role which is totally unacceptable for the defined requirements of our community policing policy.'

That two-day conference sowed the seeds of 'A Neighbourhood Police Service – Ardoyne', a report published by the Ardoyne Association in May 1996 naming Professor Mary McAleese as a 'facilitator'. It expressed deep-seated distrust of the RUC. 'Policing must change in Northern Ireland,' the report demanded. 'For many that means the removal of the RUC from their communities and the creation of a new community-based police service. It is too much to expect the people who have been brutalised by the RUC to forgive and forget.'

Further on, the report stated: 'Since 1969, 28 innocent people from this small underprivileged community have been murdered by British Security Forces. Although each death had its own horrific effect on each particular family, it also instilled fear and despair into our broader community. Our feelings of frustration were further cultivated by the sheer inadequacies and blatant lack of willingness of the system of justice to come to our aid.' The final sentence of the report asserted: 'Our community wants, needs and demands a complete new police service which has our interest and well-being at heart – events have proven the RUC cannot fit this bill.'

The debate over the future of the Northern Ireland police force was one of the most controversial by-products of the peace process. After the IRA declared its historic cease-fire on August 31, 1994, the walls of west Belfast were daubed with demands that the RUC be disbanded. It was a politically sensitive issue but it echoed her earlier pronouncements on the force and her own experience of it back on the Crumlin Road. She had repeatedly claimed after her family fled north Belfast that nothing was ever done about the machine-gunning of her home.

Like most other people in the North, she had celebrated when the Republican guns went silent. Now, as the subsequent negotiations for permanent peace staggered and slithered in a quagmire of intransigence, her voice became an intermittent plea for help to friends and contacts south of the border. On Friday February 9, 1996, it looked like it had all been for nought when the IRA detonated a massive lorry bomb near the giant Canary Wharf building in London's Docklands, killing two men and wreaking millions of pounds worth of commercial damage on the city.

'I remember Mary rang me that night,' said her friend, Harry Casey. 'She was very upset. She kept asking: "How can we get back to peace?" She was crying on the phone.'

Though she had faded from public consciousness in the South, she had retained strong connections. She frequently travelled to Dublin to meet friends, attend concerts and cheer from the stands at Croke Park, staying overnight in the Ballsbridge apartment. For three years, she served on the Catholic Church's Irish Commission for Justice and Peace. 'There was no side to her,' recalled the Commission's executive director, Jerome Connolly. 'She was emotional in the best sense; in the sense that she would feel for an issue, feel for people. That inspired and coloured what she did. She had enormous personal courage.'

She spent holidays and long weekends in County Roscommon, restoring her grandparents' house in Croghan to its original spartan simplicity. Inside, there was no carpet, no television and no telephone. On the outside, she hung a little wooden sign chiselled with the name, 'Cara Cottage'.

She worked as an external examiner in criminal law for the Kings Inns in Dublin, overseeing course standards for the barristers' academy. She was also acting as an adviser to the joint forum on legal training in the Republic. Like many Northern nationalists, her relationship with the South brooked no borders. Though she had come to view Dublin as a place apart, she never treated the island as two countries.

In the summer of 1996, when the stand-off between marching Orangemen and resident nationalists in Drumcree re-ignited the torch of civil unrest, the first phone call Mary McAleese made was to Leinster House. Since the previous year, when David Trimble and Ian Paisley had strutted down the nationalist Garvaghy Road against the residents' wishes, Drumcree had been transmuted into a metaphor for the intractability of the Northern problem. In 1996, an initial order banning the Orange march was overturned and the RUC brandished its batons to clear 'the queen's highway' of Garvaghy Road protesters. Within 10 minutes of the decision being taken, Mary McAleese was on the phone to one of the most important architects of the peace process.

'She was the first person to let me know what had happened. She was angry about the situation,' remembered Martin Mansergh, the Oxford-educated Anglo-Irish Protestant republican who served as adviser on Northern Ireland to three taoisigh, Charles Haughey, Albert Reynolds and Bertie Ahern.

Mary McAleese was moving inexorably closer to the North's political pit. After Drumcree '96, she was drawn centre-stage under the auspices of the Catholic Church. Despite his refusal to entertain her notions about women priests, Cardinal Cahal Daly invited her to join a Church delegation to the Commission on Contentious Parades. The Commission was chaired by Dr Peter North and assisted by the Presbyterian church minister, writer and broadcaster, Rev John Dunlop, and Fr Oliver Crilly, who had spearheaded a doomed initiative by the Irish Commission for Justice and Peace to end the IRA hunger-strike 15 years earlier.

After the trouble stoked by the Orange Order parades in Drumcree and the Ormeau Road (where marchers taunted nationalists outside a Catholic betting shop in which the UDA had shot five men dead), the Commission on Contentious Parades was established to defuse the powder keg of the marching season. Cardinal Daly and Dr Sean Brady, who was installed as Archbishop of Armagh in November 1996, led the Catholic Church delegation to the Commission. The other three delegates were Mary McAleese, Monsignor Denis Faul and the civil rights lawyer, Martin O'Brien. As they prepared their submission to the Commission, a dispute broke out among them as to the best approach to adopt. Monsignor Faul argued that their December presentation should bar no holds, that the message they delivered should be blunt and to the point. Mary McAleese cautioned that the Archbishop should not be seen to be 'prescriptive'. Their differences on strategy left the craggy Dungannon priest with the impression that the Queens' lawyer was bending over backwards to make concessions.

'She took all the nasty bits, all the steel and the hard stuff, out of our document but I took it all and put it in my own submission. I went to the meeting in Archbishop's House the week before the delegation met the Commission and she was practically grovelling.'

Unknown to Denis Faul, and to almost everybody else, Mary McAleese had been practising the art of compromise behind closed doors, long before the Commission on Contentious Parades. When she had asked Harry Casey on the telephone how peace could be restored the night of the Canary Wharf bomb, her question had been rhetorical. She got her answer nonetheless. It came, in the form of an invitation, from a priest who is said to 'idolise her'.

Fr Alex Reid was the Tipperary-born Redemptorist priest who had started facilitating the talks between SDLP leader John Hume and the Sinn Féin president, Gerry Adams, at Clonard Monastery as far back as 1987. Those secret meetings, held in the shadow of the peace line that runs behind the rambling old monastery on the Falls Road, had culminated in the 1994 IRA cease-fire. Fr Reid's picture had been flashed around the world in March 1988 as he gave the kiss of life, in vain, to one of the two soldiers cornered and murdered in Andersonstown during the funeral of one of Michael Stone's Milltown Cemetery victims. The newspaper photographs showed the middle-aged priest, spattered with mud, the young corporal's blood smeared on his lips, and a look of intense grief in his eyes.

With permission from the Redemptorist order, he had worked trojanly to end the violence, believing that the inclusion, or 'mainstreaming', of Sinn Féin would bring the IRA's political wing in from the cold. When the 1994 cease-fire ended with the Canary Wharf bomb, he asked Mary McAleese and *The Irish News* publisher, Jim Fitzpatrick, to join him in his Redemptorist Peace Ministry.

A former solicitor in the family law firm, Jim Fitzpatrick took over the nationalist daily paper in 1982. The son of a War of Independence veteran and a devout Catholic with a special devotion to the Clonard Novena, he had been educated by the Redemptorists in Limerick and spent three years studying for a degree at the order's Galway seminary. As managing editor of *The Irish News*, he was threatened with assassination by the IRA when he banned the paramilitary organisation's death notices from the paper's memoriam columns.

The priest, the publisher and the professor, who would become known as the Holy Trinity, began meeting in the spring of 1996. Each session began with a prayer and was conducted in the strictest confidence. Their aim was to re-establish the IRA cease-fire and so they concentrated primarily on finding common ground between Sinn Féin and constitutional nationalism. Some nationalist politicians regarded it as little more than 'well intentioned meddling'. In the more reluctant quarters of the SDLP, it evoked memories of Henry II's 'troublesome clerics' – in this world, but not of it.

Outside of the Clonard confines, Mary McAleese exploited her network of heavyweight contacts. Politicians in Dublin were vaguely aware that she was bringing opinion-makers together at private dinners in pursuit of the elusive second cease-fire. It was even whispered in Rostrevor that the Sinn Féin leader, Gerry

Adams, had been in her house. At one point in 1996, she heard that the head of personnel in Washington, Jim King, was visiting Belfast to give an address at Queens. She had met the senior civil servant in Bill Clinton's administration when Tom Kelly introduced them at the first economic conference at the White House. She immediately set about organising a dinner at home in 'Kairos' where Gerry Adams, among others, could meet the influential Boston man. But Jim King declined the invitation, considering such a get-together too sensitive in the lacuna before the new IRA cease-fire was declared in July 1997.

A major plank of Sinn Féin's agenda at the time was to push for an electoral pact with the SDLP in advance of the British general election coming up in 1997. The Redemptorist peace triumvirate played devil's advocate, tossing the proposal to John Hume's party. The bigger, constitutional party, however, baulked at the idea of creating what could be construed as a pan-nationalist front. While John Hume's initiative in talking to Adams had paid off in terms of the peace dividend, many SDLP members remained deeply distrustful of Sinn Féin and its motives. They feared that any grand alliance of nationalism would be met by a mirror alliance of unionism, which would inevitably bow to the lowest common denominator.

One evening, a senior member of the SDLP accepted an invitation to attend the Clonard talks. She listened to Mary McAleese, who did most of the talking at the meeting, advance the merits of the Sinn Féin proposal. As she listened, the SDLP member's thoughts were fixed on the possibility of a new IRA cease-fire. It never crossed her mind that this meeting would be used as a high-risk dirty-tricks weapon in the Republic's presidential election before the year was out.

The name of the SDLP member was Bríd Rodgers.

# 17

# When Harry Made His Sally

SHE WAS DRIVING HOME from Queens University in the white Mercedes Martin had given her for her birthday when the mobile phone rang. It was Harry Casey calling from Navan.

'Mary,' he said, 'please don't shoot this down now. I've a proposal to put to you. All I'm asking is that you think about it.'

'What is it?' she asked warily.

Harry took a deep breath. 'Will you stand for the presidential election?' he blurted out, his excitement bubbling down the cellular network.

Long silence.

Eventually: 'Where did this idea come from?'

Harry crossed his fingers. 'I've been talking to some Fianna Fáil councillors and I mentioned your name and they didn't rule it out,' he fibbed.

It was March 12, 1997 just hours after Mary Robinson had announced her intention to depart Áras an Uachtaráin when her seven-year term of office expired in the autumn. It was with 'great reluctance', the most popular President in Irish history disclosed in an official statement issued to the media that she had decided not to seek a second term.

The announcement presaged the end of the nation's unprecedented love affair with its first citizen. Since her surprise election in November 1990, the former *enfant terrible* had conquered the hearts of the people. Her reign was nothing short of a phenomenon. A diffident, formal woman with an iron will, she had consistently scored almost full marks in opinion poll after opinion poll. It was a watershed presidency, transforming the traditionally staid sinecure for retired politicians into an active and highly visible role.

At the time of her election, when she sensationally beat the odds-on Fianna Fáil favourite, Brian Lenihan, into second place, Harry Casey had been in Rome. Having abandoned his plans to join the priesthood after four years' study, he had completed a degree in philosophy, theology and English in Maynooth. In 1990 he was spending a year at the Irish College in the Italian capital, working for a master's degree in counselling, psychology and spirituality. On the eve of the presidential election back home, he had organised a mock poll at the college in Rome where the rector was the future Archbishop of Armagh, Dr Sean Brady. In Harry Casey's poll too Mary Robinson emerged the victor but, even then, the Longford man had another woman in mind for the pre-eminent position in the land.

The first time he had seen Mary McAleese was on the television set in a neighbour's house in 1981. The Nethercotts, who had fled South from the violence in Belfast, were watching *Today Tonight* when their sons' form teacher dropped by.

'Isn't she very articulate?' Harry had said, nodding to the presenter on the screen.

'Do you think so?' asked Elizabeth Nethercott. 'She's a friend of mine.'

One week later, Harry Casey was introduced to Mary McAleese. Theirs was a handshake that would change both their lives.

The weekend after President Robinson's announcement, Harry got into his car and drove to Rostrevor. He talked to Martin, a man with strong political opinions who did not rule out the proposition. He talked to Mary, who trotted out all the reasons why it was a crazy notion. He badgered her until she 'reluctantly' agreed to think about it some more.

Among her thoughts must have been the bad memories of her life in Dublin. The sour history with RTÉ and the NUJ, key elements in any election campaign. The three rejections at the polls: in the 1987 general election when Harry had been her election agent, and the referendums on the Single European Act and abortion. Her rancorous split from Fianna Fáil and her remoteness from the political milieu in the Republic.

Then there were the practical considerations. Did she, a woman loath to apply for any job she was unsure of landing, have a snowball's chance in hell of winning? Did she even want to be the one to try to fill Mary Robinson's outsize shoes? Could a role where style outweighed substance be expanded any further? When her erstwhile Trinity colleague was elected in 1990 the country had been crying out for symbolic reassurance. The economy had been moribund, political scandals abounded and peace in the North was still but a pipe dream. Now there was to be a vacancy in the Áras but in a climate of economic and civic well being, was there any longer a deficit in the national morale that could be requited by a figurehead?

Conversely, it was a tantalising prospect. All the indications were that Mary McAleese had reached the zenith of her career in Northern Ireland by 1997. She had tendered her application to replace the retiring vice-chancellor of Queens University, Sir Gordon Beveridge, but her name had not even made it onto the short-list. And, in the provincial backwater of Belfast, there was little scope for advancement. Besides, to return to Dublin as the Republic's premiere citizen would be the sweetest homecoming imaginable.

Over-riding all her musings, however, was the twin spectre of The Peace-Makers. John Hume and Albert Reynolds had been acclaimed as the joint constitutional architects of the 1994 IRA cease-fire. In electoral terms, they appeared invincible. And the names of both men were already being floated as alternative dream presidents.

John Hume, in particular, had acquired the status of a saint in the Republic; his battle-weary face bookending 30 years of a pacifist's crusade for justice and peace. If he wanted to be Uachtarain na hEireann, then so be it – no political party in its right mind was going to stand in his way. Despite President Robinson's caveat that her successor should be elected by the people, the body politic was willing to offer the job to the SDLP leader on a plate.

The first chink in the consensus was made by the most surprising interloper of all, Fr Alex Reid. The intensely private Redemptorist priest who had brought Hume and Adams together to kick-start the peace process and who had often telephoned Albert Reynolds in the middle of the night to bend the Taoiseach's ear, suddenly lobbed a new name into the hat.

It was in early April that the thin, stooped cleric visited Dr Martin Mansergh in his Leinster House office for one of their regular discussions on the North. In mid-conversation, the priest suddenly switched course, probing Fianna Fáil's guru about the likelihood of the party nominating Mary McAleese for the presidential election.

'He was indicating her interest in being a presidential candidate on behalf of Fianna Fáil and sounding me out about it,' remembered Martin Mansergh. 'My reply would have been that we were concentrating on the general election. Nobody would decide how they would play the presidential election until they got through the general election. I tried neither to be too encouraging or discouraging. At that distance it looked like somewhat of an outside prospect. I knew her and liked her. I thought, *in abstracto*, she would be a very good and plausible candidate. But she would have to get through the Fianna Fáil parliamentary party first.'

Mary McAleese had given her supporters the green light in April when Harry had, once again, driven to Rostrevor on his mission to persuade her. By this time, the media was speculating about the possible candidacy of Dana Rosemary Scallon, the 1970 winner of the Eurovision Song Contest who was preparing to fly to Ireland from her home in the American bible belt to test the waters. On that April evening, as Mary and Harry had walked along the shoreline of Carlingford Lough, he realised that she was not going to need much persuading after all. Her ruminations had made the quantum leap from contemplating the starting line to clearing the first hurdle. She asked Harry how she could get nominated for the election. The Longford man was jubilant when he detected her new mood. She had decided to take it on, she admitted, but only if John Hume turned it down.

Back in 'Kairos', Harry talked to Martin, teasing out the tactical manoeuvres to secure her nomination. The constitution required that presidential candidates have the backing of either 20 Oireachtas members or four county or borough councils. 'Leave the strategy to me,' Harry told Martin.

The schoolteacher drove back to Navan that night, his brain buzzing with names of people he could rope into the campaign. It was an impressive list that he mentally worked through. For starters, there was Fianna Fáil's deputy leader, Mary O'Rourke – Harry's brother had taught her two sons in school and her youngest, Aengus, played tennis with members of his family. Another Fianna Fáiler in his contacts book was the general election candidate, Mary Hanafin, who had studied for her BA degree in Maynooth when Harry was there. He would call on his local Fianna Fáil deputies, Noel Dempsey and Mary Wallace, and his family's friend back in Longford, the Progressive Democrats councillor, May Sexton. Moreover, he had an immediate entrèe to the media through his wife, Mary. On their wedding day in August 1993, Mary McAleese had addressed the couple's 270 guests at the Ardboyne Hotel in Navan. One of those who had listened to her was Harry's new brother-in-law, Liam Hayes, the former GAA star and now the editor of *Ireland on Sunday*.

Back in Northern Ireland, Mary was conducting her own market research. She talked to Fr Reid and Jim Fitzpatrick, both men immediately recognising the symbolic potency of a Belfast woman succeeding to the Áras. Martin Naughton, the Queens benefactor whose business empire was headquartered in Dunleer, County Louth, was another instant convert to the idea. Something of a Northern caucus began to evolve when her friend, the 37-year-old solicitor Denis Moloney, also came on board.

He was a man with extensive contacts, as a lawyer, a governor of St Louise's comprehensive school in Belfast and a prominent Catholic. In an *Irish News vox-pop*, he had cited the Bible as one of his favourite books and his faith as his greatest strength. A pioneer, a bachelor and a lay student of theology, the senior partner in Donnelly & Wall and legal representative of the Down and Conor diocese was generally reputed to be a Knight of Columbanus. His only sibling, Dr Maria Moloney, had been the personnel director of Harland & Wolff. Their parents, Pearl and Denis, a retired RUC superintendent, had perished in the Kegworth air disaster in 1989.

Mary McAleese next called on another friend – Tom Kelly, the public relations consultant who had withstood the unionist brickbats with her at Queens. As soon as she made her decision in April, she phoned and told him of her intentions. They arranged to meet with their families for Sunday lunch that weekend in Warrenpoint. Mary asked him for suggestions on structuring her campaign.

'My view was that Fianna Fáil was no different to any other party,' Tom Kelly recalled. 'I said if you want a nomination just track its fault lines and a good start would be the Lenihans/O'Rourke axis. After that, rural TDs, particularly those along the border, and not to forget key cumann and constituency office holders. As a Northerner, I told her to ensure she was seen to have a mainly Southern campaign base and team.'

But he turned down her request to work on the campaign. 'I told her I was really hoping Hume would seek the nomination and was committed to encouraging political support for that to happen. I declined involvement at that time but offered support in terms of contacting TDs I knew.'

In an *Irish News* interview on December 8, 1997, Mary McAleese recalled that, when 'the idea of me standing was first mentioned in the early part of the summer', her reaction was 'not to take it seriously'. 'Over the summer, pressure mounted from quite a number of sources,' she added. 'I said to them "go away and get me the evidence that quite a broad range of people could conceivably support me as a president". They did that.'

In truth, she had made up her mind well before the summer, but she was still considering her options on the best method of securing a nomination. One of Mary Robinson's strengths seven years earlier had been her detachment from party politics. It was the Labour Party that had chased her and she had repeatedly emphasised her independence as a candidate. The benefits of staying aloof were evident and, on June 18, 1997, a news story appeared, which suggested that this was what Mary McAleese had in mind too. The report was carried by *The Irish News*, Jim Fitzpatrick's paper. It claimed that the Queens professor had been approached by Fianna Fáil, Fine Gael and Labour for the presidency. She was quoted as 'adamant' that she would 'not lobby for it'.

The report, however, was inaccurate. That message was unequivocally relayed to the McAleese campaign through the medium of a Jesuit priest, Fr Edmond Grace. A former law student at Trinity College and labour law lecturer at the College of Industrial Relations in Dublin, he had first met Mary at a lunch with her fellow academic, Kadar Asmal, in the 1980s. The priest, who had been a member of the Labour Party in Trinity before joining the Jesuits, had became a good friend of the McAleese family, spending a weekend at 'Kairos' every year.

'When I read the story in *The Irish News* I was intrigued and I rang her at home,' Fr Grace remembered. 'She said there had been some interest expressed by Fine Gael and she asked me if I knew anybody in the (Labour) party and I said I could ring John Rogers.'

But when the Gardiner Street-based priest phoned the senior counsel and adviser to Labour leader Dick Spring, he got short shrift. 'He gave an emphatic no,' Fr Grace admitted. 'He had a very good argument against it. He said it would be seen as the politicians' choice – not the people's choice.'

The only thing left for the priest to do was to write to his local TD, urging him to consider Mary as a presidential candidate. That TD was Bertie Ahern, leader of Fianna Fáil and, by June 26, leader of the government to boot.

In the meantime, Mary was putting out her own feelers. On the evening of June 21, when all the auguries after the cliff-hanging general election were pointing to a Fianna Fáil-led government, she and Martin went to the National Concert Hall in Dublin for a performance by the Guinness Choir and the Carlow Choral Society. Over drinks at the interval, she bumped into Martin Mansergh, whose eldest daughter was one of the Guinness choristers. As Martin McAleese slipped discreetly away, the pair discussed the recent shooting in Lisburn of two policemen and the implications for the peace process. Then the conversation turned to the presidency. After his meeting with Fr Alex Reid more than two months earlier, Fianna Fáil's expert on Northern Ireland was not surprised by her interest in the job. By the time they returned to their seats in the auditorium, he had reeled off a number of party names she should contact to make her pitch.

Fianna Fáil, in fact, had a major dilemma on its hands. The party desperately needed to win back the presidency, whipped from under its nose by the left alliance when Bertie Ahern had been Brian Lenihan's director of elections. The trouble was that it could not produce a convincing candidate, someone untarnished by the party's record of low standards in office but with the charisma to guarantee victory. All the obvious names had been tossed around. Charles Haughey, tending his chrysanthemums in bucolic retirement, ruled himself out as he waited for the secrets of his Walter Mitty fiscal life to explode. Mary O'Rourke toyed with the idea but, finally, rejected it, preferring to stay in the hurly-burly of government. Maire Geoghegan-Quinn was a possibility, but her retirement from politics the previous January for reasons of family privacy could not be squared with the most public office in the country. David Andrews was safe and languidly statesmanlike but his Dáil seat in the volatile constituency of Dun Laoghaire could not be put at risk.

That left Albert Reynolds. The 64-year-old perma-tanned petfood millionaire was the ideal candidate, on paper. Regarded internationally as a statesman, he had been tipped for the Nobel Peace Prize, he had steered both the peace process and the economy with assuredness, he had a model marriage and seven vivacious, personable children. All the ingredients of a perfect president, or so Albert Reynolds thought.

He had relinquished the Fianna Fáil leadership after precipitating the collapse of his coalition government with the Labour Party in 1994. His bloody-minded insistence on promoting the Attorney General, Harry Whelehan, to President of the High Court in the face of his government partner's unswerving opposition had signalled the end of his 34-month stint as Taoiseach. In the immediate aftermath of his administration's downfall, Fianna Fáil had tried to hatch an agreement, with Bertie Ahern as the new party leader, to stay in government with Labour. Ancillary to the plan was a proposal that Albert Reynolds be appointed a roving ambassador for the peace process, a novel position loosely styled as a super envoy. But even as the cabinet secretary, Frank Murray, was examining the powers and status of the job, the coalition negotiations broke down and Labour chose Fine Gael and Democratic Left as its new government partners. The concept of a super envoy was put on hold.

In January 1996, Bertie Ahern and Albert Reynolds met for lunch in the dining-room of the Berkeley Court Hotel. The Fianna Fáil leader and his predecessor discussed domestic politics, the intricacies of the peace process and the most likely date of the next general election. Out of ear-shot of *The Sunday Tribune* political correspondent, Stephen Collins, and the former government press secretary, Frank Dunlop, who were lunching at a nearby table, they also discussed the presidency. In fact, Albert Reynolds was convinced this was the main item on the agenda. Afterwards, he told confidantes that Bertie had asked him to be the party's candidate for the presidential election. The lunch ended inconclusively. 'Come back and ask me if the lady in the Park decides to move on,' was Albert's reputed parting shot.

The two men again met for lunch a year later, this time in McGrattan's Restaurant, situated in a laneway opposite Government Buildings. It was early 1997 and a general election was looming. The Fianna Fáil leader urged the older man to defend his Dáil seat in Longford to maintain a national profile for the presidential election. They discussed which of Albert's children – the businessman, Philip, or the barrister, Leonie – would contest the by-election in the event of their father being elected president.

'After the lunch in '96, I said I wasn't keen,' Albert Reynolds recalled. 'He asked me to think about it. When I didn't go back to him he invited me out again in '97.'

Bertie Ahern was stewing in a political pickle. He needed to keep his predecessor on side and to be seen to have Albert's support going into his first general election as Fianna Fáil's leader. Yet the sweetener of seven years in the Park was starting to look more like a bitter pill with the growing school of thought in the party that Albert would make a disastrous candidate. There were just too many negatives.

An uncomplicated 'one-sheet' man who had once memorably resorted to the word 'crap' on the national airwaves, unaware of its scatological meaning, he was not a natural statesman. On another occasion in the 1980s, he had togged out in a cowboy outfit and crooned 'Put your sweet lips a little closer to the phone', on television. A former dancehall promoter, he was regarded as the mascot of the 'country 'n' western set' within Fianna Fáil. He had weathered controversies over his role in the Beef Tribunal and his petfood company's monetary gain from the passports-for-sale scheme. As he was limbering up for the presidential campaign he suffered public humiliation when the London High Court allowed him a pyrrhic victory in a libel action he had taken against *The Sunday Times* – awarding him a paltry penny in damages.

By 1997, Albert Reynolds had fallen foul of his past. His political judgment had been called into question when he needlessly caused a general election in 1992. It was the only one in which he had led Fianna Fáil and it had been a catastrophe, with the party losing nine seats. Most critically, he had pulled the rug from under his own government at the Beef Tribunal when he questioned the honesty of one of the most respected politicians in the country, Des O'Malley, leader of his PD coalition partners.

When the PDs coalesced with Bertie Ahern's Fianna Fáil after the general election in June 1997, Albert Reynolds was hoist on his own petard. The junior party's new leader, Mary Harney, whose full Dáil complement amounted to four TDs, warned the Taoiseach that she could not, in conscience, support Albert's candidacy for the presidency.

She was not the only one opposed to him. Others were massed in the senior ranks of Fianna Fáil itself. People like Mary O'Rourke, Rory O'Hanlon, Gerry Collins, Ray Burke, Michael O'Kennedy and the rest of the eight ministers Albert had sacked from the cabinet on succeeding Charles Haughey in February 1992. He had also dismissed nine of the 12 junior ministers in what came to be known as his Valentine Massacre.

When, in June 1997, Fianna Fáil entered into a minority coalition government dependent on the votes of three Independent TDs to stay alive, it was a gift to Albert's detractors. Now, they argued, he could not jeopardise the Longford seat. Losing it would not only have repercussions for Fianna Fáil, but for the government itself. Contrary to a headline in *The Evening Herald* three days after the government was formed, proclaiming 'Reynolds Is Presidential Front-Runner', the former Taoiseach's star was already waning. A new political movement was gestating. ABBA, short for Anybody But Bloody Albert, threatened to be his Waterloo.

But the hung Dáil was a stroke of luck for Mary McAleese.

'Things fell absolutely right for us with the tight numbers after the general election,' agreed Harry Casey.

He had been beavering away all the while on the campaign. Letters of support were pouring into the McAleese home in Rostrevor 'at my behest', he admitted. Mary herself had not been shilly-shallying either. One of the most important phone calls she had made was to her old campaign ally in the abortion referendum, Patricia Casey.

No relation of Harry's, the Cork-born psychiatrist had emerged as a hugely influential woman in the Republic in the intervening four years. As chairwoman of the Medical Council's powerful Fitness to Practice committee, she had built up an impressive network of contacts. After the initial phone call from Mary she set to work with Harry Casey, executing a blanket siege of the Fianna Fáil parliamentary party, the 114 TDs, senators and MEPs enfranchised to elect the party's nominee.

Mary McAleese was, of course, well aware of Albert Reynolds' desire to be the next president. Their paths had crossed in political and social circles, primarily at the dinner table of Mary's neighbour's son, Edward Haughey, the wealthy Newry businessman whom Albert appointed to the Seanad. And, though her friends said she 'liked Albert and admired what he did for peace', she was not prepared to gave him the *carte blanche* she felt John Hume deserved.

On July 4, Harry went back to Rostrevor to step up the campaign. Mary had just returned home from an Independence Day party at Hillsborough Castle. She was dithering; reluctant to show her hand before Hume made his decision. She had even written to the SDLP leader, exhorting him to accept the presidency. But Harry was growing impatient. The time had come, he told her, when she must declare her intentions to the Taoiseach. Together with Martin, they sat down that night and composed a letter to Bertie Ahern outlining her credentials for the Park. Then they made a copy. Mary signed both in her careful, rounded handwriting. The following morning, Harry drove to Drumcondra and deposited one missive in the letterbox of 'St Lukes', the Taoiseach's constituency office. He posted the second one from Navan on Monday morning by registered mail to Fianna Fáil headquarters in Upper Mount Street.

Though the letter only elicited a formal acknowledgement of receipt a week later, Bertie Ahern could not ignore the growing momentum of the McAleese campaign. The entire parliamentary party (bar Albert Reynolds) had, by now, received an introductory letter and a truncated biography of the Belfast woman, courtesy of Patricia Casey. She had also telephoned the Wicklow back-bencher,

Dick Roche, for whom she had canvassed in the general election. Within days of that phone call, he had approached his party leader.

'I collared Bertie in the lobby and told him Mary was interested. He said: "Oh ya, very good". I spoke to him again several times about it,' Dick Roche confirmed. 'Bertie told me twice he was staying out of it. I remember saying to him: "Christ, we're going to lose this unless you make a decision". At one stage he told me to let him know how the name was being received. It was as casual as that. Nothing more.'

As Dick Roche embarked on his own canvass of the parliamentary party, more senior Fianna Fáil members were gradually entering the frame. The first cabinet member to meet Mary McAleese was the Minister for Social, Community and Family Affairs, Dermot Ahern. A neighbour of his in Blackrock, County Louth, Kieran Taaffe, a friend of the McAleeses and vice-president of the Dublin Institute of Technology, acted as the go-between. A meeting was scheduled for the first week in July in the minister's Leinster House office. Martin McAleese accompanied his wife to the meeting.

'I explained to them about getting through the parliamentary party,' said Dermot Ahern. 'She had done a letter campaign which some TDs didn't like because they saw it as going behind their backs to their constituents. We left it on the basis that I would let the Taoiseach know she was with me and that I would talk to a number of my colleagues.'

Mary McAleese, however, was leaving nothing to chance. Within a week of the government's formation, she had phoned her former colleague on the Fianna Fáil Womens Committee, Mary O'Rourke, to request a meeting. It was to be the most critical test of her prospects. Having been mooted as a contender for the presidency herself, Mary O'Rourke was the party's deputy leader and a significant player in the decision. A sister of the 1990 candidate, the late Brian Lenihan, two of her nephews were also TDs, Conor and Brian Lenihan. Most crucially, she was now the most senior of the rehabilitated ministers axed in Albert Reynolds' cabinet bloodbath.

They met at seven o'clock on the evening of July 12 at Mary O'Rourke's home in Athlone. There were just four people present – the Minister for Public Enterprise, her husband, Enda, and Mary and Martin McAleese. They talked for two hours, the initial chitchat about Roscommon and the old days in Fianna Fáil being quickly overtaken by the impending presidential election. The Belfast woman said it was something she would like to do and she felt qualified for the job.

'I pledged my troth that night,' Mary O'Rourke remembered. 'I asked her who she knew in the party and she mentioned Dermot Ahern and Rory O'Hanlon. I told her she would want to move quickly because others were moving as well. I advised her to get her name into the public domain.'

Once again the message was relayed to Bertie Ahern. And, once again, he remained resolutely non-committal.

'I've met Mary McAleese and she's interested in standing for the presidency,' his deputy leader told him.

'So I've heard,' replied the Taoiseach.

It was a lifeline, however, which could not have escaped his notice. Bertie Ahern was facing heavy-duty embarrassment should John Hume resist the lure of the Park. Fianna Fáil had a proprietorial interest in Áras an Uachtaráin. Before the Robinson glitch, the party had held the seat for 14 unbroken years in the person of Dr Patrick Hillery. But the chances of wresting it back were looking bleak. If Albert Reynolds was to be their candidate, the election campaign could prove internally divisive and plunge the party into a media trawl of old scandals. Even worse, Albert might not win. As the Taoiseach packed his suitcase for his summer holidays in Kerry, August was threatening to be an exceedingly wicked month.

John Hume too was planning a vacation. He was off to his beloved France where, he announced, he would be contemplating his future.

Albert Reynolds, on the other hand, had consigned his sand bucket to the closet. His public assertion that he wanted to be president, no matter what John Hume decided, dropped like a bombshell.

'What other people do is their business,' he proclaimed in Belfast on August 9 after delivering a memorial lecture in honour of the civil rights solicitor, Paddy McGrory. 'My name was there, maybe unconfirmed, for the last two months. It was there for a long time back. It is not news to anybody.'

The determination of the millionaire politician could be measured by his bank balance. He had already engaged the services of Communique International, a Dublin firm of communications consultants headed up by Peter Finnegan, a former member of Fianna Fáil's national executive and party councillor in Meath. A blueprint for the campaign was devised by the core team of Finnegan, his business partner, Mary McGuire, Albert's eldest son, Philip, and the Munster MEP, Brian Crowley, working out of Communiqueé International's office in Herbert Place.

They were not deterred when, on August 20, the *Church of Ireland Gazette* warned that the nomination of Albert Reynolds by Fianna Fáil would be a reversion to 'the old and tiresome system of using the presidency as a reward for past taoisigh and ministers'.

On August 28, his team mail-shot every member of the Fianna Fáil parliamentary party with a letter from Albert, accompanied by the findings of an opinion poll he had privately commissioned at a cost of £10,000. 'As we all know,' he wrote, 'polls are more indicative than definitive in what they tell us. Nevertheless, I thought you might be interested in both the figures and the analysis.' The survey, which had been conducted on two days in early July, showed that, in a three-way presidential race between the most likely candidates at that time, the former Fianna Fáil leader would win outright. The results were 45 per cent for Albert Reynolds; 20 per cent for Fine Gael's Mary Banotti; 17 per cent for Labour's Michael D Higgins; and 18 per cent undecided.

In his letter, he promised to reward deserving citizens with an annual honours list, to promote enterprise and to be a voice for the less fortunate in society. 'It would be a great honour for me to be the party standard bearer in this election,' he wrote, 'and ultimately to apply my accumulated experience to the office of President of Ireland.'

On the face of it, the last thing Albert Reynolds needed was a new job. He was a very wealthy man who had tramped the lucrative American lecture circuit after withdrawing from frontline politics. His lifestyle was charmed, involving regular first-class travel to the Orient as chairman of a group of companies in Singapore and director of another in Hong Kong. He had declined the role of peace envoy, resurrected after the general election. Its proposed powers were ambiguous and the job would have involved a problematical relationship with his party adversary, the Foreign

Affairs Minister, Ray Burke. But he remained unsatisfied. He exuded a hunger for recognition, as if he felt short-changed in the coinage of respect for brokering the IRA cease-fire in 1994.

Albert Reynolds had good reason to believe that the Fianna Fáil nomination was his for the taking. His candidacy had, after all, been mooted by the party leader. Furthermore, he could count on the support of cabinet heavyweights like Finance Minister Charlie McCreevy, Health Minister Brian Cowen and Environment Minister Noel Dempsey, all of whom he had promoted when he was Taoiseach. Charlie McCreevy publicly endorsed him on August 31. 'I was on the back-benches for almost 15 years and Albert gave me my chance,' the Minister for Finance explained. 'I would support him now without equivocation whether he asked me to or not.'

But another cabinet member in his debt had already sounded a warning bell. It came three days after the party's director of the June general election, PJ Mara, had described John Hume as the outstanding candidate at the Humbert Summer School in Mayo. Now David Andrews, a back-bencher for 27 years until Reynolds made him Marine Minister in 1992, publicly urged him to withdraw from the race if John Hume was willing to go forward. It was read as a clear endorsement of Hume by the Fianna Fáil leadership. On August 11, Andrews admitted that he was 'extremely interested' in the position himself and that he would make a decision in the coming weeks.

Five days later, the pitch was further queered when the 61-year-old Tipperary North veteran, Michael O'Kennedy, added his name to the growing list of contenders.

'I met Bertie at Croke Park and I told him I was going to throw my hat in the ring,' he recalled. 'He said nothing to discourage me. In fairness to him, I wasn't looking for an endorsement. I felt it was a matter for the parliamentary party. It would be inappropriate to tie down the party leader. There is a convention that the leader remain neutral.'

Though he was not regarded as a winnable option, Michael O'Kennedy's declaration at the MacGill summer school on August 16 was bad news for Reynolds. O'Kennedy was one of the party's old guard. First elected in 1969, he had held the agriculture, finance, foreign affairs and transport portfolios in various governments and had been EEC Commissioner for a year in the early 1980s. The immediate ramification for Reynolds was the inevitable divided loyalties of another cabinet member he thought he could rely on. Defence Minister Michael Smith, a stalwart of the so-called 'country 'n' western' wing of Fianna Fáil, happened to be a constituency colleague of O'Kennedy.

The slow fragmentation of alliances within Fianna Fáil was manna to the Friends of Mary McAleese campaign. By now, Patricia Casey had contacted the chairman of the parliamentary party, Rory O'Hanlon, a fellow doctor and former Health Minister. They met in his Cavan-Monaghan constituency, when the psychiatrist took a detour from Carrickmacross after delivering a speech to a medical conference. O'Hanlon, who was responsible for procedures at parliamentary party meetings, told her that Mary McAleese's name was not being mentioned in Fianna Fáil circles. Next, she rang the Minister for Justice, John O'Donoghue, who shared both Casey's and McAleese's opposition to abortion. The Kerry minister had known Patricia Casey since before his marriage, when his wife-to-be had shared a flat in Dublin with her best friend. Yet another key player was Éamon O'Cuív of Galway West, a good friend of Mary's confidante in Rostrevor, the historical novelist, Siobhán Ní Dubhain. A grandson of the party's founder, O'Cuív was the junior minister to his first cousin, Síle de Valera, in the Department of Arts, Heritage, Gaeltacht and the Islands.

It was a classic example of Irish networking. Every available connective thread spun into a web, with Mary McAleese at its centre. 'We were getting bundles of letters on her behalf,' recalled one cabinet member. The government chief whip, Seamus Brennan, even received a phone-call from his dentist, an old classmate of Martin McAleese. Harry Casey augmented the saturation coverage behind the scenes. He too contacted Éamon O'Cuív, Rory O'Hanlon and Mary O'Rourke as well as Síle de Valera, Mary Wallace and Noel Dempsey. The Environment Minister replied in writing that he had passed the name on to the party leader. By the end of August, Mary McAleese had also met the Tanaiste, Mary Harney, at the introduction of Councillor May Sexton.

And yet the public remained oblivious to the Belfast academic's ambition to become president. On September 2, the *Irish Independent* published the results of an opinion poll. It showed that John Hume was still the most popular choice, with a rating of 31 per cent. Second, but a long way behind at 13 per cent, was Albert Reynolds. He was followed by David Andrews (8 per cent), Dana (6 per cent) and Michael O'Kennedy (3 per cent). Mary McAleese never even featured in the questionnaire, a mere fortnight before the nation's media would be salivating with her name.

Six days after that opinion poll, John Hume returned from France with a light suntan and an announcement to make. He had deliberated long and hard. 'It was a very difficult decision – one of the most difficult personal decisions I have ever had to take in my life,' he said. He had been encouraged to go to the Áras by thousands of well-wishers who wrote to him and by some SDLP people who felt the party would benefit from a new broom. But others had worried about the future of the peace process without Hume at the helm. His friends fretted too that the comparative sedateness of the presidency would drive the indefatigable Derryman round the twist. There had been a sinister development when it was rumoured that a British tabloid was planning to resurrect a scurrilous story about him it had binned three years earlier if he decided to go for the Irish presidency.

In the end, it was his sense of patriotism that made up his mind. He was staying put to see the peace process through. 'My whole adult life, together with my colleagues in the SDLP, has been devoted to resolving the crisis here in the North,' he said. 'That's now at a critical stage and I believe, therefore, that it's my duty to stay here and use all our energies to achieve the lasting peace and lasting settlement all sections of our people want.'

Albert Reynolds was in Cyprus when John Hume issued his statement. He packed his bags and prepared to fly home the following day.

Mary McAleese heard the news in Belfast. It resounded with the same adrenaline-pumping impact of the starter's gun. She had just eight days to convince a majority of the Fianna Fáil parliamentary party that she could swing the job for them. It would be a sprint all the way to the finish. And there would be many casualties.

# 18

# Mary Who?

THE TAOISEACH STUDIED THE letter. It was pristinely typed. He glanced again at the signature. The name had an increasingly familiar ring. Harry Casey, that man he kept hearing about lately. Looking for a meeting between the Fianna Fáil leader and Professor Mary McAleese. The letter had been gathering dust for nearly two weeks, filed in the office under L – for long finger. Might this woman be his salvation? Bertie Ahern wondered.

He sought advice.

The chief whip thought he should meet her if only for the sake of good manners. 'You've agreed to meet Dana so I think you should meet her too,' Seamus Brennan advised him.

Martin Mansergh was of like mind. 'Do,' urged the Taoiseach's adviser, 'if only out of respect to her Northern backers.'

———

The telephone rang in a house in Navan. The man who answered it listened with mounting excitement. When the call ended, he replaced the receiver, and smiled. Harry Casey exhaled a long, deep breath.

———

TUESDAY, SEPTEMBER 9. Mary and Martin McAleese climbed the granite steps of Government Buildings. None of the people they passed paid the couple the slightest heed. It was only 24 hours after the media had reported that John Hume would not be the next president. Bertie Ahern had told *The Irish Times* he intended meeting two prospective candidates for the presidency. He had named one of the two as Dana. Such was the media frenzy over the pontifical pin-up singer there had barely been a ripple of speculation about the identity of the second person.

The McAleeses were greeted in the domed marble foyer by Martin Mansergh. The Taoiseach's adviser on Northern Ireland would, as a matter of course, have scanned the previous day's edition of *The Irish News* and its front-page story that Professor Mary McAleese was 'now set to seek nomination' for the presidential election in the Republic.

Much later, she would tell the Belfast newspaper: 'By the time he (John Hume) decided against it we had done an enormous amount of homework, testing the market, testing the response. I knew at that point that it was a winnable option.'

It was three o'clock in the afternoon when they entered the Taoiseach's suite of offices. Martin McAleese took a seat in an anteroom. His wife proceeded to the inner sanctum where Bertie Ahern and Seamus Brennan awaited her. Martin Mansergh made the introductions.

'You're obviously getting a lot of support,' said the Taoiseach, a portrait of Patrick Pearse watching from the wall behind him. 'We've had a lot of letters and phone calls about you.'

He invited her to make her pitch.

She spoke for 15 minutes. Telling them about her upbringing in north Belfast, about her qualifications and experience as an academic lawyer and her behind-the-scenes work for reconciliation. Her candidacy, she said, would be a signal for peace. She had spent her life building bridges in the North.

'What about Austin Currie?' interjected one of the three men listening to her. The former SDLP housing minister at Stormont had trailed in last for Fine Gael in the 1990 presidential election.

'That was a different campaign and a different candidate,' she replied, unfazed.

But what about her reputation as a right-wing Roman Catholic?

'OK,' she said, 'I may be seen as a conservative but I also have liberal credentials.'

She sold herself as a lawyer, expert in the constitution, independent of the political parties. A fresh face. But, she warned, she could not win, could not hope to become the first president from the North, without the Taoiseach's support. Bertie Ahern reminded her that two Fianna Fáil men, Albert Reynolds and Michael O'Kennedy, had already declared their interest.

'There was no commitment, no endorsement or any departure from neutrality,' Martin Mansergh recalled.

Winding up the meeting, the Taoiseach told the chief whip to explain the parliamentary party process of nomination to Professor McAleese. 'Good luck,' he said, shaking her hand.

'You went in a no-hoper,' Martin Mansergh said as he escorted her from the room, 'and you have come out with some hope.'

'Her quarter-of-an-hour monologue on her vision of the presidency was a tour de force,' Mansergh remembered. 'Very persuasive, flowing and articulate. All three of us were hugely impressed.'

Seamus Brennan felt the same. 'It was lofty stuff about the North and society, mixed with an appreciation of the practical problems. She understood Bertie's problem. At no stage did he say '"I like this" or "you are our candidate – I'll sort it out". She knew we were impressed and she knew she had a tough battle on her hands.'

Immediately after the meeting, the chief whip brought her to his own office in Government Buildings and handed over a list of Fianna Fáil deputies, senators and MEPs, complete with their telephone numbers.

'Who do you know in the parliamentary party?' he asked her.

She mentioned Dick Roche, Dermot Ahern and John O'Donoghue.

'Get a team together and canvass the parliamentary party,' the chief whip instructed her. 'You must talk to all of them. Starting from now, you have one week to do it.'

————

Even as she was setting out her stall in Government Buildings, next door in Leinster House Fianna Fáil deputies were perusing the curriculum vitae of Mary McAleese. Harry Casey had compiled the exhaustive biography, helped by an economics graduate from Longford, Cathal McGinty. The tightly-spaced chronicle filled seven pages. It had been typed by Sandra Garry, the owner of a secretarial business in Navan who had prepared the manuscripts for Harry's three religious books. The accompanying letter read as follows.

Dear Deputy,

Firstly, a brief word of introduction! I live and work in Navan as a secondary teacher and writer of school textbooks. I am a close friend of Mary McAleese's and was her election agent when she stood in the Spring 1986 (sic) general election for the constituency of Dublin South-East.

After President Robinson officially declared her intentions not to run for a second term of office as Uachtarán na hÉireann, I visited Mary McAleese in her home and asked and urged her to allow her name go forward for consideration by those elected to serve as public representatives and who will play a large part in determining who our next President will be.

Mary McAleese is a woman I greatly admire and respect. Her intelligence and warmth, her breadth and depth of insight and vision, her capacity to inspire trust and reconciliation, and the ease which she empathises with and empowers others has to be experienced first-hand to be believed.

At 46, Mary, a gifted listener and communicator and a successful academic, public broadcaster, journalist and administrator, has the qualities of ambassadorship and leadership which the Presidency calls for. She also brings the added unique dimension which springs from profound experience of life both North and South of the border. As we stand at the dawn of the third Millennium, I can think of no better or imaginative choice for the Presidency in these days that are heavily scented with the promise of peace.

In conclusion, may I request that you nominate Mary McAleese for the Office of President. I unreservedly recommend her for the position of 'First Citizen' and will be very happy to discuss this matter further with you, should your busy schedule allow it.

Thanking you for your attention in this matter and wishing you continued success in your work as a public representative.

Gúim rath Dé ar do chuid oibre.

Harry Casey.

Next he called on his babysitter's daughter, a UCG law student called Elaine White. The day before the McAleeses' visit to Government Buildings, Harry shoved a stack of more than 100 photocopied biographies into Elaine's arms and, handing her the keys of his trusty 11-year-old car, charged her with distributing them in Dublin.

Unsure of the capital's geography and aware that time was of the essence, Elaine abandoned Harry's car in the city and hailed a taxi. Literally laden down with the weight of her mission, she offered the taxi driver an explanation.

'I'm delivering the curriculum vitae of the next President of Ireland,' she told him proudly.

'Who's that?' he asked.

'Mary McAleese.'

'Never heard of her,' the driver replied dismissively. 'She doesn't stand much of a chance.'

———

WEDNESDAY MORNING, SEPTEMBER 10. Mary and Martin McAleese were met at the Kildare Street entrance to Leinster House by Mary Hanafin. Newly elected to the Dáil three months earlier, the daughter of the anti-amendment campaigner in the 1992 abortion referendum signed the couple in at the front desk. She showed them to the bar and settled them with coffee, to await Dick Roche.

The Wicklow deputy was to be their guide for a tour of the labyrinthine TDs' and senators' offices in the House. The Belfast academic explained to each one that she was seeking the party's nomination for the presidential election. The ABBA deputies were relieved to have a realistic alternative to Albert Reynolds. Many of the 38 new members of the parliamentary party were open to persuasion. Some, however, bridled at the implicit assumption that only an unblemished outsider could carry off the election in their name; as if they were all somehow contaminated. There was a gut instinct in the party, which reached all the way up to the leader, that Fianna Fáil should, ideally, field one of its own.

Mary McAleese needed 50 per cent-plus-one of the party vote to swing the nomination and, as yet, there was no guarantee. Harry and Patricia Casey, assisted by Denis Moloney, were working behind the scenes. Martin Naughton keeping in telephone contact for up-dates on how the campaign was being received.

They had targeted the party's upper echelon and were satisfied that a third of the Fianna Fáil ministers were four square behind them. The big guns of Mary O'Rourke, Dermot Ahern, John O'Donoghue, Síle de Valera and Jim McDaid. They felt sure too of party chairman Rory O'Hanlon and junior minister Éamon O'Cuív. The chief whip, Seamus Brennan, was a distinct possibility and Education Minister Micheál Martin a strong maybe.

'They focused on 10 cabinet members,' Seamus Brennan confirmed. 'Between half and three-quarters of her support would have come from people who would not vote for Albert. The rest were people who feared a by-election or wanted a repeat of the Mary Robinson phenomenon.'

From the outset, the Friends of Mary McAleese blanked out about a dozen names on the list supplied by the chief whip. These were people who would never contemplate her candidacy. Albert Reynolds and Michael O'Kennedy for starters, followed by their respective backers. The Finance Minister, Charlie McCreevy, planned to propose Albert at the party meeting, seconded by Bertie Ahern's constituency running mate, Marian McGennis, whom Reynolds had appointed to the Seanad. Michael O'Kennedy had lined up Brian Lenihan and Mary Hanafin as his proposer and seconder, respectively. The McAleese pool shrank still further with the elimination of the Munster MEP, Brian Crowley, and TDs Denis Foley from Kerry North and Batt O'Keeffe from Cork South Central. *The Examiner* had reported, as far back as August 13, that their allegiances lay with the former Taoiseach. Ministers like Brian Cowen and Noel Dempsey were sure to back him too.

Further complicating the sums was David Andrews, who still had not made a decisive announcement about his own candidacy for the nomination. As the last working week before the party meeting drew to a close, the prize was still anybody's.

———

SATURDAY, SEPTEMBER 13. West Ham were playing the Taoiseach's favourite team, Manchester United, at Old Trafford. Sitting amid the raucous, cheering fans were Fianna Fáil's general secretary, Pat Farrell, and the party's chief whip, Seamus Brennan, a West Ham supporter.

The two men made an incongruous sight. They had brought their sons to the match as a special treat only to spend most of the time glued to their mobile phones, briefing journalists from the Sunday papers in Dublin. Forced to raise their voices above the din, they outlined all the reasons why it would be disastrous if the parliamentary party selected Albert Reynolds in four days time.

Unknown to them, two friends of the man known as the Longford Slasher had been sitting nearby in the Theatre of Dreams. They duly reported back to Albert, who surmised that Pat Farrell, the organisation's most senior official, must be working to the leadership's agenda.

Manchester United won the game by 2-1.

Back home, Charles Haughey's former press secretary, PJ Mara was attempting to pull a rabbit from a hat at the last minute. He spent the weekend trying to cajole Ray MacSharry into the race for the nomination. The wealthy Sligoman was one of Fianna Fáil's success stories. After an impressive tenure as EC Commissioner, the 59-year-old former Finance Minister known as Mac The Knife had returned to the private sector in Ireland where he held a clutch of prestigious company directorships. He and Mara had worked closely together on a constituency review in advance of the June general election. But for once Mara's powers of persuasion failed him. MacSharry refused to bite the cherry of seven years in Áras an Uachtaráin.

Before close of business, Paddy Power bookmakers were offering odds on the Fianna Fáil nomination. Albert Reynolds was the clear favourite at 7/2 on. Mary McAleese lay in second place at 5/1, followed by David Andrews (6/1) and Michael O'Kennedy (14/1). Dustin the Turkey was an outside bet at 1,000/1.

———

SUNDAY, SEPTEMBER 14. The peace of the Sabbath was shattered by Charlie Bird's excited voice zinging across the national airwaves. In a classic piece of doorstep journalism, RTE's chief news correspondent had blown open the Labour Party's secret strategy. He had tracked down Adi Roche, the articulate and attractive founder of the Chernobyl Childrens Project, and question-bombed her into admitting that Labour had asked her to contest the election.

A founding member of the Greens and daughter of a Fianna Fáil couple, all the main political parties had courted her at one time or other. Her infectious concern for the irradiated children of Belarus having won her universal respect. Her friendship with the U2 rock star, Bono, and his wife, Ali, made her the sort of funky can-do pioneer that is the stuff of campaign managers' dreams. In the past, she had addressed a Fianna Fáil Árd Fheis and an annual conference of the party's Womens Committee. Only a few months before Labour came a-courting, she had attended a fund-raising dinner in New York as Fianna Fáil's special guest.

If Adi Roche was Labour's dream candidate, she was Fianna Fáil's worst nightmare. Bertie Ahern could no longer allow the nomination race to drift along at its own precarious pace.

———

MONDAY, SEPTEMBER 15. Government minister David Andrews issued a statement *en route* home from Mother Teresa's funeral in Calcutta. In it, he announced that he would not, after all, be seeking the party nomination at the meeting in 48 hours time. The announcement had the effect of bringing the contest into sharper focus and concentrating Fianna Fáil minds.

In his Dundrum office on the same day, the former RTÉ executive, Tom Savage, received a baffling phone call. It came from a close friend of Mary McAleese, inquiring if the media guru would be prepared to direct her presidential election campaign.

The phone call reeked of eleventh-hour jitters in the McAleese camp. Hardly the action of a confident campaign, anticipating the availability of Fianna Fáil's legendary publicity machine. Was she possibly considering going it alone if she failed to secure the party nomination?

———

TUESDAY, SEPTEMBER 16. The dawn of an eventful day. By midnight, Albert Reynolds would be shafted.

Michael O'Kennedy was starting to panic. He had heard whispers that senior party members were actively conducting a vote-McAleese campaign. The former EU Commissioner rang Bertie Ahern looking for reassurance. He got none. Told to wait for a signal later in the day. While he waited he espied Mary McAleese in a corridor of Leinster House and concluded that 'the woman was walking on air'.

Albert Reynolds was uncharacteristically ubiquitous that day. Talking to TDs, totting up his final tally of support before D-day. At one stage, he was seen with Bertie Ahern in the chamber. The two men with their heads fraternally together, talking confidentially. Untroubled.

As expected, the Labour Party selected Adi Roche as its presidential candidate.

As the news reverberated round Leinster House, Michael O'Kennedy took a phone call in his Dáil office from Rory O'Hanlon. The party chairman was seeking his consent to a new format at the following morning's meeting allowing the three candidates to make speeches. O'Kennedy agreed, but he was getting angry. People had suddenly started warning him that the government could not risk a by-election in his Tipperary constituency.

In the evening he wandered downstairs to the members' bar. Seeing Dermot Ahern there, he laid into the Minister for Family Affairs.

'You're proposing Mary McAleese tomorrow,' he accused the dapper Louth solicitor.

'I am not,' Ahern defended himself.

Suddenly, all Michael O'Kennedy's pent-up anger exploded there in the bar. Rounding on his party colleagues, he lashed out: 'I thought I would have earned honesty from you,' he blurted. 'How could you let me go this far on a false campaign? I'm withdrawing my name. I will not be a candidate tomorrow.'

With that, he turned on his heel and stormed out of Leinster House. By the time he reached his Ballsbridge home he was white-faced with fury. 'You've got to go ahead with it,' his son, Brian, pleaded. 'You formally announced that you would seek the nomination and, even though I accept your political judgment that you haven't a chance of getting it, you owe it to yourself and to those supporting you to let your name go before the meeting.'

The older man finally relented, but he categorically refused to canvass. The circulars he had planned to distribute to the party ended up in the kitchen bin. Then he rang Brian Lenihan, the fellow lawyer who had volunteered to propose him. 'If you as much as canvass one vote for me tomorrow morning I will personally disown you,' O'Kennedy warned the son of Fianna Fáil's vanquished candidate last time out.

At around the same time, the party's ministers and ministers of state were beginning to evacuate Leinster House, striding purposefully across Merrion Square to the organisation's headquarters in Upper Mount Street. Ostensibly, they were heading for the regular monthly meeting of party ministers, normally held every first Thursday to review Fianna Fáil business at cabinet level. But this was neither Thursday nor any ordinary meeting. It had all the makings of a crisis summit, specifically brought forward to discuss the impending party meeting on the presidency. For Albert Reynolds, it was the night of the long knives.

Watched by a roomful of gimlet eyes, the party leader toyed with all the euphemisms in the political dictionary. Telling his lieutenants the time has come to face up to the electoral realities. In an ideal world, Bertie Ahern said, it would be nice to have one of their own contest the election. But this was not an ideal world. This was politics. A *frisson* shot through the room when he gave the nod, advising them to vote for the best candidate.

'There was a bit of a shock that he left it open,' Seamus Brennan recalled.

Over a chicken and wine supper in Mount Street after the meeting broke up, Mary O'Rourke had a premonition. 'I got the feeling Mary McAleese was going to win,' remembered the deputy leader. 'It seemed to gather pace that night.'

Even as a buoyant Dermot Ahern got on the phone to canvass the rank and file, Albert Reynolds was winding up his campaign team's final meeting around the corner in Herbert Place. He looked a happy man. His numbers showing that, in just over 12 hours, he would be confirmed as Fianna Fáil's candidate for the presidency.

'We estimated it would take just one ballot and he would win comfortably, even allowing for the 20 per cent margin of error,' recalled his right-hand man, Peter Finnegan. 'We met at nine o'clock the night before the parliamentary party meeting and we were told from the Fianna Fáil meeting in Mount Street that the nomination was not a matter for debate there. That it would not affect Albert.'

Despite the rosy arithmetic, something was niggling the former Taoiseach. In an effort to clear the decks for a stately presidency, he had been negotiating to settle his libel action against *The Sunday Times*, which he was appealing in the London courts. Lawyers for the two sides had planned to meet earlier in the day in the hope of reaching an agreement. But his legal advisers had notified Albert that the meeting was cancelled. *The Sunday Times*, he heard, had picked up on the grapevine that he was not expected to win the crunch party vote.

Meanwhile Mary McAleese was poring over her lap-top in the apartment known as 'Independent House'. Though there was no guarantee that she would ever deliver it, she carefully punched out a script designed to seduce those Fianna Fáilers still wavering. Harry had already rung her that night, insisting that she 'push for an invitation to address the parliamentary party meeting'.

When Patricia Casey phoned at midnight to wish her luck, Martin answered the phone. He told her his wife was still working on her speech. She would not finish until two o'clock in the morning, snatching three hours shut-eye before rising again at 5 a.m. for rehearsals.

Despite their woman's midnight labours, Patricia and Harry were anxious. Nobody suitable had yet been found to propose or second her in the morning. Harry had argued against Mary O'Rourke 'because Albert dropped her from the cabinet and it might look vengeful'. Dick Roche was another no-no as he was 'seen as being fractious and difficult within the party', according to Patricia. Mary McAleese had even asked her fellow Northerner, Dr Maurice Hayes, to do the honours but the Independent senator explained that he did not have a vote in the Fianna Fáil party.

'There was confusion about who would propose her,' Mary O'Rourke confirmed. 'Nobody wanted to show their hand.'

Her failure to secure two appropriate backers had set her firmly outside the party loop and threatened to leave her stranded at the starting line. As the first slivers of Wednesday morning stretched across Dublin bay, Mary McAleese was facing the real threat of defeat.

# 19

# That's Women Now For Ye!

MARTIN'S INSTINCT WAS TO flee. He confided to Dermot Ahern later that he had wanted to grab his wife by the arm and urge her: 'Come on, let's get out of here.' The couple had been standing at the door of Fianna Fáil's party room on the fifth floor of Leinster House, their faces fixed with supplicant smiles for the 112 TDs, senators and MEPs invested with the power to decide their destiny. Uneasy in the unfamiliar territory, conscious that some of those returning their salutations resented their presence; saw them as gatecrashers of the jealously guarded party.

'They looked worried,' remembered one TD.

As well they might. Despite the meticulous groundwork, the months of painstaking lobbying behind the scenes and the intensive ministerial telephone canvass the previous night, the outcome had never seemed so uncertain. As the hands of time ticked relentlessly towards 11.30 that Wednesday morning, September 17 1997, Mary and Martin McAleese grappled with rising panic.

They probably heard Albert Reynolds before they saw him. Suntanned, spruce and bursting with *bonhomie*, his face illuminated by the megawatt beam of the expectant victor. On his way into Leinster House, he had stopped to chat with reporters about the media conference scheduled to take place in Buswells Hotel after the party meeting, when he fully expected to be presented as Fianna Fáil's candidate for the presidential election.

He was not a stupid man. He knew there was a parcel of votes that would never be his: the casualties of his Valentine Massacre still smarting. He had heard their argument being promulgated that his Longford seat would be imperilled by a by-election, thus jeopardising the minority government. He had heard, and he had laughed. Sure, the party vote had dropped in the constituency by 5.3 per cent in the June general election but, with Albert installed in the Áras, he had no doubt the voters of Longford-Roscommon would come out in droves to elect his eldest son, Philip, to Dáil Eireann.

As he punched the elevator button to take him to the fifth floor, Albert Reynolds was on a high. He could have floated up the stairs, such was his optimism. Nobody – and certainly nobody called Professor Mary McAleese – was about to steal the prize from the man who had once exclaimed exasperatedly in the Dáil chamber: 'That's women now for ye!' He had done his arithmetic, and found the numbers stacked in his favour.

But even that psychological cushion could not adequately justify his mood. A seasoned campaigner, he knew no contest was over until the final vote was counted. That was why the telephone call he had received 75 minutes before the meeting had set his heart racing with expectation.

It was around 10.15am when the phone rang in the Reynolds' sumptuous house in the exclusive embassy belt of Ailesbury Road. The caller was Bertie Ahern. His attitude had been felicitous. He asked the man he succeded as party leader if he believed he would win the vote. Albert asked in turn if he would be required to make a speech. Bertie said no, he would not, that only the proposers and seconders would speak. Then the conversation moved beyond the selection, to the presidential election campaign. They discussed who would be Albert's preferred choice as his director of elections.

'Bertie rang me at about 10.15 on the morning of the meeting to ask who I would like as my director of elections,' Albert Reynolds recounted. 'He suggested Martin Mackin (later appointed Fianna Fáil general secretary) and I agreed. He asked me was I happy that I had the numbers to get me through and I said yeah.'

But, by the time Albert Reynolds stepped out of the Leinster House elevator to walk the few paces across the corridor to the packed party room, a very different fate had been sealed for him.

Before his arrival, a state of agitation had broken out in the corridor. Mary McAleese had still been standing at the door, clutching the speech she had laboured over until two o'clock that morning, when she and Martin spotted Dick Roche.

'Are you nominating Mary?' Martin McAleese anxiously asked the Wicklow deputy.

'No,' he replied, surprised, 'isn't it Mary O'Rourke?'

According to Dick Roche, 'they got a start because Mary O'Rourke was nowhere to be seen at that stage.' Inside the room, the rows of seats were filling up with members of the parliamentary party. The clock on the wall showed that time was running out fast. Mary McAleese was up against the wire, facing the shocking prospect of her name not even going before the meeting.

The next thing Dick Roche remembered was being approached, still in the corridor, by the Taoiseach and the party chairman, Rory O'Hanlon.

'Are you proposing Mary?' they asked him.

'No,' he said again, the bile of anxiety bubbling in his throat.

'Well, that panicked me,' he admitted. 'Then Rory said: "We won't have any proposers or seconders." That's literally what happened. It was confusion. It was cobbled together at the last minute.'

The decision was made by the time Albert Reynolds reached the party room. 'Rory O'Hanlon told me at the door on the way into the meeting about the proposers and seconders,' the former Taoiseach recalled. 'He said there would be an address to the party by all the candidates and there would be no proposers or seconders. I asked to go last.'

According to Dermot Ahern, one of the most energetic ministerial backers of McAleese – along with deputy leader Mary O'Rourke and Justice Minister John O'Donoghue – the decision was made for the good of the party. 'Abolishing proposers was a device to prevent divisiveness,' he claimed.

Michael O'Kennedy, the third and almost forgotten candidate, had deliberately delayed his arrival in Leinster House until 10 minutes before the meeting was scheduled to begin. Though Mary McAleese was the only one of the trio with a prepared script, the multi-lingual O'Kennedy, fluent in French and Italian, had rehearsed his address in his head. Rory O'Hanlon had already gone to O'Kennedy's proposer, Brian Lenihan, before the meeting and informed him of the plan to abolish the usual procedure. After consulting with his candidate, a bemused Lenihan reported back that his camp had no objections.

On the stroke of 11.30am, the chairman, Rory O'Hanlon, called the meeting to order, nearly 100 Fianna Fáil parliamentarians ranged in rows of chairs beneath austere portraits of the party's former presidents – Dev, Lemass, Lynch, Haughey and Reynolds. The newest addition to the portrait gallery was Bertie Ahern, who had left the Mount Street meeting the night before to go for a pint with his friend, Senator Tony Kett. Now he sat at the centre of the top table, facing the room and flanked by the three candidates: Albert Reynolds on his immediate right; Michael O'Kennedy on the left and Mary McAleese one seat away, close to the window.

It was she who was invited to speak first, not for reasons of gender courtesy but because the order was arranged alphabetically, each applicant given three minutes for the nail-biting audition. Her voice was strong and fuelled with conviction, despite the last minute drama outside the door. And the speech she delivered was a *tour de force*.

'The constitution sets a clear agenda for the presidency,' she read from her script, 'but, ultimately, the role wraps itself around the person and the signs of the times.' She talked of being a figurehead for 'a dynamic Ireland growing more complex by the day, an Ireland in which the prospect of lasting peace based on consensus looks tantalisingly close.'

When she sat down, the applause was warm and sustained. Next it was Michael O'Kennedy's turn. The Tipperary lawyer began by quoting the oath of presidential office. Then he launched into one of the most bizarre job applications in history.

'If you're thinking of voting for me for your own sake, please don't,' he cautioned his colleagues. 'If you're thinking of voting for me for the party's sake, please don't. If you're thinking of voting for me for the government's sake, please don't. If you're going to vote for me, then do it in the interests and well-being of the Irish people.'

They clapped when he was finished, but the sound was dulled by the glance of shock.

Finally, it was Albert Reynolds' turn, his hastily prepared words a regurgitation of the campaign letter he had already sent out. When he reached the part about promoting Irish business abroad, 'spectres dangled before horrified eyes', according to one observer who foresaw the resurrection of all the party's skeletons in the run-up to the election. Though his supporters gave him an encouraging ovation, some of his non-partisan listeners adjudged his address overly long and rambling.

The speeches over, it was time to vote. Each member writing the name of their preferred candidate on a sheet of supplied blank paper and walking two-by-two to the top of the room to deposit their votes. The Foreign Affairs Minister, Ray Burke, an arch enemy of Reynolds and ally of O'Kennedy, had left his vote in an envelope before departing the country on government business. MEP Jim Fitzsimons sent a postal vote from his hospital bed while his Euro colleague, Mark Killilea, made Fianna Fáil history by delivering his vote on a fax machine. The Environment Minister, Noel Dempsey, was also absent, attending the tenth anniversary of the Montreal Protocol in Canada. One of the most prominent cabinet members on the Reynolds wing, Noel Dempsey failed to register his vote.

As she watched the TDs, senators and MEPs queue up to drop their papers in the box, Mary McAleese must have been struck by her exclusion from the process. With no entitlement to vote, she had time to ponder the framed front pages of *The Irish Press* nailed to the walls, alongside official photographs of various Fianna Fáil cabinets. Prominent in many of them were her two rivals, Albert Reynolds and Michael O'Kennedy.

Nor would she have had sight from where she sat at the top table of an extraordinary vignette played out within feet of her. In the hubbub of voting, Bertie Ahern had flicked over his ballot paper, allowing Albert Reynolds to see what he had written on it. Reynolds' heart sank when he saw his own name on the paper, suspecting the party leader was so confident of McAleese's victory he could afford to squander his own vote. Brian Crowley saw it too. Sitting at the edge of the front row to accommodate his wheelchair, the MEP from Cork looked balefully at his mentor and warned Reynolds: 'You're finished now.'

Later, some would joke that it was 'the only time Bertie ever backed a loser'.

When Rory O'Hanlon announced the result of the ballot, there was no winner. Albert Reynolds was marginally ahead with 49 votes, followed by McAleese with 42 and O'Kennedy bringing up the rear with 21.

Even before the chairman declared the elimination of Michael O'Kennedy from the second ballot, two government ministers, Dermot Ahern and John O'Donoghue, were heard laughing excitedly. Sitting in the front row of seats facing Mary McAleese, Dermot Ahern looked up, caught her eye and winked. 'We knew then Albert was scuppered,' remembered the Minister for Social, Community and Family Affairs.

As the party members pored over their voting papers for the second time, a perplexed voice at the back was heard to ask: 'How do you spell McAleese?'

It was at this stage that Albert Reynolds turned to his party leader and told him no matter what resulted from the second ballot, he would not accept the nomination. But a mishmash of his enemies, of those loyal to the McAleese frontline of Mary O'Rourke, Dermot Ahern and John O'Donoghue, and a sprinkling of pro-life advocates, jettisoned any such embarrassment. When the result of the vote was announced, Mary McAleese, the blow-in from north Belfast, had won hands down: by 62 votes to Reynolds' 48. Among those who supported her was Senator Des Hanafin, her adversary five years earlier in the abortion referendum and whose daughter, the TD Mary Hanafin, had backed Michael O'Kennedy. Another party dynasty split three ways when Mary O'Rourke voted for McAleese while her two nephews, Brian and Conor Lenihan, respectively backed O'Kennedy and Reynolds. In fact, Albert Reynolds lost one of his votes in the second ballot when his friend, Senator Paddy McGowan, had to leave for a medical appointment. 'Albert was stuck to the floor,' Dick Roche recalled. 'He was very close to tears.'

Beneath his suntan, the millionaire former Taoiseach was white-faced with shock. His humiliation was an unedifying sight as he rose to accept his defeat. 'When we leave this room, we leave as a united party,' he cautioned, admitting: 'I am very disappointed to lose my last political contest.'

Afterwards, he confessed plaintively to media reporters: 'I am disappointed. I'm a human being like everyone else.'

The contrast with Mary McAleese could not have been more stark as she was swept out of Leinster House and across the street to the news conference in Buswells Hotel on a tide of celebration. Her triumph had coincided perfectly with the lunchtime news bulletins, the nation hearing almost instantly that this relatively unknown woman was to be the presidential candidate of the country's biggest and most powerful political party.

———

In Belfast, the peace talks at Stormont had been adjourned for lunch when the news came. Knots of negotiators – unionists, nationalists, loyalists and republicans – were tucking into their lunch when the canteen in Castle Buildings was electrified by the events in Dublin. An observer sat and watched the different reactions to the news as it cannoned through the room. He saw David Trimble glower, in contrast to his deputy leader, John Taylor, who looked 'intrigued, but pleased'.

The Women's Coalition, he noted, were 'cock-a-hoop', Sinn Féin 'thrilled', but John Hume, the man who had been offered the presidency on a plate, looked decidedly 'glum', disappointed for Michael O'Kennedy, his old chum from their student days in Maynooth.

Someone remarked that Mary McAleese could now claim to be the only person to have beaten both David Trimble and Albert Reynolds for a job.

———

Back in Dublin, Professor Patricia Casey was attending to her psychiatric patients at a clinic in the Mater Hospital when the news came through on the portable radio she had carried around with her all morning.

'I jumped up and down with excitement,' she remembered. 'Some of my patients thought I was mad.'

Elsewhere in the city, Mary McAleese's old friend from Trinity College, Senator David Norris, heard the news and privately wondered at her readiness to 'skewer' Albert Reynolds. 'It showed a really interesting ruthlessness,' he decided.

That night, Harry Casey drove to Rostrevor with his wife, Mary, to celebrate at the McAleese's home; the house by the lake with the Greek name for 'Opportunity'.

Michael O'Kennedy and his glamorous wife, Breda, flew to Italy for a holiday the next day. The newspapers there were carrying wire stories about the forthcoming presidential election in Ireland, focussing on the all-woman line-up of Adi Roche, Dana, Mary McAleese and Fine Gael's Mary Banotti. The O'Kennedy's were lying at their hotel poolside in Portofino one morning when their favourite waiter, Mario, dropped by to show them an Italian newspaper report on the petticoat power struggle back in Ireland.

*'Non ce nessun uomo con gnocchie in Irlanda?'* Mario asked, puzzled.

Michael O'Kennedy smiled at the waiter, lay back in the warm sunshine and savoured the translation of the waiter's question. 'Is there no man with balls in Ireland?' the Italian had asked.

# From the Commons
# to the Áras

THE OTHER DINERS WERE too sophisticated to stare. They were mostly businessmen and women, power-lunching in one of the city's best-appointed restaurants. The place exuded worldliness, with its crisp napery and discreet service. Boardroom moguls and executives favoured it for its fine food and tony address on St Stephen's Green. For the man and woman sitting apart at a table-for-two, the name of the restaurant could hardly have been more apt. They had chosen The Commons for their first meeting, to size each other up. Assessing the staying power, the gumption and the shrewdness necessary in both of them to cut a swathe all the way to Áras an Uachtaráin.

It was the week after she had sensationally won the Fianna Fáil nomination and the chattering class was still agog at the behind-the-scenes machinations, unable to resist covert glances at the woman who had done down a former Taoiseach.

The man sitting across the table from her was the Minister for the Environment, Noel Dempsey, 44-years-old and ambitious with grassroots savvy. He had briefly locked horns with Charles Haughey early in his parliamentary career but had survived to be rewarded by Albert Reynolds. Absent on business in Canada the previous Wednesday, he had been spared the spectacle of his old mentor's public execution. Now, as he studied the woman opposite him, he laid out the gameplan for her ascension to the highest office in the land.

You have to trust me and trust my judgment, even if it's contrary to your judgment, he was warning her. 'And there'll be times when you'll wonder what I'm doing.'

She nodded, accepting the ground rules. Aware that Dempsey's appointment as her election director was, in effect, the fundamental golden rule of the blueprint. He had spearheaded Brian Lenihan's by-election campaign in Dublin West, the vacancy created by the death of the new TD's father who had been the party's candidate in the 1990 presidential election. But, when Fianna Fáil's general secretary, Pat Farrell, had offered the poison chalice to the Minister from Trim, both men had known there was an ulterior motive. Roping in a high-profile Reynolds' loyalist would act as ointment on the sores of the vanquished camp.

They were almost finished lunch when she mentioned, almost *en passant*, that there was something she should tell him. 'I want you to know this but it's only for your information so it doesn't come as a surprise if anything comes from it.'

Then she told him about her involvement in the Redemptorist Peace Ministry and the secret negotiations to re-establish the IRA cease-fire. His heart-beat quickened. He saw it as a trump card, a direct connection with the most important events in the island's history for 30 years. But his heart sank as quickly when she insisted: 'I don't want this used at any time.'

Noel Dempsey was impressed at that first meeting. 'I knew we had a very good candidate,' he recalled. The way he saw it, Fine Gael's Mary Banotti was the solid, experienced parliamentarian; Adi Roche (Labour, Democratic Left and the Greens) was the 'sexy' candidate, a charity doyenne untainted by politics; Dana, the orthodox Roman Catholic and media novelty. Despite being the candidate of the two government parties, Mary McAleese was at an immediate disadvantage, resented by many traditional Fianna Fáil supporters for having gutted Albert Reynolds and largely unknown to a young apathetic electorate.

The international news agencies evaluated the all-woman line-up in a lighter vein, with the Press Association branding it the 'Spice Girls Election'.

Three days after her lunch with Noel Dempsey, Mary McAleese officially launched her election campaign in the Shelbourne Hotel, flanked by Bertie Ahern and Mary Harney.

'It is a dream for an active presidency which will meet the future and build bridges with hope and confidence,' the candidate heralded her vision for the assembled scribes. But her promises of bridge building were deemed only secondary to her new streamlined appearance. Gone was the scatty professor with the familiar make-do hairstyle and safe string of pearls. This was a planned glossy package designed for six weeks of intensive media exposure. Her hair shone with a new honey brown tint, sleekly styled to accentuate her good bone structure. A palette of MAC cosmetics, the make-up favoured by top fashion models, painted the photofit of a modern, attractive woman capable of projecting a positive image for the country.

'I was astounded by how good she was that day,' Noel Dempsey remembered.

'I thought that, if we got a fair run, she was almost a certainty. The more TV and radio and press coverage she got the better. That would be crucial. The Church relationship and conservative values were her banana skins at that stage. If Dana hadn't been there Mary would have been the target of the anti-Church element.'

In fact, the backlash also came in reverse, from the traditionalist quarter who saw her new incarnation as unholy treason. Six months before she became a candidate for the presidency, Mary McAleese had written a stinging attack on the Vatican. It appeared under the headline, 'It Won't Wash With Women', in the March 15 edition of the English Catholic paper, *The Tablet*.

'Most intelligent men and women can recognise sexist cant, no matter how nobly dressed up, no matter how elevated the speaker,' she had railed.

'So when the Holy Father admits the Church just might have been a teensy-weensy bit sexist at times, we wait for the next obvious statement "that the Church is going to take a long, hard, scholarly look at itself. It's going to try to understand how its own thinking, its very own understanding of God, has been skewed and damaged by 2,000 years of shameful codology dressed up as theology and, worse still, God's will". But the statement does not come. Instead the big gun, the howitzer of infallibility, is armed and aimed.'

She endeared herself even less to those whom liberals would have considered her natural bedfellows by diagnosing the Pope's thinking as being riddled with 'woodworm' and accusing 'defenders of the Vatican line' as sounding 'more and more like Communist Party apparatchiks hawking redundant clichés'.

Alienating the Church's dwindling doctrinaire constituency, however, constituted more of a weapon than a wound in electoral terms. This, after all, was a much-changed Republic from the one she had left a decade before. Secularism had grown in tandem with prosperity, toppling old taboos in its stride. Mary McAleese's volatile position on divorce, for instance, reflected that change. In a radio interview, she said: 'I looked at the last referendum and I saw the kind of divorce law that was eventually introduced here 'a very cautious, very careful law. And I think it's fairly compatible with my own view.'

That about-turn incensed at least one of her previous admirers. Writing in *The Brandsma Review*, editor Nick Lowry, at whose book launch she had unleashed a vitriolic attack on Garret FitzGerald during the 1986 divorce referendum campaign, counselled his readers to vote for Dana.

Describing Mary McAleese as 'an enigma', he surmised: 'One can only presume that she has fudged her earlier principles in the interests of *realpolitik*, hoping to follow in Mary Robinson's footsteps, and land a prestigious international job after her stint in the Park.'

Dana provided a ready-made patsy for the brickbats from Church dissenters. The evangelical anchor-woman for Mother Angelica's bible-belt television station in Alabama had already made history by being the first candidate to secure a presidential nomination from the county councils. The 45-year-old recording artist of such hits as *Everything is Beautiful* and *Something's Cookin' in the Kitchen*, was indebted to numerous Fianna Fáil councillors in Donegal, Kerry, Wicklow, Longford and Tipperary North. Noel Dempsey, whose Environment portfolio embraced the local authorities, was only too happy to see the zealous Derry woman enter the fray, thus deflecting attention from his candidate's background in Church affairs.

Dempsey and the Taoiseach had more immediate concerns. The first opinion poll of the campaign, conducted by Irish Marketing Surveys and published by the *Irish Independent* three days before McAleese's opening gambit at the Shelbourne, showed her trailing the favourite, Adi Roche, by three percentage points. That finding was unsurprising for the relatively unknown Belfast candidate in the teething stages of the campaign. What really worried the Fianna Fáil top brass was that she was only attracting support from half of the party's core constituency throughout the country. Patently, the bitterness over the shafting of Albert Reynolds had not gone away.

In time-honoured tradition, Fianna Fáil organised a blitzkrieg of the organisation. The ink was hardly dry on the poll results when an early morning meeting convened at party headquarters in Mount Street. It was decided that both Bertie Ahern and Noel Dempsey should send personal letters to each comhairle ceanntair exhorting cumann members to get out and canvass for the candidate. The following Wednesday, the two men urged the parliamentary party, at a meeting in Leinster House, to 'gear up', warning them direly that too much was at stake.

In public, the focus was off Mary McAleese and trained on her Left-alliance rival, Adi Roche, the early front-runner. It bore all the hallmarks of a deliberate smear strategy when, on the first Sunday of the campaign, newspaper stories depicted the founder of the Chernobyl Childrens Project as an unapologetic bully. Some of her former colleagues in the Cork-based CCP were anonymously quoted as saying she was dictatorial and 'Stalinist.'

A genuinely kind-hearted woman with an effervescent personality but a virgin in the maelstrom of politics, Roche was deeply hurt by the stories. They were quickly followed by reports that her older brother, Donal, had been compulsorily retired from the Army 28 years earlier.

'The next night after the smears, I met Mary McAleese at a reception for Boutros-Boutros Gali at the College of Surgeons and she was very nice to me,' Adi Roche recalled.'It wasn't for anybody to overhear. It wasn't Mary feeling sorry for Adi. It was her making contact with another human being who had suffered pain.'

More legitimately, Roche was satirised for her fuzzy, happy-clappy view of the presidency. Out on the canvass one day, she was captured by television cameras jiggling in her chair and tapping her foot to a Luka Bloom song, beside a mortified Labour leader, Dick Spring. The image lent credence to the impression of a huggy-wuggy space cadet itching to turn Áras an Uachtaráin into a kiddies' playground and a travellers' halting site at the first opportunity. In fact, the entire contest looked like descending into irredeemable dippiness.

'The thing I found most difficult was the pretence that it wasn't a political campaign,' recalled Mary Banotti, whose efforts to trumpet her electoral track record were continually frustrated.

Any attempt at a serious discussion about different people's visions of the presidency was interpreted as being mean and nasty.'

Having started with 38 per cent support in the first opinion poll, Adi Roche's ratings dropped to 22 per cent by early October and continued tumbling to 13 per cent by the middle of the month and two weeks before the election on October 30.

Her elimination meant the focus swung back onto Mary McAleese. Initially, the flurry of resurrected quotes conveying her opinions on everything from contraception to life in Dublin made little impact. This was a getting-to-know-you period when the squeaky-clean, all-woman line-up had newspaper colour-writers despairing of any real action. An *Irish Independent* headline on a sketch by Miriam Lord said it all when it pleaded: 'Oh for a candidate who drinks and fornicates.'

It was a phase which coincided with the resignation from both the cabinet and the Dáil by the Minister for Foreign Affairs, Ray Burke, in a sordid scandal over payments-to-politicians. A scandal which threatened to rebound on the McAleese campaign by fixing the emphasis on Fianna Fáil's skeletons and a poll finding that 48 per cent of voters believed Bertie Ahern had handled the affair badly.

Inevitable tensions with the media were already bubbling beneath the surface of the McAleese campaign, and they exploded in Noel Dempsey's sitting-room on the night of October 9. He was home from the hustings unusually early, satisfied with a job well done earlier in the day when Mary McAleese had outlined her manifesto for the Áras at a rally in Cork. She had pledged to represent the 'forgotten Irish' abroad, to blaze a trail for enterprise, to open the residence to the public and to visit Irish peace-keepers on UN service around the world.

It was a tired but relaxed Noel Dempsey who collapsed into an armchair that night, free, for a change, to watch television with his family.

'Is this a party political broadcast?' he asked his children, staring at Mary Banotti's face smiling back at him from the screen.

They told him it was not, it was *Prime Time*. The RTÉ current affairs flagship was broadcasting one of the candidate profiles it was serialising during the campaign. At that, the minister went ballistic. His candidate had filled him in comprehensively on her fraught relationship with the national station and he had adjudged the *Prime Time* profile of her as 'tough but fair'. But suspicion of the media is endemic to politicians, and to Fianna Fáil in particular, so much so that it could be mistaken for party policy. Now Dempsey raged at what he saw as the soft-focus Hello-type treatment of Banotti, her main competitor. He immediately sought a meeting with RTÉ's top rank.

It was speedily arranged for nine o'clock the very next morning in a conference room at Montrose. Present from the McAleese campaign were Noel Dempsey, his deputy election director Pat Farrell, and Martin Mackin, the Dundalk-born co-ordinator of the campaign's media centre in Lower Mount Street. Across the table were seven of RTÉ's most senior executives – director general Bob Collins, managing director for organisation and development Liam Millar, director of radio Helen Shaw, manager of audience research Tony Fahy, director of public affairs Kevin Healy, director of television productions David Blake-Knox and director of news Ed Mulhall.

The station's managing director of television and Mary McAleese's former boss, Joe Mulholland, was not present.

Noel Dempsey fired the opening salvo of 'a very stormy meeting' when he asked if any of the executives had seen *Prime Time* the previous night. Six of the seven said they had not. (Ed Mulhall had seen the programme but he arrived late for the meeting). 'That's it,' spat Dempsey in disgust, making to leave the room. 'There's no point in talking to you people.'

'Let's talk this thing through,' coaxed Bob Collins, managing to restore a semblance of calm.

'Last night's programme was like a party political broadcast,' Noel Dempsey fulminated. 'The ultimate manifestation of the bias in RTÉ's coverage of the campaign.'

Much of his criticism was directed against the station's news coverage, specifically two items on the Boutros-Boutros Gali reception at the College of Surgeons and a student debate with his candidate at UCD. He also complained that Adi Roche and Mary Banotti had appeared on *Questions & Answers* together instead of each candidate featuring individually.

The RTÉ executives counter-argued that the station was striving to achieve balance and fairness in its coverage and a commitment was given to consider a request by Pat Farrell for regular meetings with Kevin Healy. The director general then gave an undertaking that the *Prime Time* profiles of McAleese and Banotti would be studied and contrasted and a report would be made to Fianna Fáil by that afternoon.

Despite RTÉ's eagerness to facilitate the Fianna Fáilers that morning, the relationship between Mary McAleese and the media was to be a continuing undercurrent of mutual animosity for the rest of the campaign. The candidate's sharpness in dealing with individual journalists hinted that, 16 years on, she still bore a grudge over her treatment in *Today Tonight* and her banishment from the NUJ 13 years earlier. She told a friend she was savouring the prospect of arriving at RTÉ for the first time as President and being officially greeted by her former *Today Tonight* adversary, Joe Mulholland.

One of her campaign team noticed that 'the only time I would see her palpably uncomfortable was whenever she came to the security barrier at RTÉ.'

Noel Dempsey attempted to reason it out with her. 'The person they were writing about was not the person I knew but, having said that, at various times during the campaign you could feel the friction,' he recalled. 'There was a certain amount of professional tension. I suggested to her to try to remain calm, that there was no point in crossing swords and falling out with the people who were covering the campaign.

Despite his pleadings, the relationship would only deteriorate further in the last three weeks of the campaign. But even that would pale beside the full-frontal political attack about to be unleashed on the 46-year-old university don. The first half had been a picnic compared with what was to come. From here on in it would be fought in the most pernicious atmosphere that ever attached to a presidential election, the fall-out potentially catastrophic.

# A Tribal Time-Bomb

DEREK NALLY WAS AN old-fashioned policeman. An advocate of tough law enforcement who still liked to hold doors open for the fairer sex, he had retired from the Gárda Siochána by 1997. Not the sort of man familiar with reverse gender balance, Nally was an unlikely mascot for a burgeoning masculist movement in Ireland.

A mascot he became nonetheless when, riding on Dana's coat-tails, he joined the hitherto all-woman presidential contest with the support of five county councils. At the launch of his campaign in Jurys Hotel, Dublin on Tuesday October 7, he presented himself as 'A Man For All Seasons'. It was clever marketing, conjuring up the vision of a mature and manly trouble-shooter who brooked no nonsense. Inspector Morse meets Joe Public and wows a media jaded by a deluge of X-chromosomes. As the whistle-blower who tipped off the political correspondent, Geraldine Kennedy, that her phone was being tapped by the Fianna Fáil administration in the 1980s, Derek Nally was obviously on the side of the little people. That image was further boosted by his track record as the founder of Victim Support, a lobby that believed the law granted greater rights to criminals than to victims. Among the first stream of volunteers to lend the organisation a helping hand had been Trinity College's young Reid Professor of Criminal Law, Mary McAleese.

Six days after he unveiled his campaign, Derek Nally was scheduled to appear as a panellist on RTÉ's *Questions & Answers*, the same television programme that precipitated Brian Lenihan's downfall seven years before. Most of Nally's core campaigners hailed from his hometown of Bunclody. They were political amateurs, memorably christened 'the Bunclody Ramblers' by the broadcaster,

Joe Duffy. Of his five-man kitchen cabinet, the director of publicity, John Caden, boasted the most prominent national profile. A former producer of *The Gay Byrne Show*, he was a close friend of Eoghan Harris, having shared the latter's socialist ideology in the febrile atmosphere of Montrose in the late 1970s and on into the 1980s. The same Workers Party philosophy that had permeated RTÉ and that Mary McAleese had scorned.

At Caden's request, Harris had drawn up a blueprint for Nally, as he had previously done for Mary Robinson in the 1990 presidential election. His 'Strategic Issues in the Presidential Campaign' urged the 'token man' to play up his security track-record, on the premise that the public wanted a return to a traditional presidency. It so impressed the candidate that, on the afternoon of Monday, October 13, Harris and Nally were closeted together preparing for that night's television programme. Mary McAleese, Geraldine Kennedy and Sean 'Dublin Bay Rockall' Loftus were to be the other panellists.

One of the chief reasons Harris had hooked up with the Nally campaign was his regard for the former cop's abhorrence of the IRA. Now, as they worked, they pored over the previous day's edition of *The Sunday Business Post*. A self-styled anti-nationalist, Eoghan Harris had been riveted by the paper's report of a leaked document from the Department of Foreign Affairs, which portrayed Mary McAleese as sympathetic to Sinn Féin. The gist of the memo, written by a senior official in the Department, Dympna Hayes, for the attention of Seán O'hUigínn, head of the Anglo-Irish section, implied that the Belfast woman was soft on Sinn Féin at a time when there was no cease-fire in place.

'To be honest, her whiney Northern victim voice irritated me at that time more than her politics,' Eoghan Harris admitted. But now *The Sunday Business Post* story, which had all but been ignored by the national dailies on Monday morning, infused him with a new fervour. 'Before the programme that night I prepared Derek Nally to make it the central issue of his campaign,' he said. *En route* to the RTÉ studios in Donnybrook that night, the candidate expressed himself very pleased with the Cork spin-doctor, declaring him 'a genius'.

The confrontation between the policeman and the professor made gripping television. Referring to the leaked document, Nally challenged McAleese to state her position on Sinn Féin, drawing gasps from around the country when he drew a link with the cold-blooded murder of Detective Garda Jerry McCabe in County Limerick the previous year.

'I do not believe that one single person should have shed one single drop of blood in this country for the things they have shed them for,' replied the government's candidate. 'I have always been strongly opposed to violence.'

Around the time the programme was being transmitted, the fax machines in Dublin's newsrooms were spewing out a formal statement by Derek Nally criticising her for her alleged support of Sinn Féin. 'Like me,' it read, 'most Irish people would never vote for Sinn Féin, peace process or no peace process, because they have been carrying on a murder campaign for 25 years. One of their victims was Garda Jerry McCabe. That is why they get two per cent of the vote in the Republic.' The statement ensured widespread coverage in Tuesday's newspapers. The Nally camp was ecstatic.

Over in Mount Street, Noel Dempsey was not unduly troubled. He was, in fact, planning to turn the furore to his candidate's advantage. 'I was quite happy that she was a nationalist from Northern Ireland and that she had a nationalist view and never hid it,' he recalled.

Mary McAleese was pressing the flesh in Tipperary on the Tuesday, with a glad-handling hustings style reminiscent of Charles Haughey in his prime. No matter what rarefied mountaintop or remote hamlet she visited, she invariably managed to dredge up some ancestral connection to the place. When Noel Dempsey failed to contact her on the mobile phone that Tuesday, the director of elections left a message warning her not to comment on the controversy.

'I have to say I had ulterior motives because I knew how she felt about keeping the Clonard thing quiet while I thought it would not be the worst thing in the world if it came out,' he confessed with a wry smile. 'I hoped it would gather legs over the coming days and she would come out and talk about it.

'But down in Tipperary that day she was asked about it by reporters and she said she was asked to do it (join the Redemptorist Peace Ministry) by the priests in Clonard and that's the end of it. I was pretty annoyed about it, I have to be honest,' continued Dempsey. 'I said to her the next day: "You said you would listen to me." But then I found out that the message had never got through to her.'

Mary McAleese's aloof attitude to the controversy could have inflicted even greater damage on her prospects than the story itself. Her salvation came from, of all places, the very quarter that had whipped up the controversy in the first place, the Nally campaign.

John Caden was driving to Dublin with the former policeman on Tuesday when his mobile phone rang. The caller was Sean Flynn, an editorial executive in *The Irish Times*. Flynn asked Caden if he would write an article for the next morning's edition on the McAleese/Sinn Féin controversy. Caden agreed and ran off the article back in Dublin before heading to Trinity College for a student debate featuring the candidates.

And that was when the Nally campaign began to unravel.

The Trinity motion for debate read: 'Is the next President going to be a clone of Mary Robinson?' It had been the burning question at the outset of the race to the Park but, by Tuesday October 14, it had been superseded by the wrangle over Mary McAleese's opinion of Sinn Féin. Derek Nally got into his stride immediately, turning the debate into an attack on his former friend's party political allegiances north of the border. Her repeated denials, however, started to suck the wind out of his sails and, when a student intervened from the floor, he finally accepted them.

Afterwards, as the audience began to drift from the hall, a visibly angry McAleese approached Derek Nally and John Caden. She told them she knew about the article that had been submitted for the next morning's *Irish Times*. 'If you have any decency at all in you you'll pull it,' she insisted.

They did not. 'The thrust of the story in terms of a presidential election,' Caden had written, 'is that Mary McAleese, in an unbuttoned private conversation, expressed views, which are strongly sympathetic to Sinn Féin at a time when they were still carrying on a terrorist campaign.' In light of Nally's concession in

Trinity the night before, the final paragraph howled dissent within the Nally camp. 'Derek Nally does not accept the McAleese denial,' John Caden wrote.

The article acted like a boomerang. Instead of upping the ante on McAleese, as was intended, it hinted at an intriguing split in Nally's campaign headquarters on the Naas Road. By the next day, John Caden had quit. With the pressure piling on Nally and, ergo, easing off McAleese, it was beginning to look like a mere glitch in the government candidate's advance on the Áras. That was until Gerry Adams re-ignited the issue on Thursday morning when he featured on Pat Kenny's radio show to promote his book, *An Irish Voice: The Quest for Peace*. Asked whom he would support in the election, the Sinn Féin leader said that Mary McAleese would get his first preference, followed by Roche, Banotti and Dana. He would not give a vote to Derek Nally. The Fine Gael leader, John Bruton, responded with a statement in which he questioned the candidacy of someone 'endorsed by Sinn Féin' on a government ticket for the presidency.

But, by that afternoon, Mary McAleese had got another lucky break.

In a telephone interview on the *News At One*, Eoghan Harris launched a vituperative attack on her.

'I mean, let there be no huggermugger about it,' he said, 'my main reason for supporting Derek Nally is he was the candidate likely to most point up Mary McAleese's weakness. I would vote for Donald Duck if they opposed Mary McAleese. I think she would make a very dangerous and tribal president.'

Sending shock waves across the country by branding her 'a tribal time-bomb', he went on: 'Mary McAleese is clearly an unreconstructed Northern nationalist who will drive all kinds of tribal baggage with her. When she's elected President of Ireland nobody will be able to control Mary McAleese. She's an arrogant and self-sufficient candidate who's using the Southern election to advance her career. She's not a Sinn Féiner of course. Let me say she's not a Sinn Féiner, she's a Mé Féiner.'

The venom of Harris' attack proved to be a double whammy, eliciting sympathy for the Belfast woman while inflicting collateral damage on the other campaigns. Probably the most innocent casualty of the entire affair was Mary Banotti. The 58-year-old Euro MP and grand-niece of Michael Collins, divorced from her Italian husband, was a widely-respected parliamentarian and champion of tug-of-love custody rights. Her biggest *faux pas* had been on *Questions & Answers* when she suggested Fianna Fáil had been so desperate to find a woman candidate the party had to go looking outside the jurisdiction. Had she been pressed on the weaknesses of her profile going into the campaign, the sister of Fine Gael's deputy leader, Nora Owen, might have foreseen some negative comment about a divorcée as a prospective president. There had been none, however, and the most dramatic incident for her had been when her campaign car had been involved in a serious road accident in Tipperary. Yet, she was to be punished by association.

According to Eoghan Harris, it was for Banotti's benefit that he had climbed on board the Nally bandwagon.

'In my case, I thought he could come in third,' Harris revealed, 'and (I) hoped that, in any event, a campaign fought with an anti-nationalist subtext might polarise opinion between Fianna Fáil and Fine Gael. And that Nally might come in third, ahead of the Labour candidate and that his transfers might elect the Fine Gael candidate.'

But, by that Thursday night of October 16, the Taoiseach was strongly suggesting in public that the Foreign Affairs leak had come from Fine Gael; a veiled accusation stoutly denied by the Fine Gael leader. It did not look good for him, though, when Fianna Fáil let it be known that Eoghan Harris had joined John Bruton and his adviser, Roy Dooney, for lunch in a south city restaurant a week before the leak. They had been spotted by the Health Minister, Brian Cowen, who had been sitting at the next table. Three of Bruton's advisers subsequently issued statements denying any involvement in leaking the documents.

By the end of the week, several cuts had been inflicted, but few of them on the intended target, Mary McAleese. The Nally campaign, which had made most of the running, was left in disarray and would never regain its momentum. Mary Banotti had virtually been eclipsed from the public's consciousness by the intense attention on her main rival. While Mary McAleese surged ahead in the polls, John Bruton's popularity dived from 60 per cent to 43 per cent.

Noel Dempsey reckoned the campaign was 'turning back in our favour'.

But even as his spirits began to rise, unseen hands were already priming the biggest bombshell of all.

Eileen Gleeson was one of the first to feel it exploding. It was Saturday night, October 18, and the headline in the early edition of *The Sunday Business Post* screamed out at Mary McAleese's press co-ordinator. Gleeson, a 36-year-old publican's daughter from Booterstown in Dublin, was not a woman easily fazed. She ran her own public relations company with a blue-chip client list and a reputation for hardball crisis management. Now, as she dialled the number of the Burlington Hotel and insisted on speaking to the manager, she knew the latest revelations could spell doom. When the hotel manager picked up the phone, she told him to go immediately to the function room where the SDLP was hosting a private dinner attended by Mary McAleese. She told the manager to get the Minister for the Environment out of there, fast.

While she waited for the director of elections to come on the line, Eileen Gleeson re-read the newspaper story. It was every bit as explosive as she had thought at first glance. Written by the paper's political editor, Emily O'Reilly, it contained extensive new detail on the memos leaked from the Department of Foreign Affairs. The story was based on two conversations between Mary McAleese and Dympna Hayes the previous January and May, and a third conversation in April between the Department official and the SDLP councillor, Bríd Rodgers.

'On a personal level Ms McAleese has no interest in participating in the upcoming (British) elections in 'any shape or form' in the absence of an SDLP-Sinn Féin joint election platform', Dympna Hayes recalled from the January conversation. 'The most interesting angle will be the direction of the nationalist vote. Ms McAleese is of the view that Sinn Féin will gain a lot of ground from the SDLP.'

By the time of the next conversation, over dinner in May, the general election was over, having swept in Tony Blair's Labour tide.

'She was very pleased with Sinn Féin's performance in the general election and confident that they will perform even better in the local elections,' Hayes wrote. 'She expects Mick Murphy, the Sinn Féin candidate in Rostrevor, her own constituency, to pick up a seat this time.'

The memo went on to record a chance encounter between McAleese and the Sinn Féin leaders, Gerry Adams and Martin McGuinness, on a flight from London just days before the conversation took place. 'Both of them were in great form and had thoroughly enjoyed their visit to Westminster. (A well known and highly successful consultant from Touche Ross whom McAleese has known for many years was seated beside her on the plane and proceeded to ignore her for the rest of the journey after hearing her exchange with the Sinn Féin leaders).'

Quoting the Belfast woman as unfavourably comparing 'the tired old faces' of the SDLP with the 'young and fresh' candidates of Sinn Féin, the civil servant summed up the other woman's attitude as tantamount to a vote of confidence in the IRA's political wing. 'Now, for the first time, many middle-class voters, especially first generation middle-class nationalists like herself, will be able to countenance voting for Sinn Féin as continuing to support John Hume while, at the same time, landing a more direct swipe at the British government. She believes that the (John) Major government, because of their dependence on the Unionists, have actively set out to keep Sinn Féin out of the process and that they bear all the blame for the present impasse.'

Eileen Gleeson's heart was pounding as she read the lengthy extracts from the memos. She had known Mary McAleese since the early 1980s, when they were both active in Fianna Fáil's Women's Committee, and they had grown closer this past month, travelling together on the campaign tour. As the candidate's press officer, the task of damage limitation fell within her remit. The synopses of the McAleese conversations were just about manageable, but the real sulphur billowed from Dympna Hayes' conversation with Bríd Rodgers.

The Gweedore-born gaelgóir was one of the most respected nationalist figures in Northern Ireland. A former chairwoman of the SDLP, she was nominated to the Republic's senate by Garret FitzGerald in 1983. At the time of her meeting with Dympna Hayes in Lurgan on April 3, the woman who shared a constituency with David Trimble was one of the SDLP negotiators at the all-party talks in Stormont. When Mary McAleese's name cropped up in the course of their conversation, the SDLP veteran mentioned that she had met her recently. Rodgers was remembering her secret meeting with the Redemptorist Peace Ministry at Clonard Monastery.

'Referring to this group as the "Triumvirate", Ms Rodgers described their main object as promoting a new nationalist consensus which owes more to Sinn Féin than the SDLP,' Hayes reported back to her boss in Iveagh House. 'All three are in regular touch with the Sinn Féin leadership and are, in reality, pushing the Sinn Féin agenda.'

Therein lay the killer punch; the nightmare scenario of a closet Republican apologist being sponsored by the Irish government for the State's most noble office. The magnitude of the bombshell crystallised as Eileen Gleeson summarised the most damning aspects of the newspaper story for Noel Dempsey. He rapidly assessed their options, and decided to do nothing in haste. The story would not hit the streets until the morning and it was unlikely the media would ambush the candidate in the meantime. No, he concluded, best not to react rashly. They would stick to the original schedule and meet, as already arranged, for Sunday lunch at the K Club.

Sunday, ironically, was Bodenstown day, a place of venerable pilgrimage by both Sinn Féin and Fianna Fáil to the County Kildare village for the annual Wolfe Tone commemorations. Mary and Martin McAleese were due to attend the ceremonies in the morning, before heading for Galway and a major rally at 8pm in the city of the tribes. It made sense, therefore, for the inner sanctum of the campaign team to re-group at the nearby K Club.

Owned by Michael Smurfit, one of Ireland's richest men, the palatial golf and country hotel was probably the most exclusive club in the country. The lunch had been planned as a pit stop to review the campaign to date and to flesh out the strategy for the final phase. But, by the time they gathered in the Yeats Room, a private haven fitted with state-of-the-art security and hung with several million pounds worth of paintings, it had acquired the status of a crisis summit. There were five people present: Mary and Martin McAleese, Noel Dempsey, Eileen Gleeson and Martin Mackin, the 33-year-old former teacher. On one wall of the room hung an ostentatious plaque noting that 'John Bruton dined here with Dr Michael Smurfit on his first day as Taoiseach'.

The campaign team appreciated the joke as they took their seats at the silver-laden table. There was little else to laugh about; precious little time for light-hearted banter. They got straight down to business. The Foreign Affairs leak was the only item on the agenda.

'Before the campaign started, you said you didn't want the Clonard thing to come out,' Dempsey reminded his candidate. 'Now, there are people mentioned in that,' he went on, stabbing the newspaper on the table, 'and it's up to them to speak out.'

But Mary, like the others, believed that the revelations had changed everything. Irate that someone was hijacking confidential civil service documents for political purposes, she argued that it was time for her to speak out. The other three backed her, believing it would look sinister if she refused to comment on the story.

But Noel Dempsey was adamant. It was his call, he told them, and he was ordering her to play dumb.

'I decided that Sunday she would say nothing because it was a document relaying an opinion by others,' he explained. 'There was no primary evidence. We didn't know what other documents would be released. If she answered that one she would have been swamped by it. If she started commenting she could have spent the whole campaign trying to contradict people's opinions of Mary McAleese. I felt it was up to the people who were being quoted or the people who were leaking documents to take it a step further and clarify it.'

There was one problem. A function-room had been booked in the Skeffington Arms Hotel in Galway for a press conference to be held before the Fianna Fáil/Progressive Democrats rally across Eyre Square in the Great Southern Hotel. There was no way the candidate could field a barrage of questions about her reported Sinn Féin sympathies without directly responding to the allegations.

According to Noel Dempsey and other campaign members, she was spared by nothing less than Lady Luck. Fortuitously, it transpired that Mary and Martin McAleese had a private appointment for 'family matters' before the drive to the west.

'I discovered they were going somewhere else and I changed the plan,' Noel Dempsey confirmed.

The deputy director of elections, Pat Farrell, had left for Galway earlier in the day in an advance party that included former Army officer Wally Young, the campaign's events co-ordinator. It was the latter who was deputed to put up notices in the Skeffington Arms and to telephone various reporters notifying them that the 7.30pm press conference was being abandoned.

RTE's western correspondent, Jim Fahy, got the call on his mobile phone. The candidate was running late, he was told. She would be going directly to the Great Southern and, more than likely, she would talk to journalists after the rally. Fahy, a solid reporter hugely respected by his peers, was philosophical.

'RTE had been trying to get a reaction to the leaks during the day and this was the first opportunity we got,' he recalled. 'I thought if that was to be the case, so be it. I wasn't under any great pressure from my news desk to deliver a report from the rally. We were really trying to find out if she would be reacting. I went there with a camera crew intending to ask her on the way in if she had any comment to make.'

Jim Fahy, in fact, was to file one of the most electrifying news reports of his career that night.

At 8.20pm, Noel Dempsey, now in Galway, received a phone call from the candidate's car, alerting him that she had arrived in the city. He went to stand on the front step of the hotel, in a greeting formation with the PD Minister, Bobby Molloy, and two Fianna Fáil junior ministers, Éamon O'Cuív and Noel Treacy. The planned protocol was for Mary McAleese to leave her car at the corner of Eyre Square and walk to the Great Southern escorted by a bagpiper. What happened next, however, depends on whose version of events is believed.

'Bobby Molloy, Éamon O'Cuív and Noel Treacy went down to meet her and surrounded her with 30 or 40 people who were determined we would not get near her to ask questions,' Jim Fahy remembered. 'I asked her three or four times for her reaction and then why she was reacting like that. I was pushed aside, as was my cameraman. There was a lot of jostling. It was like a rolling scrum.

'I caught her eye and I saw in that look an absolute determination to get straight from the car to the hotel as quickly as possible. There was a press of people who were forming a human tunnel for her route to the hotel. We went through the revolving door and started up the stairs. The same kind of tactic was used to get her up the stairs. There was a certain amount of pulling and tugging. My jacket was being held by somebody from behind. Some of my colleagues told me afterwards it was Noel Dempsey. We got to the top of the stairs and she was ushered into a small anteroom.'

An *Irish Times* journalist, Catherine Cleary, recalled Dempsey 'rugby-tackling' the RTÉ correspondent. But the Environment Minister remembered the episode differently.

'I was standing on the steps waiting to greet her when I saw a posse of media heading down to the corner,' he said. 'When the car arrived she was surrounded by media. I came down to the bottom of the schamozzle. She was visibly shaken when she got into the room. She had to get a glass of water and calm herself down.'

Shortly after Mary McAleese rose to address the rally in one of the hotel's function rooms, Noel Dempsey was approached by a Fianna Fáil activist who told the minister he had overhead Jim Fahy discussing the events in a telephone call to his newsdesk. Dempsey immediately left the rally and, from an upstairs room, dialled RTÉ's phone number in Dublin.

'I will be watching the news programme,' he warned, 'and, if there is anything wrong or libellous, I will take action.'

Despite the threat, that night's *Nine O'Clock News* was sensational, showing the candidate resolutely tight-lipped amid scenes of utter mayhem. It was a disaster for Mary McAleese's campaign.

One person who watched the unfolding scenes on her television screen was Professor Patricia Casey. She and the other affiliates of 'The Friends of Mary McAleese' had retained a direct link with their candidate through Liam Murphy, a member of the campaign team and the Catholic bishop's representative for secondary schools in the Meath diocese.

'I was worried it was all going to fall apart,' Patricia Casey recalled. 'Harry Casey rang me that night and I rang Mary the following morning. She told me she had been silenced by the campaign managers.'

If Noel Dempsey was depending on senior SDLP politicians to come to the candidate's rescue, his hopes were dashed. Monday wore on with a deafening silence from north of the border, broken only by Lord Alderdice, the Alliance Party leader, who called on Mary McAleese to withdraw from the Republic's election. Bríd Rodgers was in a quandary. Apart from her party's policy of detachment from elections in the South, she felt that, were she to speak out in support of McAleese, she would be undermining Dympna Hayes' professional reputation. So, instead of issuing a public statement, she wrote a private letter explaining her dilemma. She addressed the envelope to Professor Mary McAleese, c/o Fianna Fáil Head Office, Upper Mount Street, Dublin.

Around the same time, another Northern nationalist was sitting down to write to the candidate. Though now a private individual, he knew she would instantly recognise his signature. His name was Rory McShane, the fiancé she had jilted 21 years earlier. He had become a highly successful solicitor and wealthy man in the intervening years. Married with children, his firm acted for Newry & Mourne District Council and in numerous criminal law cases spanning the two communities. Still a member of the SDLP, the former captain of Warrenpoint Golf club had become involved in a voluntary peace organisation called 'Jigsaw' after a restaurant he owned in Newry had been blown up twice by the IRA because, they claimed, it was frequented by off-duty policemen and soldiers. In the letter he wrote to his former sweetheart, Rory McShane encouraged her to withstand the blizzard of accusations that she was 'soft' on Sinn Féin. Before sealing the envelope, he slipped in a personal cheque as a contribution to her campaign fund.

Among her other financial backers were Jim Fitzpatrick, who donated £2,000, her Uncle Eddie, whose company, Connors Fuels, gave £1,000, and the most generous of all, Martin Naughton, with a personal contribution of £5,000 plus £6,000 from his company, Glen Dimplex. The County Louth multi-millionaire had also hosted a fund-raising lunch in Dublin's only two-Michelin-starred restaurant, Patrick Guilbaud's, on October 14 for the campaign coffers. Similarily, Patricia Casey would host a dinner for 120 of her medical colleagues in the Davenport Hotel on the Saturday night before polling day.

But financial support alone was not enough to weather the avalanche of controversy which followed Sunday night's events in Galway. On Monday October 20, the campaign moved to the Aran

Islands for a dollop of picture postcard photo-opportunities. But the idyll was not to be. A statement, issued the previous night by Fr Brendan Callanan, the provincial of the Redemptorist Order, insisted that Mary McAleese was 'implacably opposed to violence'. The candidate, however, was still under Noel Dempsey's gagging order as news spread that her father had signed the nomination papers for a Rostrevor neighbour and former IRA prisoner, Mick Murphy, during the local elections in the North. Reporters on the campaign trail were increasingly bewildered by her reticence.

Back in Dublin, Noel Dempsey got a phone call from the Fianna Fáil back-bencher, Eoin Ryan, Mary's old running mate in Dublin South East in the 1987 general election. 'Eoin rang me and said the feedback he was getting was that she was coming across as arrogant because she wouldn't answer questions. I got on the phone to the Aran Islands and spoke to Wally on the mobile. I told him to tell Mary to explain to the journalists about the Redemptorist Ministry.'

The press briefing was held in a school hall in Kilronan, constituting a series of one-to-one interviews with various journalists. Catherine Cleary was one of them. 'Mary McAleese was sitting on a chair in this room and the journalists had to hunker down in front of her,' she recalled. 'There was a crowd of her supporters there and they were very hostile. There was a lot of booing and hissing from the crowd when she was asked how she felt about being criticised by the nationalist community. I have to say it was the most bruising interview I ever did. She frequently challenged you on your research. She was flushed and angry. It was such a contradiction to see her being so pleasant to people and yet being so unpleasant to reporters. I suppose, looking back on it, she had a lot of balls to put it up to us because most politicians would be currying favour with the media.'

Jim Fahy, who also travelled out to the islands with the entourage, remembered her being 'very cool, calm and collected' that day. 'She was under a great deal of pressure and she held unflinchingly to the line.'

She explained her composure-under-fire six weeks later in an interview with *The Irish News*. 'During the worst parts of the campaign, when some of the things that were being written and said and alleged were happening, I just had this very strong inner conviction that the truth would out,' she said. 'I had lived here, don't forget. I had worked in RTÉ. I had lived through some very difficult times here. I had a fair insight into the kinds of things that I might come across. I had myself psyched for that, so to some extent when it happened, I was able to deal with it.'

She did not mention, however, that members of her family back in the North were compelled to review their personal security arrangements because of the controversy. 'Her family were under police protection in the North because of all the publicity,' according to a member of the campaign team. The three McAleese children were continuing to attend school in Rostrevor in the absence of both their parents. Martin McAleese acting as liaison between his wife and the campaign team. 'Martin was very protective of her,' Noel Dempsey recalled. 'He thought I was driving her too hard.'

On leave of absence from his dental practice, he provided a bulwark against the growing disgruntlement of journalists. 'The spikier she would get, the more pleasant Martin was to us,' according to Catherine Cleary.

But there was one more drama to be played out in the stand-off with the media. John Alderdice's intervention the previous day gave license to the hitherto silent nationalists in the North to come out in her favour. After fervent behind-the-scenes appeals by such Friends of Mary McAleese as Denis Moloney, both John Hume and Bríd Rodgers issued clarifying statements. The SDLP leader defended Mary McAleese's politics and her role in the peace process. Bríd Rodgers' statement was more circumspect, simply 'deploring the spin' that had been put on her comments. She did not deny their veracity.

Tom Kelly, Mary's PR ally at Queens who had declined her invitation to work on the campaign for the party nomination, also answered the distress signals. The SDLP's director of communications in Newry/Armagh penned a trenchant defence of the candidate in a major article published by *The Irish News* on Tuesday October 21. 'Never has McAleese espoused violence, never has she said she speaks for Sinn Féin (though it would be legitimate for her to do so), in fact all her on-the-record comments stated very clearly her opposition to all forms of violence,' he wrote.

The article effectively flushed out other Northern nationalists in her favour, most notably her own MP, Eddie McGrady, who issued a statement the following weekend.

'Whether or not McAleese mooted the idea of a nationalist pact in discussions with SDLP representatives depends on who you believe,' according to Tom Kelly. 'I have no doubt the subject may have been discussed generally in the context of SDLP/Sinn Féin relations. It was, after all, something that was very much part of the Sinn Féin agenda at the time. However, I think it's unlikely that McAleese was a strong advocate and that any airing of the initiative would have been in the context of a post-violence situation which is something we have all thought about.

'When the Foreign Affairs leaks were damaging Mary, I encouraged public statements from various Protestant ministers in her support and had them released to RTÉ. It was important to do this because very genuine and sincere people were not only hurt by the allegations or inferences drawn from the leaked memos but were actually exposed to physical risk.

'Locally, the South Down SDLP groups felt very uneasy, particularly around Rostrevor and the border area,' Kelly recalled. 'They were very uncomfortable with the SDLP silence on the issue of Mary's political allegiance when she said on RTÉ that she supported the party and had offered the local branch her own home office during McGrady's election. She had, in fact, attended a local SDLP meeting before the elections and explained her difficulty as pro-vice chancellor in playing an active role in an overt way but offered private local support. The officers of Rostrevor branch were angry at the failure of the SDLP hierarchy to speak out and they asked me to draw up a public statement of support on their behalf. I drafted a release and issued it to the press. It teased a few more SDLP-elected speakers from the woods.'

The newspaper publisher and member of the Redemptorist 'triumvirate', Jim Fitzpatrick, also issued a personal statement. 'Our sole purpose in the Peace Mission was to facilitate discussion and dialogue and we did not engage in the promotion (of) any particular political agenda,' he declared. 'This was a genuine and sincere initiative and it is both hurtful and malicious to suggest any subversive motivation by any of the individuals involved. Professor McAleese is an honourable and trusting individual who is totally committed to peace and these smear attempts are uncivilised in the modern, democratic Ireland.'

All of which was manna to Noel Dempsey. As the controversy assumed new dimensions, pointing the finger of anti-patriotism at whoever was willing to endanger the peace process by leaking the memos, it began to work in favour of the McAleese campaign. Mary McAleese had still not put the allegations to bed, however. There had been no satisfactory or comprehensive rebuttal from the candidate herself. That needed to be done before the whole affair could be left behind, and Dempsey saw his opportunity in RTÉ – the colossus that had been his bête noir since the start of the campaign. *Prime Time* was badgering him for an interview with the candidate.

'I felt the tide was turning and we had to take the opportunity and go on,' he remembered. 'But Mary didn't want to go on that night. She had moved on from Galway to Limerick and the interview was to be done by Eamon Lawlor in a hotel there on Tuesday night.'

Her suspicion of the media, inherited from her experience in journalism, combined with Fianna Fáil's prickliness to form a cocktail of near paranoia. The candidate stuck her heels in, refusing to appear on *Prime Time* for fear of being 'set up'. Martin Mackin was duly despatched to Montrose to view the taped introduction to the interview. He reported back to Noel Demspey that the item 'had pluses and minuses'.

'It was my call and I made the decision,' the campaign manager confirmed. 'She was going on.'

Once again, her appearance made compulsive viewing. The nation's television screens bristled with the candidate's ill-concealed tension. In one of those extraordinary twists peculiar to politics, it worked to her advantage, projecting a woman under siege because of her Northern nationalist heritage. It may even have pricked consciences in the Republic as a subliminal reminder that many Northerners believed they had been abandoned by the South. When Eamon Lawlor asked her if she was 'intimate' with Gerry Adams, the question seemed to confirm the impression of a woman unfairly treated.

The £350,000 McAleese campaign was back on the rails. By Saturday, her lead in the opinion polls had stretched to 37 per cent, eight points ahead of the nearest contender, Mary Banotti. An article by the Unionist MP, Ken Maginnis, in *The Irish Times* on Thursday, October 23, created scant ripples with its warning that Mary McAleese was 'an unlikely bridge-builder'. There was, however, one loose end that still needed to be tied up. In the throes of the Foreign Affairs controversy, Mary McAleese had claimed that she was receiving messages of support and good-will from 'many' Unionists. Only one had, so far, raised his head above the parapet. Virtually unknown in the Republic, Councillor Harvey Bicker's statement of endorsement only served to undermine her contention. But, on the Sunday before the election, one of the heaviest-hitters of all, John Taylor, deputy leader of Ken Maginnis' party, made an unexpected foray when he spoke out in her favour. Describing her as 'an out-and-out nationalist', the man who, a decade earlier had tabled 10 questions about her in the House of Commons, declared that she was 'by no means a Republican sympathiser'. She was, according to Taylor, 'a most able person, quite easy to work with'.

On Tuesday October 28, an *Irish Independent* poll showed her running clear of the rest of the field at a whopping 49 per cent. But that extraordinary rating was relegated to off-lead news status throughout the day as regular radio bulletins delivered breathless details of a development in the gárda investigation into the leaked Foreign Affairs documents. The story of how a former Fine Gael ministerial adviser had been arrested in his home at 7.20 that morning by members of the National Bureau of Criminal Investigation choreographed with the winding down of the campaign. The man was released without charge after 12 hours interrogation at Lucan garda station.

That night, all five candidates appeared on *Prime Time* for the wrap-up before RTÉ's moratorium the next day, the eve of the election. Despite the best efforts of her driver, Denis Lawlor, to ensure she had plenty rest during the campaign (he even bought a compact disc of Andean pipe music in a supermarket to lull her to sleep in the car), Mary McAleese was suffering a severe dose of influenza. Only the cosmetics applied in RTÉ's make-up department concealed the swelling on her face caused by a reaction to the antibiotics she had been prescribed. Yet, of the five, she looked like the winner that night.

Her campaign team's optimism continued to soar on Wednesday, as the final hours of a fraught six-week campaign ticked away.

With no vote of her own in the Republic, Thursday would be the first free day Mary McAleese would have had in over a month. Her husband was planning a round of golf with Noel Dempsey in Portmarnock on the morning of the election while the candidate was looking forward to an afternoon shopping with her press aide, Eileen Gleeson. But, before retiring to bed that night, there was one last thing Mary McAleese needed to do. She picked up the telephone receiver and dialled a number in Northern Ireland.

'I got your letter,' she told the person at the other end, 'and I understand. Maybe we'll get together for a cup of coffee when all this is over.'

'That would be nice,' Bríd Rodgers agreed.

# Home Rule

LIGHTS BLAZED FROM THE windows of the apartment as the car pulled up outside. The driver killed the engine, silencing the excited voice on the radio. His passengers made no objection. They had heard all they needed to know.

A shiver of winter cold ran through the car as the family flung open the doors and hurried towards the lights. They could hear voices, see the shadows flitting inside, beckoning them. The children ran ahead.

Martin McAleese squeezed his wife's hand. She looked at him, radiant eyes filled with triumph. They moved together into the room.

A champagne cork popped. There were wineglasses and teacups and platters of sandwiches everywhere. Faces wreathed in victory. She saw her mother, white-haired and proud, accepting congratulations. Her father, tall and stoic and fit to burst. Her best friend from Rostrevor, Ailish Farrell; her brothers and sisters and their children; Denis Moloney from Belfast; Dick Roche beaming; the Jesuit priest, Fr Edmond Grace; Clement Leneghan, the baby of the family, leaning into the television set in the corner, studiously working out percentages on a notepad. They were all here.

The poise that had set her apart from the other candidates threatened to crumble. Only her powerful instinct for self-preservation held her together. The television announcer was saying that the 47 per cent turnout had been the lowest ever recorded in a presidential election. Her own vote falling significantly short of previous winners'.

But none of that mattered now. What mattered was that 574,424 people throughout the Republic believed she was the best choice. Her 45.2 per cent share of the first preference vote far out-stripping Mary Banotti's 29.3 per cent. What mattered was that she had won.

Soon they would leave for the formal declaration at Dublin Castle, driving in cavalcade from the apartment they called 'Independent House' in the heart of the Dublin 4 constituency that had rejected her a decade before.

'I want us to share as a nation the adventure of this, the most dynamic country in Europe, heading into the next millennium, ' she would tell them in her victory speech at the Castle. 'And I believe this will see the Irish people taking a central role as key players not just on the European stage but globally. It will mark, I believe, the true age of the Irish because I believe we are an unstoppable nation now very definitely in our stride.'

It had taken a strong nerve to come back. Her single-mindedness flouting the past to become the first Ulster president-elect. A woman who had lived under the threat of paramilitary execution about to embark on seven years of round-the-clock security, pomp and ceremony. She had been hurt, but unsurprised, by the viciousness of the campaign. She too had trampled on the feelings of others in defence of her good name, bridling at the anguish caused to her family. 'Mary Poppins with a chill at the core,' was how one newspaper had described her.

Ever since the day the Leneghans had fled their home in north Belfast, she had striven to make her mark. To establish an identity for herself independent of the Northern Catholic tag that bound her tribe. Setting out on a course of ambition that would inevitably draw the ire of others. Even within her own community there were those who accused her of jumping on bandwagons for selfish interest. Some who would say she never created an original space of her own.

But she had proven them wrong. She was a history-maker, at last. The daughter of the ghetto about to be crowned first citizen in the greater part of a divided island. Guardian of a constitution she believed inadequate for its failure to outlaw religious discrimination. Many of the friends celebrating her victory in the apartment were finding affirmation of their own place too in the very fact of her success. As she looked around the room at them, her gaze came to rest on Patricia Casey. The psychiatrist had come bearing a basket of crab sandwiches and a home-made mackerel pâté for the party. But her face was set in sadness.

Mary made her way across the room to her friend. 'What is it?' she asked gently. The other woman laid her head on the president-elect's shoulder, and sobbed. She told her she had come to the apartment directly from Our Lady's Hospital for Sick Children in Crumlin where she had left her five-year-old son, Gavan. He was seriously ill, undergoing heavy, invasive medical treatment, and she did not know if he would get better. The two women stood together, holding hands for 15 minutes, a capsule of grief in the midst of jubilation.

When it came time to leave, Mary McAleese draped a shimmering velvet scarf over her shoulder for the delectation of the media cameras massed in wait for her at Dublin Castle. She kissed her parents, waved goodbye to her friends, and reached for her husband's hand. Just then, the door of the apartment swung open and Harry Casey bounded in, all but hidden by the bouquet of yellow roses in his hands.

The school teacher held the flowers out to the woman he had long dreamed of becoming Uachtaráin na hÉireann. The buttery yellow of the roses, the colour of homecoming, lit up her face as she took them from him.

'We've done it, Harry,' she smiled.

# Index

## A

# K

Kavanagh, Fr Myles 10, 146
Keane, Colm 64
Keane, John B 85
Keane, Moss 28, 30
Keating, Michael 40
Kee, Robert 78
Keenan, Dermot 1
Kelly, Gerry 8, 9
Kelly, Nuala 78
Kelly, Tom 121, 122, 136, 151, 156, 157, 210, 211
Kennedy, Geraldine 82, 196, 197
Kennedy, Joe 144
Kenny, Pat 63, 200
Kerr, Myrtle 108
Kerr, Rev Cecil 70, 108, 109, 117, 132
Kett, Tony 183
Killilea, Mark 184
King William of Orange 16
King, Jim 151
Kinley, Howard 64
Kinsella, Patrick 66
Kirby, Terence 59
Küng, Hanz 141

# L

Lampen, John 142
Lawlor, Denis 213
Lawlor, Eamon 212
Lawlor, Patsy 78
Leahy, Dr Paddy 49
Lee, Simon 118
Leichty, Joe 143
Lemass, Seán 74, 183
Leneghan, Bridget 68
Leneghan, Claire (Senior) 10, 13, 14, 32, 33, 109, 215
Leneghan, Claire 18
Leneghan, Clement 18, 215
Leneghan, Damien 18
Leneghan, John 7, 8, 18, 38, 109,115

Leneghan, Kate 18, 109
Leneghan, Nora 18, 109
Leneghan, Paddy 9, 10, 11, 14, 18, 20, 21, 22, 23, 126, 215
Lenihan, Brian 64, 157, 163, 174, 177, 182, 185, 189
Lenihan, Brian (Senior) 153, 158, 163
Lenihan, Conor 163, 185
Leonard, Hugh 38
Linehan, Mary 88
Little, Joe 55, 56
Loftus, Sean 'Dublin Bay Rockall' 197
Logue, Christopher 4
Lord, Miriam 193
Lorimer, Sir Desmond 144
Lowry, Nick 79, 132, 191
Lyle, Sir Nicholas 115
Lynch, Jack 75, 183

# M

MacBride, Seán 39, 78, 88
MacCartan, Pat 40
MacConghaíl, Muiris 44, 49, 50, 56
MacGréil, Dr Micheál 40
Macken, Fidelma 139
Mackin, Martin 181, 194, 204, 212
MacSharry, Ray 175
MacStiofán, Seán 47
Magee, Dr John 139
Maginnis, Ken 213
Maguire, Annie 78, 93
Main, John 131
Major, John 203
Mallie, Eamonn 76
Mallon, Seamus 121
Mandela, Nelson 41
Mansergh, Martin 148, 155, 158, 169, 170, 171
Mara, PJ 166, 175
Martin, Micheál 174
Mateer, Philip 118